REINVENTING RELIGION

REINVENTING RELIGION

Beyond Belief and Scepticism

PETER MOORE

REAKTION BOOKS

To Janet and Gerald,
with love and
gratitude

Published by Reaktion Books Ltd
Unit 32, Waterside
44–48 Wharf Road
London N1 7UX, UK
www.reaktionbooks.co.uk

First published 2020
Copyright © Peter Moore 2020

Printed and bound in Great Britain by
TJ International, Padstow, Cornwall

A catalogue record for this book is available from the British Library

ISBN 978 1 78914 325 6

CONTENTS

PREFACE

I t is my hope that this book will be of interest to all or any of those, religiously affiliated or not, who accept that questions about religion must, in the very nature of the case, remain open. My general rule of thumb is that religion should be treated in the same way, and be subject to the same rules of rational discussion, as any other sphere of human interest or activity. Even though there is much about religious experience that transcends mere reason, religion itself is a human phenomenon, and its doctrines, practices and institutions are all human constructions. Religions have not come about through alien invasion. At the same time, the rich resources of the world's religions suggest that human beings are on the edge of a vast hinterland not dreamt of – or simply ignored – in the philosophies of those sceptics and rationalists claiming to have, at last, the full measure of humanity. In any case, if the highest forms of religion are those in which life is lived to the full, which often means those which are the riskiest and most challenging, then its lowest forms will be those that pander to our insecurity, our suspicion of others, our rejection of life's gifts or our lust for certainty.

Despite the ambitious title, there are many important aspects of religion not touched upon in this book, or touched upon only briefly. But this is an 'ideas' book, not a 'facts' book. It will have succeeded in its aims if it gets people thinking both critically and creatively about religion in any of its more specific contexts.

The Select Bibliography includes a range of books covering the particular 'dimensions' of religion and also representing different sides of the various arguments about religion. Some of these endorse the approach to religion taken in this book, while others illustrate approaches of which I have been critical.

INTRODUCTION

T his wide-ranging study of ways of being religious has a particular critical focus. In the course of reviewing various aspects of religious life, I explore some of the misconceptions about religion that are prevalent not only among sceptics and those hostile to religion but among large numbers of religious people too. What religious people themselves say and do about religion will often confirm the doubts and criticisms of those who are non-religious or anti-religious. Thus religion very often proves to be its own worst enemy. Religious adherents will not take any more kindly to my suggestions than the sceptics and critics, and so it is quite possible that I shall do little more than irritate both sides – rather as two opposing political parties, for example, might be equally irritated by the ideas of some radical environmental group. The aim of the book, however, is not simply to criticize certain ways of thinking about religion, or of actually being religious, but rather to excite interest in the subject and to encourage people to ask constructive questions about it.

It is hardly novel to claim that those who are critical of or sceptical about religion, or perhaps just one religion in particular, have not really understood it. This is a complaint found in many sacred texts and also in much secondary religious literature. In many cases, those who criticize a particular religion or form of religion do so through commitment to some other form of religion. 'Infidel' and 'unbeliever' were, and in some quarters still are, common terms of abuse, applied not so much to those without religion as to those who profess a different (and therefore false) religion.

In recent centuries, however, a new constituency has emerged – the constituency of those who are sceptical about any form of religion, of those who are sceptical about religion as such. This generalized scepticism does not necessarily entail outright hostility to religion. Some will certainly identify religion as a main cause of human suffering and confusion in this world. But many sceptics are quite ready to acknowledge the positive achievements and personal benefits of religion. For most sceptics, however, religion is something incompatible with, and now largely discredited by, a modern, scientific understanding of the world.

Even so, scepticism and hostility are not the most difficult of the challenges facing the religious apologist. More challenging still is the fact that beyond the constituency of the sceptical are many people who, rather than being sceptical or critical of religion, are more or less indifferent to it.[1] Religion simply does not seem to speak to them in any way. Such people do not represent themselves as defiantly 'humanist' or 'secularist', as the actively sceptical or critical will often do. Rather, they simply cannot see the point of religion. Religion, whatever role it may have played in the past, is now, for them at least, an irrelevance. Thus as well as making a case for religion as compatible rather than incompatible with science, and as potentially if not always actually a benign force within human life, the religious apologist has to make the case for taking religion seriously in the first place.

It is all very well telling people that their views about religion are misguided. But on what basis is criticism of any particular view of religion to be made? What is at issue here, of course, is informed criticism, not simply the assertion of a contrary view, still less the mere rehearsal of prejudice. Informed criticism of someone's religious beliefs or behaviour is liable to take place at two levels: ideas, rituals and particular kinds of behaviour can be judged at one level by universally (or widely) accepted general criteria, and at another level by criteria internal to this or that particular religious tradition. Thus one could condemn the persecution of the Rohingya people by the Burmese authorities (who explicitly identify themselves as Buddhists) both as a violation of human rights (regardless of religion) and as behaviour contrary to the principles of Buddhism.[2] Of course, if such behaviour were to become customary among Burmese Buddhists, and perhaps even to be endorsed by Buddhist authorities, then a sociologist of religion could be entitled to say that such persecution was now part of Burmese Buddhist culture, and to that extent part of the totality of the Buddhist tradition. But non-Buddhists as well as some Buddhists themselves would still see a conflict with basic Buddhist principles as well as with general ethical ones.

Any religion claiming that its doctrines and practices are rationally worth following must by this same token also accept the possibility of these doctrines and practices being subject to rational criticism, whether from within or from outside its own domain. Indeed, one of the ways in which religions evolve, and reform themselves, is through criticism based either on their own first principles or on new insights or discoveries common to human society as a whole. What this book is chiefly concerned to challenge, however, are not particular religious doctrines or practices, but rather certain views *about* religion, whether these views are held by religious believers themselves or by religious sceptics or academic commentators. Indeed, the kinds of views about religion challenged in this book are just as likely to be held by religious believers as by religious sceptics. The two parties agree on what religion is; what they disagree about is the truth or the value of religion.

What sceptics are likely to be ridiculing and rejecting, and believers to be recommending and defending, is a dualistic view of religion as a relationship between supernatural powers in heaven above and human beings on earth below – a relationship conducted through interventions, transactions and obligations and sanctioned by hope of reward or fear of punishment. The following passage might well serve as a summary of what believers and sceptics agree is the nature of religion:

Religion . . . is expressly premised on the idea of an external, supernatural source of moral authority. In the standard case it is held that the agencies which possess this authority are personally interested in having humankind conform itself to their purposes; and the religions in which they figure further teach that petition and sacrifice can influence those purposes. All the faiths employ prayer, ritual and sacrifice to achieve this, the last ranging from the repetition of religious formulae to slitting the throats of sacrificial victims. Unless an outlook premises the existence and interest of one or more supernatural beings, and claims that the utmost importance attaches to believing in them and responding to their requirements, it cannot be called a religion.[3]

This could be branded the 'standard view' of religion. It is the standard view that is attacked and the standard view that is defended. Relatively few people question the validity of the standard view itself.

The standard view is richly represented in the past history of religions and by the character of much of religion in the world today. Many people, religious and non-religious alike, assume that this is essentially what all religion is about. It is the kind of religion which millions of people nowadays continue to endorse, but which millions of others reject as intellectually incoherent, scientifically discredited or morally repugnant. What I am suggesting in this book is that this standard view of religion, whatever merits it may have had for past generations, fails to do justice to the real nature, and full potential, of religion (at all times and not just for people today).

The survival and even resurgence of religion in modern times is sometimes said to refute the claims of psychologists, sociologists and other experts that religion has been marginalized and will eventually be extinguished by secular modernity and modern science.[4] It is equally possible to argue, however, that many of the forms of belief and practice current nowadays are themselves the product of a secular and scientific mentality. Many of the more childish ideas about God, creation, salvation and so on proclaimed by 'believers' and ridiculed by 'unbelievers' are not so much relics of a primitive religious past as products of an age that has lost those traditions of knowledge and discrimination through which to think properly about religion.

Although the aim of the book is to question certain widely held attitudes to religion rather than any particular religious doctrines or practices, the criticism of general attitudes cannot always be clearly differentiated from the criticism of specific doctrines or practices – as the example of the Burmese treatment of the Rohingya people perhaps demonstrates. Inevitably, therefore, some of the criticisms made of how religious and non-religious people think about religion will at least raise questions about particular religious doctrines or practices. One would, for example, have to be an extreme cultural relativist not to think it appropriate to question the truth or value of those doctrines in Aztec religion that required mass human slaughter as part of its veneration of the gods.[5] Nor, to give a recent modern example, would civilized non-Muslims, along with many Muslims themselves, hesitate to condemn as both morally pernicious and profoundly un-Islamic the mentality of those Pakistani mobs who clamoured for the execution of a Christian woman for allegedly insulting the Prophet Muhammad.[6]

The horrors condoned or perpetrated by religious people, sometimes in the name of their religion, seem to some sceptics and critics reason enough not to have anything more to do with religion. But many of the people who are alienated by religion have backed away from it not because they have no interest in or instinct for religion but, on the contrary, because none of the forms of religion with which they are familiar seem able to satisfy this interest or instinct. This is why any worthwhile critique of religion should also be asking how it is that religion fails or disappoints so many people nowadays, and whether there are not, within the rich resources of the religious traditions, forms of religious experience, understanding and practice that avoid the narrow and narrowing forms of religiosity all too prevalent in the modern world.

Throughout this book I have kept the language as simple and straightforward as possible. The twelve chapters can be read either in sequence or, in any order, as self-contained essays. The first chapter, 'Religion Undefined', cautions against relying on any neat definition of religion, and recommends instead an approach that respects the irreducible diversity of religion and its various continuities with other human interests and concerns. Chapter Two, 'Overcoming Belief', questions the emphasis placed by religious and non-religious people alike on believing and beliefs, and suggests that belief is as liable to constrict as to nourish the religious life. Chapter Three, 'Religion as Practice', comments on the extremely varied range of activities performed in the name of religion – some of them purely instrumental, some of them expressive, some of them experimental, but many of them as purposeless as play or pleasure. Chapter Four, 'Religion as Theory', warns against over-determined and narrowly literalist interpretations of religious doctrine, emphasizing the provisional and pluralist nature of much religious teaching. The chapter mostly concentrates, however, on misconceptions about the nature and role of myth and symbol in religion. Chapter Five, 'In Experiences We Trust?', considers the claim that the ultimate explanation or justification of religion is to be found in those extraordinary foundational or confirmatory experiences associated with mystics, yogins, shamans, prophets and so on, but also suggests that such experiences can easily become the basis of what has been called 'experientialism' or 'spiritual materialism'. Chapter Six, 'Here Be Authorities and Institutions', reviews the sources of authority in religions (texts, leaders, experiences), and shows how religions easily become self-enclosed systems and institutions capable of stifling rather than supporting the religious aspirations of their members. Organization and institutionalization nevertheless constitute an inevitable dimension of religions as social entities.

Chapter Seven, 'No Good Being Religious', questions the nature of the commonly invoked link between religion and morality (and the consequent confusion of holiness with goodness). One of the chief arguments of the religious sceptic is that one does not have to be religious in order to be good. But who says that religion has anything more to do with 'being good' than has any other human activity? Chapter Eight, 'Idolatries Ancient and Modern', suggests that idolatry in religion comes less from venerating images and the like than from uncritical devotion, and even enslavement, to the ideas, practices and institutions that are meant to liberate and enlighten. Arguably, the ultimate idolatrous object is religion itself. Chapter Nine, 'Universality in Particularity', considers the tensions between the localizing and the universalizing tendencies in religions. In considering the plurality of religions, it argues not that 'all religions are one' but rather that each of them should be valued for its unique contribution to a common human legacy. Chapter Ten, 'The Cosmological Connection', aims to show that religion cannot be relegated to some safe space beyond rational or scientific criticism, as well-meaning apologists sometimes attempt to do. As 'maps for living and dying', religions embody coherent worldviews for the whole of life that should be able to hold their own against any of the secular worldviews or scientific cosmologies. Chapter Eleven, 'Losing Our Religion?', explores various modes of disaffection with religion, asking what it is that people risk losing when they lose religion. It suggests that to have doubts or reservations about religion is no reason for refusing some measure of participation in them. In thus participating, one is drawing upon the resources of the religious traditions that belong not to a particular group but to the whole of humanity. Chapter Twelve, 'Reinventing Religion', proposes that religions are best defended, and best criticized, as human constructions – constructions built up as responses to what is understood as the sacred or the transcendent. Religion can be thought of as the organization and application of our human response to the questions the universe, just by being there, poses for us all.

The majority of readers will follow the arguments in this book without needing to be aware of debates current in religious scholarship. The academic reader, however, may be alert to some of the methodological questions attending this scholarship. For this reason it is worth anticipating three points of criticism to which this book might well be subject, mostly relating to the use of the term 'religion' itself. To begin with, it may be pointed out that despite my reluctance explicitly to define religion, I do at least operate with an implicit definition, and that this is clearly one based on Western conceptions of the subject. Second, it may be observed, the concept of religion is itself a product of Western culture (as also would be any proposed definition of religion), one deriving from the post-Enlightenment study of religions. In many other cultures there are no real equivalents of the term 'religion', 'religious' ideas and practices not being separated out from all the other aspects of life. And third, even if we accept the inevitability and usefulness of the term 'religion', it may be further objected that the term encourages one to think of the various religions too substantively, that is to say, as monolithic entities with their own fixed identities, so that one is led into making monolithic statements of the form 'Buddhism teaches such-and-such,' or 'Christianity differs from Buddhism in this or that respect.' In reality, it will be urged, there is no such thing as Buddhism or Christianity, for example, but rather a plurality of Buddhisms and Christianities, or perhaps only a variety of groups and individuals all of whom identify themselves (or are identified by others) as 'Christians' or 'Buddhists'. In recent scholarship about religion, indeed, there are some who argue that religions – as distinct from particular religious ideas, practices, institutions and so on – do not exist in any real sense, being purely abstractions created in the minds of those who attend to those more particular things.[7]

Taking the last point first, what I would argue is precisely the opposite: that religions very much do exist, that they are constructions with distinct identities every bit as real as, for example, the existence and identity of the United States, the British monarchy or Amazon.com. Their real existence is not undermined by the fact that they are ever changing, or by the fact that they are abstract as well as physical entities, or by the fact that they depend for their very real existence in large part on the activities and intentions of human individuals. Indeed, many of the problems associated with religion come precisely from the fact that they do 'exist' in these various ways.

As regards the point that the concept of religion is an essentially Western one, one can accept this and yet still argue that it is a useful and even indispensable term for the study of those ideas, practices, experiences and institutions, universal throughout human history, whereby human beings have sought to relate themselves to a wider order of reality than the one immediately present.[8] The concept of religion is certainly not the only concept invented in Western culture in the last few centuries that has allowed people all over the world to understand universal aspects of human life more clearly. What, if anything, is peculiar to the Western mentality is the idea that one is forever trapped inside one's own culture, unable to make valid statements about any other. Taken to its logical conclusion, this kind of cultural relativism would prevent one even being able to study one's own past history. The past may indeed be a foreign country where they do things differently,[9] but noticing these differences is, surely, already a step towards understanding them. Naturally there is always a danger of imposing the categories and values of one's own culture on the cultures of others, but this risk is justified by the opportunity of enlarging one's ideas about humanity by finding cognates and parallels in these other cultures. Arguably, the greater danger comes from individuals in one culture refusing to look beyond its borders, or from stewing too long in its own narrow repertoire of ideas. It is precisely this kind of mentality that leads people to define their own religion partly in terms of their fear and ignorance of the religions of others.

This brings us back to the first of the objections itemized above. There are undoubtedly implicit conceptions of religion at work in this book. The identification of ideas, practices, experiences and institutions as the four basic 'dimensions' of religion is, perhaps, a clear sign of this. But a conception of religion is not quite a definition of it, definitions being less open or flexible than conceptions. A conception is more like a tool, a definition more like an artefact.

Behind the academic debates about conceptions and definitions of religion lies a question that in one way or another confronts anyone who thinks seriously about religion: can one hope (or even wish) to reach any real understanding of religion without making judgements about its truth or value? What might well be motivating those academics who object to the identification of 'religion' as a legitimate category, or to the use of 'religion' as the name for any kind of cultural entity or social institution, is a desire to avoid having to deal with questions about the truth of religion, or about the role of religion within their own and others' lives. Few if any of them would make equivalent objections to the use of the terms 'art', 'science', 'law' and other familiar cultural labels, all of them problematic in one way or another but none of them without real objects or legitimate uses.

ONE

RELIGION UNDEFINED

I t is an assumption all too easily made that anyone seeking to write a book on religion must be in possession of a definition. Definitions of religion, however, come in many forms and are more likely to prove troublesome than useful. A definition of anything will often tell us more about its author, or its author's preconceptions, than about the subject being defined. Many so-called definitions of religion are mere appropriations of the word to suit a particular argument, point of view or theory. In Henry Fielding's novel *Tom Jones*, for example, Parson Thwackum barely allows the word 'religion' to apply to any form of it apart from his own. The fact that there are many sects and heresies in the world, he says, does not make religion manifold: 'When I mention Religion, I mean the Christian Religion; and not only the Christian Religion, but the Protestant Religion; and not only the Protestant Religion, but the Church of England.'[1] Strictly speaking, this is a specification rather than a definition, but it shares with many definitions the attempt to wrap up the complex reality of life within a misleading simplicity.

At least the parson is making his prejudices explicit. Those who take definitions seriously, however, expect more from them than merely a statement of the author's starting point, however much broader this might be than Parson Thwackum's. They expect some kind of formula that separates the phenomenon (or phenomena) of religion from other phenomena with which it (or they) might be associated, or confused. Alternatively they expect some kind of insight into the essence or meaning of religion. The trouble with definitions of the first kind is that they tend to isolate religion from the very real connections it has with other human concerns, and with definitions of the second kind that they often turn out to be theories of religion in disguise. Perhaps definitions should come at the end of a book, if at all, and should ideally be the work of the reader rather than the author.

A review of some of the more influential definitions will nevertheless be useful in bringing home to us the diverse ideas about and attitudes to religion current in our culture, as well as in demonstrating how the various academic disciplines inevitably tend to privilege one aspect of religion over others. In many cases a particular definition of religion, although one-sided in itself, can prove a useful corrective to a definition which is one-sided in another direction. It will in any case be instructive to consider here a few examples.

The psychologist William James, whose particular interest in religion was in 'immediate personal experiences', defines religion as 'the feelings, acts, and experiences of individual men in their solitude, so far as they apprehend themselves to stand in relation to whatever they may consider the divine'. James is not saying that this is all there is to religion, since it is out of religion that 'philosophies, theologies, and ecclesiastical organizations may secondarily grow'.[2] His definition, rather, seeks to identify what for him is the basis or heart of religion, rather than to capture religion in all its complexity. In this, his definition is similar to several others. But it also illustrates the tendency of many definitions to kick the definitional can further down the road. In James's case, surely 'the divine' itself stands in need of definition. What is more, in referring to a person's 'consideration' of the divine, James implicitly includes ideas as well as feelings or experiences in his definition of religion.

A more fundamental but no less question-begging definition of religion in terms of personal experience is that of the eighteenth-century German theologian Friedrich Schleiermacher, for whom

'the essence of religion consists in the feeling of absolute dependence.'[3] This definition is not merely theistic (like James's definition)
but is specifically theological. It also anticipates James's emphasis
on 'passivity' as one of four principal marks of profound religious
experience (the others being ineffability, transience and noetic
character). Again, in Schleiermacher's as in James's definition it is
difficult to disentangle feelings from ideas, and in this respect Paul
Tillich's definition is both more accurate and more inclusive:
'Religion is the state of being grasped by an ultimate concern, a
concern which qualifies all other concerns as preliminary and
which itself contains the answer to the question of the meaning
of our life.'[4]

Tillich's definition exemplifies the tendency among scholars with greater knowledge of the diversity of world religions to
provide definitions that make room for non-theistic traditions
such as Buddhism, Jainism or Taoism, as well as for what Tillich
himself calls 'quasi-religions'.[5] These include secular ideologies
and their practical manifestations, such as communism, fascism
and nationalism.[6] Some critics have seen broad definitions like
Tillich's as overly comprehensive, avoiding the error of producing
a culturally provincial definition at the cost of including so much
in addition to religion as to raise all over again the question of
what is to count as a religion. Other writers have sought to avoid
this kind of problem by subsuming the concept of religion (itself
arguably a culturally provincial one) into the broader concept of
'worldview'[7] – a term to which I shall return in due course.

The definitions cited so far avoid any too specific conception
of the divine or of ultimate reality, presumably in the interests of
remaining as generic or as neutral as possible. For it is a manifest
defect of many of the more precise definitions that they mar-
ginalize certain types or examples of religion, if not excluding
them altogether. Just as in the world of publishing and book
reviewing, the use of the term 'non-fiction' suggests that 'fiction'
is what counts first or most, so in the worlds of religion and (until
relatively recently) of much religious scholarship do references
to 'non-theistic' or 'non-Christian' religions tend to imply that

theism and in particular Christianity somehow constitute the normative or even the most authentic forms of religion. This was, of course, Parson Thwackum's unashamed opinion.

Tillich's definition of religion, like those of James and Schleiermacher, clearly affirms the importance of experience, but unlike theirs makes it explicit that religion consists as much in ideas as in experiences. Other definitions give far more prominence to the ideas that drive religion, sometimes to the extent of making ideas, or beliefs, the core of religion. Perhaps the most concise example is anthropologist E. B. Tylor's definition of religion as 'Belief in Spiritual Beings'. This succeeds not only in narrowing religion to 'belief' but in narrowing the object (or objects) of belief to 'spiritual beings'. On the other hand, the role of experience is still recognized, at least to the extent that believing in something, or someone, is itself a form of experience. As an example of a more specifically intellectualist understanding of religion, one can cite the overtly theological definition offered by Tylor's contemporary James Martineau, for whom religion is 'belief in an ever-living God, that is, in a Divine Mind and Will ruling the Universe and holding moral relations with mankind'.[8] Since Tylor's and Martineau's day, definitions of religion in terms of ideas or symbols have become more sophisticated.

What is often lacking in definitions of religion is any explicit reference to ritual or behaviour. R. R. Marett, another nineteenth-century anthropologist, states that religion, psychologically regarded, is 'a form of experience in which feeling-tone is relatively predominant', and that what drives people into a relationship with the supernatural being is 'awe', which he identifies as a 'compound of fear, wonder, and negative self-feeling'. But he emphasizes a behavioural as well as an emotional and intellectual response to religious awe: 'My own view is that savage religion is not so much thought out as danced out.'[9] Marett thus links religious feelings as much with religious acts or activities as with religious ideas. William James, it is true, also includes 'acts' (unspecified) among the personal responses to the divine, but these do not necessarily correspond to the formal and communal rituals that come to the fore in other definitions. James Frazer emphasizes the active elements in religion in a definition that is also an explanation of religion. Religion for him is 'a propitiation or conciliation of powers superior to man which are believed to direct and control the course of Nature and of human life'.[10] For Anthony Wallace, similarly, religion is 'a set of rituals, rationalized by myth, which mobilizes supernatural powers for the purpose of achieving or preventing transformations of state in man or nature'.[11]

The desire to formulate a neat definition of anything inevitably tempts one into identifying some particular element that explains, or is the basis of, all the others. In the case of religion it may be certain types of experience, particular beliefs or ideas, or some kind of ritual act or behaviour. For some commentators, however, the key element in religion is a moral code or the moral instinct. Thus Immanuel Kant confidently proclaims that 'Religion is (subjectively considered) the recognition of all our duties as divine commands.'[12] Matthew Arnold defines religion, more vaguely, as 'ethics enkindled, lit up by feeling' or as 'morality touched by emotion'.[13] For Emile Durkheim, the moral element in religion is more social than individual. Religion for him represents the objectification of the shared values of a community: 'The religious force is only the sentiment inspired by the group in its members, but projected outside of the consciousnesses that experience it, and objectified.'[14] How different the emphasis here is from that of Durkheim's near-contemporary A. N. Whitehead, for whom 'Religion is what an individual does with his own solitariness . . . Thus religion is solitariness; and if you are never solitary, you are never religious.'[15] Definitions that locate religion in the head, so to speak, or which confine it to the privacy (or solitude) of the individual, both reflect and reinforce the tendency in Western culture to think of religion mainly in terms of individual choice or personal commitment.

The definitions presented hitherto are all definitions of religion as such or of religion in general; they are implicitly or explicitly predicated on the assumption that there is a single 'something' to be defined – a something to which a carefully formulated 'one size fits all' definition will be applicable. There is, however, an important distinction to be observed between the definition of 'religion' (religion as such or religion in general) and the definition of 'a religion' (a religion as a historically actualized or culturally manifested entity). Especially in more recent times, scholars of religion are inclined to regard substantive (essentialist) definitions as highly suspect, and instead to offer functionalist definitions of 'a religion'. The latter emphasize how religions work as historical, social or institutional entities. The modern academic study of religion, therefore, favours definitions of religion that emphasize its social aspects or functions. Sociological (or sociologically oriented) definitions of religion also tend to be 'safer' in that by concentrating on the observable social (and psychological) functions of religions they steer clear of attempting to identify, let alone evaluate, the object, origin or truth of religion. A much-quoted example is Melford Spiro's succinct definition of a religion as 'An institution consisting of culturally patterned interaction with culturally postulated superhuman beings'.[16] This might nevertheless be judged as little more than a sophisticated version of Tylor's substantive definition.

Perhaps the best-known sociological definition of (a) religion is the one offered by Durkheim, who describes a religion as 'a unified system of beliefs and practices relative to sacred things, that is to say, things set apart and forbidden – beliefs and practices which unite into one single moral community called a Church all those who adhere to them'.[17] The most convincing definitions of religion are those which, as in the examples cited from Spiro and Durkheim, seek to bring the discrete elements of religion together, even if one of them tends to be given priority. Likewise, for J. Milton Yinger, (a) religion is 'a system of beliefs and practices by means of which a group of people struggle with the ultimate problem of human life'.[18] A definition from Clifford Geertz spells out yet more explicitly the component dimensions of religion. A religion, he says, is

(1) a system of symbols which act to (2) establish powerful, persuasive, and long-lasting moods and motivations in men by (3) formulating conceptions of a general order of existence and (4) clothing these conceptions with such an aura of factuality that (5) the moods and motivations seem uniquely realistic.[19]

What is noteworthy about the definitions cited from Durkheim, Yinger and Geertz is that all of them make use of the term 'system'. This term can be applied to many things – to languages, ecosystems and transport networks, for example. A system is a complex whole comprising a number of distinguishable but interconnected elements or functions. It is the interaction of these elements or functions that makes a system more than simply the sum of its parts. Few if any systems are completely self-contained, and any given system is likely to interact or connect with other systems. Thus a transport system is likely to have an interface with another transport system as well as with, for example, the electrical system that provides lighting and motive power and the monetary systems that allow passengers to purchase tickets. There are, of course, closed systems whose behaviour is more or less predictable – the mechanism of a clock or watch, for example. But even a clock has to be wound up, or powered, from outside the system. Other systems are open systems, meaning that their behaviour and development are continuously subject to the unpredictable effects (positive or negative) of various external factors.

Religions (and the various denominations within them) are also instances of systems, and hence susceptible to systemic analysis. They are organized social entities that behave systemically, both internally and in their interaction with other cultural systems – for example, with political or educational systems. The systemic nature of a religion is as important a fact about it as are any of its particular elements. A systemic approach to religion encourages us both to appreciate the internal complexity of religions, or of any particular example of a religion, and to pay attention to the connections and continuities that link religious interests and activities with other human concerns.[20]

The internal complexity of religions, and of other cultural systems, can be usefully schematized in terms of 'aspects' or 'dimensions', terms which suggest that the parts can only be fully understood in relation to the whole. When we characterize a description or analysis of anything as 'one-dimensional' we declare its failure to comprehend the complexity that any proper account of its plural aspects or dimensions must accommodate. Even the standard two-dimensional characterization of religion as a 'system of beliefs and practices' acknowledges not only that religion comprises more than a single dimension but that the two dimensions in question are mutually conditioning. Beliefs affect practice, and practices affect belief. But whereas a one- or even a two-dimensional model of religion is liable to oversimplify the picture of a religion, dimensions can also be multiplied beyond necessity. The enumeration of more than a small set of dimensions is likely to obscure rather than illuminate its subject matter. The point of identifying dimensions is to provide a template, at once generic and neutral, within which the more particular (and culturally specific) elements of religion can be plotted, just as the dimensions of height, length and depth provide a template within which a variety of physical objects can be described or measured.

A good example of a four-dimensional structure for the analysis of religion, found in a number of textbooks, is the neatly alliterative quartet of creed, cult, code and community. In the case of the first two terms, the terminology is too culturally specific. 'Creed' sounds too Western, too Christian even, to serve as an appropriately generic term. The term 'cult' misleadingly implies worship as the paradigm religious activity.[21] The third term, 'code', arguably mistakes for a distinct dimension what is better seen as an example of the interaction of the two basic dimensions of theory and practice. The term 'community' is perhaps the only satisfactorily identified dimension here. What is perhaps most deficient in this set of dimensions, however, is that it neglects the dimension of religious experience.

In this book I recognize four broad dimensions: those of experience, practice, theory and institution (this latter term covering membership, organization and authority). Each of these dimensions embraces further, more specific elements, the life of a religion consisting in the complex and ever-changing relationship between them. Scholars and other observers may give priority to one dimension over another, for this or that particular purpose, but in reality these dimensions are inseparably interdependent. To take just one example, a thoroughgoing appreciation of sacred architecture would require one to understand how the shape and decoration of religious buildings reflected and at times stimulated changes in liturgical practice and popular piety, just as changes in the latter reflected and stimulated developments in doctrine. The development of sacred architecture is also influenced by demographic and political changes, not to mention advances in architectural construction and new artistic fashions. One has only to think of how changes in the design and decoration of medieval church buildings, evolving from the secular Roman basilica after the legalization of Christianity, led to new architectural spaces built to accommodate increasingly elaborate liturgical performances and the various practices associated with pilgrimage and the cult of relics. It might even be possible to show that there were connections between the shape and decoration of sacred buildings and the interpretations people give of the religious experiences they have within them.

The dimensional analysis either of religion in general, or of particular religions and denominations, can help free us from the temptation to search for some elusive essence or centre of religion or of some particular religion. At the very least the dimensional approach to religion encourages us to think of religious individuals – those who actually live by a religion – not simply as 'believers' but also as 'practitioners', 'experiencers' and 'adherents'. To live by a religion is to be engaged with ideas, experiences, practices and institutions, but the specific form these take and their mutual relationship will vary from one religious tradition to another, and within a given tradition from one period, culture and denomination to another. The dimensional approach also encourages us to see how religion varies from one adherent to another. For some adherents their religion may be largely a matter of ideas, for others chiefly a matter of practice. For some it may be focused on certain types of experience, while for others it may be valued mainly at the social level. Of course the views held about a religion by those who are actually living it will not necessarily be in harmony with the views of those merely observing it. And yet these observers must take into account, as facts about the religion they observe, the range of views that its various adherents actually express. One important question here is how the views and attitudes of individual adherents should be weighed against the 'official' statements about a religion made in sacred texts or by its leaders and representatives at any given time.

The broadly inclusive dimensions of theory, practice, experience and organization clearly characterize any and every kind of cultural system or institution. They do not in themselves identify what is (or may well be) *sui generis* about religion or serve to differentiate religion from other cultural systems or human concerns. It is the further specification within each dimension, and the relationships between these, that provides this differentiation. These deliberately broad dimensions simply provide a basic framework for the more detailed work of analysis and comparison. Superficially viewed, the observed structural similarities between, say, a religious tradition, an education system, a charitable foundation and an international bank might serve not only to dissipate the illusionary search for some essence or paradigm of religion but to obliterate everything distinctive about religion, everything that justifies the existence and use of this word in the first place. The value of these generic dimensions, however, is not only that they create a context for even-handed comparative analysis (of just the sort that people would expect if banks, charities or schools were being compared for any reason), but that they make explicit the systemic character of religions and the connections religions have with other cultural systems and institutions.

Thus a dimensional analysis of religion serves to remind us that religious systems are no different from other systems in respect of a host of general features – in respect of their complexity, their historical development, their internal politics and their relations with other systems. But to say that religions, as systemically complex human institutions, behave no differently from any other cultural system is to make no judgement about the truth or falsity of religious doctrines, the value or efficacy of religious practices, the authenticity of religious experiences, or the social and ethical effects of religion. Some religious people, however, will want to say that even if there are features of religions that sociologists and others are able to analyse and evaluate as they do any other kinds of human institution, it cannot be assumed that religions are exclusively human structures. Some of them, or even just one of them, might be in some sense divinely initiated or inspired.

Now if a religion really were considered to be divinely guided, how could one identify, and demonstrate to others, which elements of it were so guided and which elements were not? What is more, if systems and structures like religions can be divinely guided, why not other human institutions and systems too? After all, this is what many religious people themselves have (very selectively) claimed – as when a ruler, or the progress of a war, or the history of a nation, is held to be under divine guidance. What is more, those who claim their religion to be divinely guided or inspired (and to this extent at least partially exempt from the usual empirical and rational analysis) are quite likely to regard religions other than their own (or at least most of them) as all too human in their origins and evolution. By contrast, those who would see a guiding spirit at work in all religions (or at least in many if not most of them) are also likely to see this spirit in non-religious institutions as well as in explicitly religious ones. Either way, we come back to the point that religions, in so far as they are systems and institutions, cannot be treated any differently from the way any other cultural systems or institutions are treated. All are equally human, just as any of them might be said to be under some kind of 'divine guidance' (assuming that this idea makes sense in the first place).

The question nevertheless remains as to how religion is to be specified if not actually defined within human culture, and thereby differentiated from other human concerns and interests. In recognizing or identifying this or that idea, practice or experience as 'religious', however, we are under no more obligation to provide a neat or final definition of 'religion', or of 'a religion', than we are to give precise definitions when recognizing or identifying in any idea, practice, experience or institution the presence of, for example, art, science, politics or sport. We may argue constantly about what religion is or ought to be, but this is no different in kind from the arguments we also have about what art, science, politics or sport are or ought to be. Generally speaking we know when we are in the presence of these things, even when we hold back from applying labels and judgements. Why should we be under the obligation to define religion any more precisely than we are to define art or science, or politics or sport? This is not to say that questions about the definition of any of these things are invalid or uninteresting, but only that we can proceed with an examination of any of these concerns, and indeed engage with them in our personal lives, without the need for questions of definition to be settled in advance. One is not challenged at the door of an art gallery, science lecture, political meeting or sports venue for some definition that will explain or justify one's presence there.

Arguably we should, wherever possible, avoid the substantive 'religion' and rely more on the epithet 'religious'. Rather than struggling to define religion, or a religion, in such a way as to satisfy all interested parties, including the actual adherents of religions, it might well be easier to define what a religious idea is, as distinct from a philosophical or a scientific one, or a religious practice as distinct from a medical or educational practice, or a religious experience as distinct from an aesthetic or a psychic experience. If so, we must also accept that these things are not necessarily to be defined exclusively in terms of their presence or pursuit within a recognized religious tradition or institution. Religious ideas, practices and experiences are liable to crop up outside as well as within explicitly religious contexts.

A SOLUTION to the problem of the definition of religion more radical than the strategy of simply avoiding or postponing definition is the attempt to abolish the use of the term 'religion' altogether. Scepticism about the value or even meaning of the word takes many forms. A tendency to avoid the term is found among some religious people themselves, usually because of its popular associations with a particular type or manifestation of religion – with intolerance, narrow-mindedness, irrationality and all those other characteristics perhaps best summed up in the term 'religiosity'. Thus descriptions of someone as being 'very religious', or 'very pious', are not always intended as compliments or endorsements. Of course, those who do in fact display these characteristics are happy to describe themselves as 'religious' and perhaps to ask others if they too are 'religious'. In many contexts, however, the question 'Are you religious?' comes uncomfortably close to resembling trick questions such as 'Do you still beat your wife?' Whatever answer you give, you end up misrepresenting yourself.

The term 'religion' may be avoided where it is too closely identified with theistic religion, with obedience to or dependence upon God or the gods. For example, it is often said that Buddhism is not a religion but a philosophy, or a 'philosophy of life'. (In fact there is no less supernaturalism and reverence for supernatural beings in Buddhism than there is in any other religion.) Or it may be that Judaism, for example, is not a religion but a 'way of life'. 'Religion' sounds constraining and even life-denying, or too closely identified with the affirmation of creeds and doctrines, whereas 'way of life' sounds freer, richer and altogether more positive in its associations. So pervasive are the negative or at least narrower associations of the word 'religion' that it is likely that many if not most religious people, given the choice, would prefer to describe their own tradition as a way of life or even a philosophy of life than as a religion. It is rather like being asked whether one would prefer to come for a healthy meal or for a wonderful gastronomic experience.

One term sometimes proposed by those allergic to the term 'religion', or critical of religion particularly in its more organized or institutionalized forms, is 'spirituality'. In itself this somewhat vague term refers to the more intense or inward kinds of religious life, and to the practices and experiences associated with such a life, which makes it in many respects synonymous with the term 'mystical'. This certainly is how it is used in many religious traditions. If there is a contrasting term, it would probably be 'religiosity'. For many people, therefore, the term is less a substitute for 'religion' and more a name for what are considered the most valuable forms or essential features of religion. In more recent contexts, however, the term 'spirituality' has come to be used in a way that is, implicitly or explicitly, critical of religion understood as a socially organized (and sometimes politically connected) system of beliefs and practices. Spirituality is seen as the pristine pearl too valuable to be left imprisoned within the dull and often ugly oyster of 'organized religion'. And so people are liable to say that while they do not subscribe to any religion, and may even say that they are against religion, they do nevertheless follow a spiritual path or affirm a spiritual view of life. What many of those affirming a religion-free spirituality often fail to appreciate, however, is that the great 'spiritual' figures in all religions have lived their lives nourished by the traditions and disciplines of organized religion.

Whatever reasons religious people themselves may have for avoiding the term 'religion', scholars too have come to question it. On the one hand are those who consider the subject matter real enough but the term 'religion' unsuitable as a generic label for it, and on the other those who question the existence of the alleged subject matter itself, seeing not just our commonly assumed ideas about religion but religions themselves as cultural constructs. Let us consider each of these positions in turn.

Although its precise etymological origins are unclear, the word 'religion', from the Latin *religio*, derives from the social obligations and outward observances of Roman religion.[22] This, along with its close historical connections with Judaism and Christianity (including the fact that many leading thinkers on religion have come from a Judaeo-Christian culture), renders 'religion' unsuitable as a generic term in the eyes of many modern scholars.[23] Such scholars additionally point out that in many cultures there is no obvious or comparable word for religion, or that religious concerns are not demarcated from other concerns as they tend to be, or have come to be, in the Christian (and secular) West. What outsiders may pick out as religion is an integral part of a total culture. But while many scholars have come to question the term 'religion', they have difficulty in avoiding it because it is so deeply embedded in our language and there appears to be no obvious alternative. Indeed, for them, the subject matter of religion appears comparable to the status of the works of Shakespeare in the quip that these works were written not by Shakespeare but by another person of the same name.[24] In having its origin and development in a particular cultural context, however, the word 'religion' is just like any other word. Nor is the generic usefulness or authenticity of a particular word or concept undermined by the fact that it has no existence or equivalent in some cultures. No doubt those who first visited or settled in the Galápagos Islands lacked the concept of, or a word for, 'evolution'. All generic terms have specific origins that they never quite shake off, but allowances can be made for this in critical judgements. This is true not only of 'religion' but of the term 'magic', which is often contrasted with religion,[25] as well as of terms such as 'holy', 'sacred', 'spiritual', 'divine', 'supernatural', 'transcendental' and many others.

It it is naive and unrealistic to imagine that we can do without a generic word for the undeniably varied forms of engagement with supernatural powers and transcendental realities intended by the word 'religion'. The fact is that no one has yet come up with a more acceptable alternative generic term for the phenomenon or phenomena in question. There is a lot to be said for the relatively new term 'worldview', the main virtue of which is that it includes, without generating borderline cases, any theory about the place and role of humanity within the universe, irrespective of whether or not any kinds of supernatural being play a major or minor or indeed any role whatsoever. If one is interested in religion mainly for its ideas, and for its relationship with other philosophies or cosmologies (such as are excluded by some definitions of religion), then 'worldview' is an ideal term within which to subsume the various religions together with all those ideologies, quasi-religions and philosophies of life on which the term 'religion' does not sit comfortably, if at all. But religions, as I have emphasized, are far more than just belief systems or philosophies of existence, and so, whatever its merits as a generic term in its own right, its use as a substitute for 'religion' represents as much a narrowing as it does a broadening of the subject matter.

Definitions of anything ideally serve to separate the relevant from the irrelevant, and to give us a benchmark for making judgements of one kind or another. There will always be borderline cases, but these can function as much to confirm as to confound distinctions made between different kinds of things. Some things just cannot be defined, or cannot be defined in a way that will clarify rather than confuse our understanding of them. Religion, along with other fundamental human interests – art, science or sport, for example – appears to be one of these undeniable things. According to one ancient writer, Plato's definition of man as a 'featherless biped' was challenged when Diogenes the Cynic arrived bearing a plucked chicken. Like plucked chickens, religions are of natural origin and human construction combined, while even a casual reading of history shows us just how tightly interconnected religion has always been with politics, philosophy, science, art, sport and much else, none of which are very easy to define. Meanwhile, serious people from very different religious traditions continue to recognize in one another's traditions the presence of what they affirm in their own as the religious, the spiritual, the sacred or the transcendental.

TWO

OVERCOMING BELIEF

P eople generally define religion, or think of religion, as consisting of both beliefs and practices. More often than not, however, it is the beliefs that are thought to come first – as indeed they do in the familiar phrase 'beliefs and practices'. Not only do the beliefs come first, but the practices are thought to come as a result of the beliefs. Holding or affirming certain beliefs is what many people think of as the basis or even essence of religion: for example, believing in God or the gods or believing in their existence. On this view, those who fear or love or worship God or the gods do so as a consequence of believing in them, or of affirming their existence. Likewise, on this view, Buddhists practise meditation because they believe in enlightenment, or because they believe that enlightenment is a possible attainment. Religious practices, in other words, are seen as dependent on beliefs, if not as the direct applications of beliefs.

In line with this, religious people are typically seen, and very often see themselves, as being, above all, 'believers'. To be religious is to believe, or to believe in, this or that doctrine. By the same token, when people describe themselves (or others) as not religious, what they usually mean is that they (or others) lack or reject the beliefs, along with the belief-inspired behaviour, of those who *are* religious. Thus non-religious persons are commonly described as 'non-believers' or 'unbelievers', or in more secular terms as 'sceptics'. For many people, whether religious or non-religious, religion starts, and very often also ends, in the head.

This emphasis on belief, in so far as it gives priority to the intellectual dimension of religion, is a phenomenon of modern times. Throughout most of human history, and in many places still today, belief (in the sense of intellectual affirmation) was not the principal basis or justification of religion. Practice, experience and community are dimensions of religion no less important, and in many ways more important, than the intellectual or theoretical dimension. Thus as well as being 'believers', or instead of being 'believers', religious people should be seen as practitioners, experiencers (and experimenters) and adherents: members of communities or followers of traditions. It is true that in some religious traditions creedal statements and intellectual formulations have been given more importance than in others, and this is especially the case with Christianity. Since theories and definitions of religion have mostly emerged in the Christian West, with Christianity itself taken as the model for the nature of religion in general, it is hardly surprising that belief-centred views of religion became so dominant, among religious and non-religious people alike.

The emphasis on belief, however, not only reflects a one-sided if not impoverished view of religion. It also fosters a false understanding of belief itself. What one might call the religious tendency to believe in beliefs reinforces the tendency to define religion as a whole in terms of beliefs. We can begin to understand how these tendencies have come about by taking a closer look at the term 'belief' itself.

TRACING THE USAGE of the English words 'belief' and 'believe' back through European language and literature is very revealing of trends in the history of ideas. The verb 'believe' derives from the Middle English *beleven* or *beleuen*, the prefix *be-* having replaced the prefix *ge-* of older English forms such as *gelefen*, *geliefan*, *gely-fan*. There are parallel words in other languages. These words have the meaning of 'holding dear'. In modern German *belieben* still means to hold dear, to value or to prize. The Teutonic root from which they all stem, *leub* or *leubh*, means 'to like' or 'to love', and from it we get familiar modern words such as the English *love* and the German *liebe*. The now archaic English word *lief*, meaning 'dear', derives from the same root through Middle English *leef* and Anglo-Saxon *leof*. From the same root comes the modern English word 'leave', via the Anglo-Saxon *leaf*, 'permission'. The older, literal meaning here is 'pleasure', so that the expression 'by your leave' means 'with or by your permission', or more literally 'by or at your pleasure'. Related Latin forms include *libet*, 'it pleases', and *libido*.

What is important here is that the original sense of the word 'belief' is not (yet) the modern one of holding something to be true or hypothesizing as to its truth. The same applies to the unrelated Latin verb *credere*, with *credo* typically translated as 'I believe'. Literally 'I set my heart on', *credo* has, like *believe*, originally more to do with pledging allegiance or committing oneself than with asserting the truth of propositions. Nearer to the modern idea of belief was the Latin word *opinio*, a supposition, the source of our word 'opinion', which now tends to express merely a preference or 'point of view'. Someone may say, apologetically, 'It's only my opinion,' or more critically, 'That's just *your* opinion.' It would sound rather odd to talk of a deeply held opinion. The phrase 'public opinion' often implies something fickle or biddable. The term 'opinionated' speaks for itself. Belief is accorded greater status than mere opinion. What belief originally meant was something involving primarily the heart, will or passions, a word that made sense mainly in contexts having to do with personal loyalty and commitment, or with any of the varieties of love. One of these contexts, and probably the main one, was religion.

But the word 'belief' undergoes a gradual shift in meaning. Originally expressing a range of personal attitudes connected with love, loyalty and personal commitment, it gradually acquires a more impersonal, propositional meaning. To represent this schematically, we might say that there is a shift from believing, or believing in, a person, first to believing in a person's word (generally), then to believing in a person's particular utterance, and finally to believing the truth of statements or propositions considered independently of the person uttering them. At this point the usage of the noun 'belief' becomes ambiguous. It may refer to the personal 'act' of believing, or believing in, someone or something (which is more or less a continuation of its original meaning), or it may refer to some proposition or doctrine that is a possible *object* of belief (for anyone). This in turn leads to talk about choosing, willing or even trying to believe something. It is this sense of belief that is parodied by Lewis Carroll in *Through the Looking-glass*, when the White Queen upbraids Alice for not trying hard enough to believe the impossible:

> Alice laughed. 'There's no use trying,' she said: 'one *can't* believe impossible things.'
>
> 'I daresay you haven't had much practice,' said the Queen. 'When I was your age, I always did it for half-an-hour a day. Why, sometimes I've believed as many as six impossible things before breakfast.'[1]

This passage has been quoted by critics of religion to illustrate the kind of mental gymnastics supposedly performed by religious believers in asserting ideas or doctrines seemingly at odds with common sense or scientific knowledge.

Religious apologists too have sometimes taken pride in the supposed irrationality of their beliefs, often citing in support of their position (as if an irrational position could ever find support) a 'maxim' wrongly attributed to the early Christian apologist Tertullian (*c*. 160–225): 'I believe because it is absurd.' Tertullian's original statement, 'It is certain, because impossible,' is not actually a statement about 'believing' at all (nor was it intended as any kind of maxim). By the seventeenth century the 'maxim' had been personalized into 'I believe because it is impossible' (*credo quia impossibile*) and then further distorted by the rationalist philosopher Voltaire into 'I believe because it is absurd' (*credo quia absurdum*). Voltaire's version was intended to parody the mindset of religious people, which ironically it all too often accurately represented, and still does.[2]

In its original sense, belief was closely related to faith, which translates the Greek *pistis* and the Latin *fides*, the theological meanings of which relate more to religious experience than to intellectual formulation. In religious contexts especially, however, faith tends to get lumped together with belief in the modern, propositional sense. As Mark Twain cynically remarks, 'Faith is believing what you know ain't so.'[3] For the more hostile critics of religion, of course, faith means something more sinister than hypocrisy – unquestioning and often fanatical belief in the truth of irrational doctrines:

> Faith is an evil precisely because it requires no justification and brooks no argument . . . If children were taught to question and think through their beliefs, instead of being taught the superior virtue of faith without question, it is a good bet that there would be no suicide bombers.[4]

Belief in its original range of meanings – faith, trust, love, loyalty – is an essentially personal activity or impulse. One can have faith only in persons, not in propositions. One cannot genuinely love or put one's trust in propositions, or be loyal to them. Nor can one believe someone else's beliefs any more than one can remember someone else's memories. But when belief becomes objectified or reified – when believing turns into the affirming of truths or propositions – then the way is open to an understanding of beliefs as impersonal propositions that are available for anyone to affirm or deny. Other people's reified beliefs, like other people's reified memories, can then be adopted at second hand.

It is beliefs as propositions that people have chiefly in mind when defining or thinking about religion, and in many cases when practising it. Beliefs are those ideas, principles or propositions which, or in which, we believe. We use the noun 'belief', and especially its plural 'beliefs', to turn the personal activity of believing into something impersonal, 'a belief' being understood as an idea or proposition that can be considered, adopted, rejected, criticized and so on, independently of any particular person's investment in it. This means that, in religion as in other areas, people may go through life accepting or rejecting ready-made beliefs (or entire belief systems) off the peg, so to speak. Belief in this abstracted and impersonal sense is about as different from the original act or experience of believing as selecting a frozen fish fillet from a super-market shelf is from catching a living fish swimming in the sea.[5]

Implicit within the modern word 'belief' is the familiar distinction between 'belief in' and 'belief that'. The usage of belief *in* something or someone is closer to the older sense of belief, the personal and volitional sense. The usage of belief *that*, on the other hand, expresses the later, propositional sense of belief. The coex-istence, and sometimes confusion, of these two usages reflects the fact that belief in either sense presupposes a believer. There must always be a believer, either to believe in somebody or something, or to believe that this or that is the case. In practice, however, the distinction between 'belief in' and 'belief that' is not clear-cut. In many contexts the expression 'believe in' is used in the sense of 'believe that'. Thus to say that one believes *in* ghosts is more or less the same as saying that one believes *that* ghosts exist. In other contexts, ranging from belief in astrology to belief in democracy, *belief in* suggests something more than simply the propositional sense of belief (belief that such and such is the case). To believe in democracy is not, trivially, merely to acknowledge the existence of democracy or democratic institutions, but rather to affirm that democratic institutions should exist, that democracy is something to be valued and upheld (even when, indeed especially when, its institutions do *not* exist).

On the other hand, the question 'Do you believe in God?' is taken by most people nowadays to be a question about belief understood in the propositional sense (that is, 'Do you believe that God exists?'). Other terms, such as trust or faith, will be used to signal the element of personal commitment or attachment (to God) such as characterized the original usage of the word *belief.* Naturally the older sense of belief survives in much of our belief talk. When you tell someone you believe in them, this is the older sense unalloyed. In many situations, however, *belief in* and *belief that* are not easy to differentiate. In a court of law, for example, believing or disbelieving a witness's statements is partly a matter of assessing these statements in the light of the evidence (believing that) and partly a matter of trusting in the individual's character and reputation (believing in).

So pervasive in modern culture is the propositional sense of belief that we may find it difficult to imagine that things were ever different. People in earlier epochs did not go around believing or asserting that God or the gods existed (or did not exist) in the way that many religious believers and non-believers are wont (or assumed) to do nowadays. That they do so nowadays is in part due to intellectualizing tendencies within religion itself and in part a response to sceptical and scientific attacks upon religion, in which the agenda is set up in terms of factual and theoretical propositions.

In a now predominantly secular culture, religious people seek to engage with sceptics and critics by deploying what purports to be a language of universal and neutral rationality, involving belief-statements, truth-claims, evidential appeals and so forth. This works its way into every stream of popular culture, from the sublime to the ridiculous. Thus it is no surprise to come across questions on the Internet about whether the ancient Greeks ever climbed Mt Olympus to see if there were any gods there, or about what happened when they discovered there were none there.[6] Those who pose this kind of question have not stopped to consider that devotees of the Olympian gods, whatever the nature of their belief in these gods, might have regarded any such expedition as an impiety. Nor, perhaps, are they acquainted with the many examples from Greek mythology of mortals coming to grief by getting too close to the gods. It is not so much the ancient Greek 'believers' as the modern Internet sceptics who are casting the Olympian gods in their own image. For the ancient Greeks, religion was more a matter of belief *in* their gods as manifested in natural forces and human psychology than belief *that* the gods existed as empirically verifiable entities.

In earlier periods, as in much of the world still today, talk about God or the gods was roughly on a par with modern talk about democracy or evolution. In our own times, the number of those who would seriously examine or challenge the ideal of democracy or the theory of evolution is far outweighed by the number of those for whom these things are simply taken for granted. It is also fair to say, however, that in Greek as in other ancient societies there were always those who expressed sceptical views about the existence (or, perhaps, the reality or the power) of the gods, just as there were philosophers and other writers who asked questions about what kind of beings the gods were, and so on.[7]

An ironic twist in the process of the reification of religious belief is that the adherents of this or that religious tradition or community are expected, or even required, to affirm this or that set of beliefs as part of their personal commitment to the religion in question. Where this requirement is institutionalized, and even enforced by the institution in question, we can talk about a particular belief or doctrine being or becoming a dogma – something that has to be believed. The idea of being expected, or obliged, to hold this or that particular belief is no less grotesque than being expected, or obliged, to like or to love some particular person or thing. Thus it is inevitable that religious people are commonly represented as, or are expected to be, dogmatic, uncritical or narrow-minded in their views about life, largely because it is assumed that they have let others do their thinking for them. A person who does not conform to this image is often made out to be uncharacteristically open-minded for a religious believer. 'She's a Catholic, but not at all dogmatic,' someone might say. Of course, popular views about religion and religious adherents can be just as dogmatic or narrow-minded as the views of some religious adherents themselves. That this is so is part and parcel of the process of the reification of religious belief.

HOW, THEN, are we to locate and value belief within the life of religion? In religion, as in other spheres of human life, belief (believing) and beliefs (ideas, doctrines, theories) are surely indispensable. The beliefs which, or the beliefs in which, religious believers are assumed or observed to believe are naturally identified with the doctrines of whatever religion is in question, or at least are identified as personal versions of a religion's official creeds and doctrines. All religions have formal doctrines of some sort. And surely, it will be said, all religions *need* doctrines, as part of the way in which they articulate and communicate their practical teachings and way of life. What, then, is so misguided about religious people believing, or believing in, these doctrines? Why should we hesitate to describe beliefs as doctrines or indeed doctrines as beliefs? Why should we refrain from describing religions as creeds or faiths, or even as 'belief systems'? When we talk about Buddhist or Christian beliefs, are we not talking about the same thing as Buddhist or Christian doctrines? Such questions bring us to the heart of the issue, compelling us to scrutinize both the nature of the doctrines in which one might believe and the nature of believing itself.

To illustrate the pitfalls of belief in doctrines, let us take as an example the Hindu Vedanta doctrine of the identity of the individual self with the universal self – or, more accurately perhaps, the doctrine of the non-duality or non-difference (*advaita*) of the individual and the universal self. What would it mean for someone to believe, or believe in, this doctrine? One might read about it, hear about it, be attracted to it, investigate its linguistic and other expressions, follow it up through its various exponents, engage in practices likely to reveal its truth, and so on. This process might eventually result in one's realization of the truth of the doctrine (or one's rejection of it). But simply believing in the truth of this doctrine in the abstract would not bring its truth home to one personally, although one might be foolish enough to assume that it can be realized simply by being affirmed. One might, of course, rightly come to recognize that some other person had realized it – a teacher of some kind, or a follower of such a person – but the danger here is that one might then substitute acknowledgement of another's realization for the need to realize it oneself. The language of belief is not necessarily obstructive of one's realization of religious truths or realities, but it is all too easy to substitute for personal engagement with religious ideas and practices the mere representations of these things in the form of doctrines and of a belief in doctrines. Although doctrines are necessary, they are also dangerous because all too easily they become objects of belief. Believing in the universal Self is one thing, believing in doctrines about the universal Self another.

The dangers posed by what might be called the wrong kind of believing are not limited to any particular religion or type of religion. These dangers occur wherever religious adherents allow beliefs to become ends in themselves. Graham Greene, writing about Roman Catholic believers, could be talking about believers from any tradition, *mutatis mutandis*, when he refers to

> the piety of the educated, the established, who seem to own their Roman Catholic image of God, who have ceased to look for Him because they consider they have found Him. Perhaps Unamuno had these in mind when he wrote: 'Those who believe that they believe in God, but without passion in their heart, without anguish of mind, without uncertainty, without doubt, without an element of despair even in their consolation, believe only in the God Idea, not in God Himself.'[8]

As I shall endeavour to show in the next chapter, the doctrines of a religion are not there simply to be believed or believed in, but rather to be lived and lived in. Religious doctrines, somewhat like scientific theories, are not static entities to be fixed, framed and uncritically revered for ever after. Doctrines are human constructions, the product of much thought and experience but also capable of yielding further ideas and insights. If they are not treated in this way, they are likely to become barriers to both thought and action.

What is more, to treat doctrines as beliefs in a narrow, propositional sense creates problems for 'believers' and 'unbelievers' alike. Those who are drawn to, or simply interested in, a particular tradition may feel they cannot identify with it, or participate in it, if they do not or cannot accept without question or reservation all the doctrines of this tradition. It would be like joining a club without signing up to all its rules and regulations. They have been encouraged to think that belief or beliefs must be the clinching factor, and that full subscription to the doctrines of a tradition is the necessary condition for any meaningful relationship with that tradition. But suppose the clinching factor were not belief but something closer to love or faith, or perhaps simply profound attraction or sincere interest? Would not people who hesitated or refused to join others in a church, temple or meditation hall on the grounds that they did not or could not subscribe to the relevant beliefs be acting as oddly as people who, say, hesitated to visit an art gallery or concert hall on the grounds that they did not subscribe to the aesthetic theories associated with the works being exhibited or performed?

A corresponding dilemma might well confront existing adherents of a religion who, if they cannot believe in some particular doctrine wholeheartedly or without reservation, might see themselves, or fear being seen by others, as insincere or hypocritical. It is just as likely, however, that the unwavering certainty about this or that doctrine proclaimed by some religious believers in fact manifests a form of repressed doubt. And it is probable that many others in fact harbour the kinds of doubts or reservations to which Unamuno refers. The real question here is why in any case belief should require or imply absolute certainty. What would be so bad about people half-believing, or even trying out a belief – make-believing if you like – rather than swallowing a doctrine or belief whole, uncritically and with no further question? This idea of provisional belief (which one might also call 'constructive belief') is not far removed from the sentiment informing Anselm of Canterbury's famous statement: 'I do not seek to understand so that I may believe, but I believe so that I may understand.'[9] Likewise, for one who is puzzled or sceptical about Cubist art, it would surely be more constructive to visit an exhibition of Cubist art, in order to test one's responses to it, than to avoid putting oneself in the presence of such art. Should religions not make greater room for, or at least more readily acknowledge the existence of, what has been called non-doxastic faith – the kind of belief that is sincere but provisional, uninformed but desirous of being informed, that in fact represents the realistic position of all those who do not have direct, mystical knowledge of religious truth?

The Buddhist tradition provides a clear example of how belief, both as doctrine and as commitment, can exist in healthy balance with the kind of scepticism and experimentation that characterizes most forms of constructive human activity. Anyone familiar with Buddhism knows that it has a very strong intellectual tradition, both philosophical and scholastic. But there is also a place for belief, both 'belief that' and 'belief in'; right view (*samma ditthi*) and right intention (*samma sankappa*) are the first two stages of the eightfold path to enlightenment. In particular, faith or trust in the Buddha as teacher is recognized as having an important role in the initial stages of the path. All of this, however, is balanced by a healthy scepticism about the value both of received views and of intellec-tual formulations, a major obstacle on the path being identified as the clinging to idle or speculative views. In Buddhism, as in other traditions, many adherents do undoubtedly become *believers* in the narrower sense I have been questioning, fixated on this or that aspect of Buddhism, or indeed believing in 'Buddhism' itself. Buddhism, like any other tradition, has generated ideas and doc-trines which, or in which, people are all too eager to believe in some absolute way. Yet the tradition is clear that the doctrine (*dhamma*) is more like a method or a path than a set of fixed or ready-made answers. One can find similar views in other traditions concern-ing the relative, provisional or instrumental nature of religious doctrines. The Jaina tradition, with its principle of *anekāntavāda* ('many-sidedness'), stands out, perhaps even more than the Buddhist tradition, in making scepticism about the finality of any doctrinal statement an integral part of its approach to religious truth.[10]

CRITIQUES OF 'wrong' as distinct from 'right' ways of believing are commonplace in most religious traditions, but generally are not intended to challenge the value of belief itself. In many contexts belief is positively valued, especially those forms or expressions of it involving love, loyalty or trust, or what is often called faith rather than (mere) belief. There is, however, a more radical critique of belief, which looks beyond the danger posed by doctrine as belief to the dangers inherent in the activity of believing itself. The same critique can be levelled at belief in other areas of human life, science and politics being perhaps the two most obvious. Let us look finally, then, at the idea that belief as such can spell trouble.

Of course there are things we must believe, usually tacitly or unconsciously, in order to go about our daily lives and to make the best of them. And of course belief in people and in causes (especially those involving the needs of others) is good, even when people or causes let us down. But both *belief in* and *belief that* can be impoverishing as well as enriching. Believing can act as a barrier to true thinking, or constitute a form of idolatry that obscures openness to the immediacy and complexity of the real world. This would of course apply to non-religious and anti-religious belief just as much as to religious belief. One is reminded of this in Tom Stoppard's play *Jumpers*, where (in Act 2) his character Professor Moore (named, it seems, after the philosopher G. E. Moore) suggests that atheism could be thought of 'as a sort of *crutch* for those who can't bear the reality of God'.[11]

Worst of all is when people start believing other people's beliefs, or, what is slightly different (though often connected), when they start believing unreservedly *in* their own or others' beliefs, or in some institutional expression of those beliefs (doctrines). Of course a particular belief or the effect of a particular belief might be benign or at least neutral in character. But it is not so much the thing believed or believed in that is likely to be damaging (for example, 'capital punishment' or 'organic gardening'), but rather the particular attitude represented by the believing – that of an uncritical acceptance that rules out objections and alternatives. Belief here is the conviction that one has arrived at a solution to a question that one does not need to think about further. The tendency to rigid and unquestioning belief is likely to be reinforced when beliefs are shared within a community that sees itself as 'under siege' from those with different views of the world.

That there is something wrong with any unexamined or uncritically held belief, even when it is a 'true' belief, is pointed out by the Danish philosopher Søren Kierkegaard:

> There is a view of life which conceives that where the crowd is, there is also the truth, and that in truth itself there is need of having the crowd on its side. There is another view of life which conceives that wherever there is a crowd there is untruth, so that (to consider for a moment the extreme case), even if every individual, each for himself in private, were to be in possession of the truth, yet in case they were all to get together in a crowd – a crowd to which any *decisive* significance is attributed, a voting, noisy, audible crowd – untruth would at once be in evidence.[12]

What is frightening about a slogan-chanting crowd is not so much the particular sentiments expressed but the mentality represented by the chanting.

So far I have been giving a critique of the misuse of belief. But what if belief itself, belief as such, were the problem? According to the Indian teacher Jiddu Krishnamurti, 'a mind that is filled with beliefs, with dogmas, with assertions, with quotations, is really an uncreative mind; it is merely a repetitive mind.' Much of the motivation for clinging to belief comes from fears of loneliness, failure, emptiness. It is to escape from such fears that 'we accept beliefs so eagerly and greedily'.

> And, through acceptance of belief, do we understand ourselves? On the contrary. A belief, religious or political, obviously hinders the understanding of ourselves. It acts

as a screen through which we are looking at ourselves. And can we look at ourselves without beliefs? If we remove those beliefs, the many beliefs that one has, is there anything left to look at? If we have no beliefs with which the mind has identified itself, then the mind, without identification, is capable of looking at itself as it is – and then, surely, there is the beginning of the understanding of oneself.[13]

Of all the critics of belief, Krishnamurti stands out as the one with the most radical and challenging views. His criticisms also raise logical or at least logistical questions, and even the suspicion that refusing belief of any kind can itself become a dogma. Certainly for some of the followers of Krishnamurti, a teacher who eschewed systems and did not want followers, the rejection of beliefs and doctrines becomes in itself a perverse kind of belief or doctrine. Surely a healthier approach is to see religious doctrines for what they are, namely as human constructions and expressions in response to significant events and experiences. Bearing in mind that we are not talking about belief in the trivial or mundane sense necessary for the decisions of daily living, the easiest option is to say that whether belief is good or bad depends upon who or what is the 'subject' or 'object' of belief.

Krishnamurti's strictures on belief nevertheless offer a welcome corrective to uncritical thinking about belief. Leaving aside the specific case of religious belief, there are many people who regard belief as somehow a good thing in itself. The trouble with so-and-so, one will hear it said, is that he doesn't believe in anything. Or, in a more question-begging way, people may think of belief as inevitable. You've got to believe in *something*, they may say. But to concede this is already to open the door to alternatives. *Have* you got to believe in something? Is it possible that belief is *not* in itself a good thing? Is it possible to do *without* belief? Is there something in the nature of belief and believing that makes it a bad (or at least potentially dangerous) thing, however unavoidable in the real world, rather than a good thing, and which ideally we should be able to do without? A key question, in any case, is this: does the value of belief depend on what is believed or believed in, or does it depend on something in the nature of belief itself?

Perhaps the best advice, then, is to be wary of believing and of beliefs – both one's own beliefs and those of others. All too often belief is belief at second or even third remove. One would do well to avoid believing in this or that creed, formulation or doctrine as constituting some fixed, final or unquestionable truth. Religious doctrines are abstractions, and as such can also be distractions – distractions from real things that really matter. It is fine and proper to believe in whomever or whatever deserves or demands our belief, faith or loyalty, but not so fine merely to believe in their abstract representations. Above all, just as one should avoid being in love with love itself, so one would do well to steer clear of believing in belief itself. Those who do so (as all of us do to a greater or lesser extent) are like someone in need of a holiday who spends all their time collecting and reading travel agents' brochures without ever leaving home.

THREE

RELIGION AS PRACTICE

Karen Blixen, in her autobiographical memoir *Out of Africa*, recalls an occasion when a servant, Kitau, came to her, after only three months of service, asking for a letter of recommendation to take to a local Muslim employer. Asked why, he explained that he had decided to spend three months with a Christian followed by three months with a Muslim, so that by observing 'the ways and habits' of each he could make up his mind which of the two religions to adopt. As Blixen wryly comments, 'I believe that even an Archbishop, when he had had these facts laid before him, would have said, or at least have thought, as I said: "Good God, Kitau, you might have told me that when you came here."'[1]

This anecdote nicely illustrates two important points about the relationship between theory and practice in religion. The first is that one's actual behaviour will more often than not fall short of the ideals and principles by which one professes to live, and sometimes indeed will blatantly contradict them. This is hardly news, but it does underline the point about the limited value of believing per se. Thus one might affirm a belief in the virtue of charity while remaining persistently uncharitable in one's own behaviour. The second point is the more important: namely, that it is possible to adjust one's behaviour to a set of ideals or principles without any real connection or long-term commitment to them. One might perform charitable acts out of self-interest or to signal one's virtues to others rather than out of any genuine concern for or empathy with others. These two points reduce to the questions of hypocrisy and insincerity, which are often cited by people as reasons for their alienation from religion or for their cynicism about it. That religious people do not practise what they preach, or that they do good only to impress others or because they are fearful of divine punishment or an unhappy rebirth, are familiar accusations made by critics of religion. Such criticisms, of course, are not uniquely applicable to religious people.[2] There is also the more basic point that people fail to live up to their ideals and obligations through weakness of will rather than insincerity or hypocrisy. The parent addicted to nicotine who tells a son or daughter to give up smoking is not necessarily a hypocrite.

That it is by one's actions rather than by what one says or believes (or says one believes) that one should be judged in life is a maxim applicable in religion no less than in any other sphere. This can easily lead to various kinds of anti-intellectualism or at least to scepticism about the role or importance of ideas and beliefs. Ideas and beliefs are nevertheless crucial to understanding the way people act in the world. People generally have motives for the actions they perform, and actions planned or performed are typically explained or justified in terms of ideas or beliefs of some kind. Thus when we focus on any kind of religious practice we shall do well to pay attention also to the ideas associated with it. As we saw in the previous chapter, however, the role of ideas and beliefs in religion is often given too much emphasis or the wrong kind of emphasis.

Many if not most definitions of religion make reference to practices as well as beliefs, but this is often with the implication that the practices represent expressions, or applications, of the beliefs. Things are not always that simple, however. In some cases beliefs, doctrines or theories may actually arise from or depend upon practices rather than vice versa, while in other cases practices may be more or less independent of any particular ideas or beliefs. Alternatively, a particular practice might be compatible with any one of a number of different beliefs. In yet other cases it is difficult to see how a particular practice could possibly have any accompanying or directing belief. The same variety of relationship between ideas and practices is found in contexts other than that of religion. For example, although many a technological invention has come about through the application of some prior theory, it is just as often the case that the theory comes after the invention. (One must of course distinguish theories about how a particular technology works from the motives and observations that lead people to develop this technology in the first place.) If human beings had had to wait for the right explanatory theory before the development of any technology, probably none of us would be here now. This, incidentally, is why we should not conflate the distinction between science and technology. People who talk about the 'wonders of science' are usually talking about the wonders of technology.

No theory, of course, can guarantee its successful practical application, or indeed any practical application at all, and it is a commonly heard complaint that something which works in theory has failed to do so in practice. Equally, there are many effective technologies and remedies that work perfectly well without anyone (yet) knowing how or why they work. So strongly do some scientists feel about the need for a justifying theory that they are sometimes prepared to say that a particular result or technique ought not to work even if it actually does work (or seems to work).[3] Either there is no theory to account for a particular technology working, or the technology appears to be in conflict with a theory that precludes the possibility of its working. An instructive example here might be the skill (if indeed it is a skill) of 'water-divining' (or dowsing) used by many hard-nosed companies to locate subterranean water supplies despite the fact that no theory is yet available to explain how it works (if it really does work), and despite the fact that most scientists insist that it cannot work.[4] The point is this: in a culture in awe of scientific explanation, and which assumes that everything must have a scientific explanation, the idea of a practice for which there is no theory, or no acceptable theory, is unsettling.

In religions we find a wide range of practices, some of which are indeed direct applications or expressions of particular doctrines, principles or historical events, but others of which have no justification in terms of any particular idea, belief, theory or event. More often than not, religious practices are rationalized or justified retrospectively, and the justifications or explanations may change in step with changes in the practices themselves. Changes in practice will sometimes reflect changes in doctrine, but in many cases religious practices change for reasons that are themselves practical, and not necessarily practical in any religious sense. Religions are not hermetically sealed from the world around them. One religion may adopt or adapt the customs, rituals or buildings of another religion, and such adoption or adaptation will in turn lead to further developments in practice. For example, religious funeral rites and customs may be shaped as much by practical circumstances, or by secular law and custom, as by any particular doctrines about death or the afterlife.

The idea that religious practices are typically applications of religious theory may well be encouraged by an ambiguity implicit in the term 'practice' itself. This ambiguity is nicely illustrated in Quentin Crisp's response to the u.s. immigration official who asked him whether he was a practising homosexual: 'Practising? Certainly not! I'm perfect.'[5] When someone is said to practise a craft, profession or religion, what is normally meant is that the person is pursuing a particular livelihood or following a particular way of life. In this sense a practising Hindu, Jew or Catholic is more like a doctor practising medicine than a music student practising piano pieces. To practise something is simply to do it, whether well or badly being another matter. At the same time, just as doctors can become more or less competent in their profession, or more or less attentive to the needs of their patients, so can those who practise a religion become more or less skilled or attentive in various respects. One can be a more or less skilled Buddhist meditator, a more or less learned rabbi, or a more or less effectual parish priest.

If the dimension of 'religious practice' includes everything that is done in religion, or by religious people, then some important distinctions need to be drawn. Here I shall identify three main categories, or levels, of religious practice under the headings of *actions, activities* and *behaviours.* The first term, *actions,* covers forms of practice which can be defined as specifically religious in character, in the sense that they make sense only within a given religious context (even when they have originated in other contexts). Prominent, and sometimes predominant, among such practices are those types of religious action generally referred to as rituals. Rituals can be individual or communal, regular or occasional, official or popular.

It is ritual that people tend to have chiefly in mind when they think about religious practice. In fact, ritual is commonly regarded as the defining form of religious practice. Ritual is undoubtedly central to religion. Yet ritual is not exclusive to religion; it also occurs outside religion, and in almost every sphere of life. It may well be the case that ritual finds its richest forms in the context of religion. It may even be the case that rituals that occur outside the sphere of religion are implicitly religious, at least in the sense that they are indications of the human need to find meaning in life and to mark key events in life – both of which needs are given explicit expression and justification in religion.

Specifically religious practices are not confined to ritual, however. No less important in the history of religions are those actions that are better described as techniques. This term covers those physical and mental practices which relate to the cultivation of various kinds of heightened or concentrated awareness – practices variously known as meditation, contemplation, prayer, yoga and so on. If such practices are defined as techniques rather than as rituals, however, there is no absolute distinction between these two forms of religious practice. For one thing, many of the techniques in question embody the kind of symbolic ideas and actions typical of ritual elements. Moreover, it is also the case that formal rituals and mental techniques have a common creative or re-creative function. Rituals are a way of receiving and re-ordering the world according to a particular religious worldview. Techniques are a way of recreating or remaking consciousness, again in conformity with a particular religious worldview. If there is one word that is emblematic of the continuities between ritual and technique, it is 'prayer'. This word is used to cover a whole spectrum of practices, from some of the simplest religious acts, such as 'petitionary' prayer, through the rituals of 'intercessory' prayer, to techniques associated with the cultivation of higher states of consciousness, as in the case of 'contemplative' or 'mystical' prayer.[6]

The second category of religious practice comprises activities that, while not being religious per se, can be described as religious when they are pursued in the name of religion, or when they are in some way motivated by religion or pursued in conjunction with activities that *are* specifically religious. Two contrasting examples would be charitable work and warfare. Neither of these is specifically religious, or religious in itself, and in many if not most cases they are activities pursued or supported without religious motivation or justification; and yet often they are sanctioned by religion or pursued in the name of religion. For some religious people, such religiously motivated secular activities are a more important part of their religion than any kind of ritual practice. For many critics of religion, the fact that such (important) activities are not exclusively religious will be part of their argument for the redundancy (if not falsity) of religion. But secular critics are not always consistent in their evaluation of religiously inspired secular activities. Religiously inspired warfare is frequently cited as evidence against religion, whereas religiously inspired charitable work is less readily cited as evidence in favour of it. But if one does not have to be religious in order to be charitable, it is also true that one does not have to be religious in order to engage in acts of violence against one's fellow humans.

The distinction between religiously motivated secular activities and what I have called specifically religious actions, in the form of rituals, does not mean that the boundaries between them are always clear-cut. Consider again the case of warfare. People have had mixed motives for going to war. Some have done so out of patriotism, others because of the adventure, excitement and opportunities it presents. But there have also been those who have seen participation in warfare as a moral or religious duty (to alleviate the suffering of others, rid the world of evildoers, fulfil a prophecy in their sacred texts, and so on). In many cultures, moreover, warfare has incorporated explicitly religious or ritual elements. One might cite Emperor Constantine's dream, or vision, of the chi-rho symbol he was instructed to put on the shields of his soldiers,[7] or the case of the third-century Sri Lankan king, Dutthagamani, who went into battle with a spear to which a relic of the Buddha was attached.[8]

The third category of religious practice, distinct both from specifically religious actions and from activities pursued in the name of religion, includes what we may call the customary habits and behaviours of religious people, including their responses to particular events or circumstances, and not least their interactions with others – behaviour which might (and arguably should) give us the best clue to their religious commitment or worldview. It was to this kind of customary or habitual behaviour that Karen Blixen's servant Kitau evidently attached great importance. Apart from anything else, this category includes or overlaps with that whole range of attitudes and responses classed as moral or ethical. The ethical (or unethical) behaviour of religious people is certainly the kind of religious behaviour by which observers and critics of religion are most likely to judge religious people. A professed Roman Catholic who never goes to mass but always helps neighbours and strangers will be judged more favourably, by those within and outside the faith alike, than one who regularly attends mass but who is never kind to others. This suggests that what may be thought most characteristic of a religion (participation in rituals and the like) is not what will be thought most important about those who are members of that religion. Even so, this is far from saying that there is no positive connection between a person's ritual activity and a person's customary behaviour.

Indeed, no absolute distinction can be drawn between what I have called customary religious behaviour and either of the other two categories of religious practice. For one thing, religious rituals and other specifically religious acts can themselves become part of a person's customary behaviour. One might, for example, habitually recite a prayer or perform a ritual of some kind before a meal. Again, certain kinds of religiously motivated but otherwise secular activities can become habitual or customary, or indeed institutionalized within a religious setting, as when a person joins a religious association dedicated to social welfare of some kind.

The value, or otherwise, of all three of the categories, or levels, of religious practice identified above, and by implication the value of the religious traditions in which religious practices are rooted, nowadays tends to be judged by the purely secular criteria that have become the lingua franca for judging everything. Thus the activities of religious individuals, the decisions of religious leaders and the customs of religious institutions all tend to be understood, and hence judged, not by their own criteria but by reference to secular values and interests. Consider, as a comic but telling example, the case of the overseas visitor to Canterbury Cathedral who, finding access to certain parts of the building restricted because of the Easter services, was overheard to complain how inconsiderate it was of the cathedral authorities to put on so many services at a time of year when large numbers of tourists were around. What is more, in the modern West the tendency to judge or justify religious behaviour and activity mainly if not entirely in secular terms is evident within as well as outside religious institutions.

DESPITE THE IMPORTANCE of the customary behaviour and religiously motivated secular activities of religious people, it is rituals that, as the most distinctive forms of religious practice, have attracted the greatest attention – the attention both of those seeking to understand religion and of those who are most critical of it. Defining ritual is a task almost as tricky as that of defining religion. Like many of the generic terms used both within and about religion, the term 'ritual' has religious origins. Specifically it referred to the actions accompanying the words ('rites') prescribed in Christian worship.[9] As a generic term, however, the word can be confined neither to Christianity nor to religion as a whole. There are rituals not only in every religious tradition, but in almost every other sphere of human life. Some secular rituals may have had religious origins, but it is equally true that many religious rituals have their origins outside religion.[10] The ubiquity of ritual in all departments of human life should help people understand, and appreciate, the importance of ritual within religion.

A minimal definition of ritual might be that it consists in a prescribed sequence of symbolic actions and accompanying words that serve to enact, enable, celebrate or reinforce personal beliefs and communal values. Rituals differ from mere routines or procedures, which (like rituals) are repetitive but (unlike rituals) are nothing more than a means to an end and not representative of anything else. For similar reasons rituals must be differentiated from those other specifically religious practices I have defined as techniques, such as those that are important in the mystical and contemplative strands of religious traditions. These methods and techniques may well incorporate ritual elements, not least especially when performed publicly or collectively. One has only to think of the ritualized techniques of ecstatic prayer practised by the so-called 'whirling dervishes' of the Sufi Mevlevi order, or the states of transic possession induced through the rituals of the Haitian Vaudun tradition. In themselves, however, they are not rituals, their practice being determined not by the times and seasons of a religious calendar, but by the efforts of individuals seeking knowledge of or engagement with supernatural beings or transcendental realities.

We can further define the nature of religious rituals by identifying three basic functions of ritual: the instrumental, the performative and the demonstrative. The balance between these functions will vary from one ritual to another. The instrumental function of ritual intends some particular effect or outcome, whether in this world or in another. A ritual could be considered exclusively instrumental where its effect is thought to be achieved automatically, through the form of the ritual itself (*ex opere operato*). Such purely instrumental rituals typically belong in the sphere of magic rather than religion.[11] The instrumental function in religious rituals is typically indirect, dependent on the power of some supernatural being. Thus a ritual intended to bring about a specific result or effect through the power of the ritual itself (or through the power of the priest or specialist conducting it) would be a magically instrumental ritual, whereas a ritual in which a god is asked to supply rain would be a religiously instrumental one (although a failed request might be attributed to ritual incompetence rather than divine absence or displeasure).

If ritual is instrumental in so far as it relates to some expected or desired external result, then it is performative when some change in the role or status of a person, community or state of affairs is conferred or confirmed in or by the ritual itself. So-called rites of passage (secular or religious) provide obvious examples here: for instance, one is married just by going through the ceremony, so that one can be married insincerely or even against one's will. Rituals are performative in so far as they are self-fulfilling, just as some of the statements we make in ordinary speech are self-fulfilling. It was the philosopher J. L. Austin who identified as 'performative utterances' those statements in a language which do what they speak, so to speak. A simple example would be an utterance such as 'I name this ship *Queen Mary*.' Performative statements, and gestures, occur within many secular or religious ceremonies, which is why it is important to identify a performative as well as an instrumental function within ritual.

This leaves, finally and perhaps most importantly, the demonstrative function within ritual. This function is manifest in so far as a ritual expresses, enacts or celebrates a particular religious need, narrative or occasion. The various forms of congregational song would offer simple examples here. In most religious rituals, the demonstrative function will be combined with the instrumental and the performative functions. For example, rituals centred on the veneration of supernatural beings will express praise, gratitude or joy but also seek (instrumentally) blessings or interventions of some kind. At the same time such rituals will establish or confirm (performatively) the faith and solidarity of the worshippers.

By not observing these kinds of distinction both within and between rituals, it is all too easy for observers to misread the nature of rituals or the intentions and expectations of those who participate in them. Mary Douglas comments on how anthropologists have drawn false as well as cynical conclusions from the fact that the rain ceremonies of African Bushmen coincide with the onset of the rainy season, or from the fact that the annual Dinka ceremony to cure malaria occurs in the month in which the disease is expected to abate. 'Old anthropological sources', she writes, 'are full of the notion that primitive people expect rites to produce an immediate intervention in their affairs, and they poke kindly fun at those who supplement their rituals of healing with European medicine, as if this testified to lack of faith.'[12] As she points out, religious rituals are not generally, and certainly not exclusively, about changing the course of events. Rather they are about praising, celebrating or coming to terms with some change in the world, or in the circumstances of a particular individual. They are about 'framing' some event or circumstance within a larger worldview.

Ritual has been variously criticized as wasteful of time and resources, as cruel where it involves the taking of life, and sometimes as a distraction from, if not betrayal of, the true goals and values of religion. One of the epithets commonly applied to ritual is 'empty', meaning either that ritual is empty of sense or that it is empty of (intended) effect – that is, ineffectual. Criticism of, or scepticism about, ritual in religion is as likely to come from religious as from non-religious or anti-religious people. Indeed religious people, being 'on the scene' so to speak, have been among the fiercest critics of ritual. The Buddha, for example, condemned the elaborate Vedic sacrificial rituals of his time not only because they involved the cruel and costly slaughter of animals but because, in his view, they simply did not and could not produce the benefits claimed for them. But to criticize this or that ritual or type of ritual is not, of course, to criticize ritual per se. Buddhism has had its own rituals (from the time of the Buddha onwards), and so have the Protestant reformers who criticized the Catholic mass and the cult of saints as blasphemous or superstitious.

It may well be that critics of religion and religious reformers are justified, on either religious or secular grounds, in many of their criticisms of ritual. Thus one might reasonably claim that a particular ritual had become too elaborate, too costly or too obscure; and rituals, like any other human constructions, can be changed. But it is no good complaining about the existence or nature of ritual as such, which is what critics usually have in mind when they dismiss ritual as empty, ineffectual or irrational. Such critics must face the fact that ritual is unavoidable – and not only within the sphere of religion. Ritual is found in almost every sphere of human life, for example in law and politics, in military life, in sport and the arts, and in the habits and customs connected with eating and drinking, friendship, courtship and sex. Human beings are ritual animals, which is something that probably derives from their being linguistic animals. Those who reject this or that ritual, or even ritual as such, will often come to adopt or invent new rituals, albeit usually avoiding this particular term to describe them. Secular people are generally happier with the word 'ceremony', although this word too has religious origins and associations.[13]

Restricting the use of the term 'ritual' to religious ritual is a further example of the misguided tendency to segregate religion from other spheres of human life. To think of ritual in this way is to rob ritual of much of its life-blood. For the power and effect of ritual in religion depends on its links with the way people live life as a whole. The movements, gestures and materials of religious ritual and ceremony are not intended to be incompatible with those of ordinary life. Much of ritual is ordinary human activity heightened or slowed down. The dignified and deliberate activities of daily life can themselves have a liturgical quality. In those societies in which religion has not been pushed into a corner, there are obvious continuities between the gestures, speech and bearing of people at home or in public places and how they behave in a church, temple or synagogue. By contrast, it is in societies in which religion has been marginalized that we find people feeling uncomfortable or behaving awkwardly in religious settings. What ritual does is to dramatize the ideas, images, feelings, gestures and rhythms of everyday life in repetitive, amplified and other memorable forms, typically within the context of particular times and spaces. Ritual is to daily life as poetry is to prose, one might say, and this would apply as much to secular as it does to religious ritual, although the 'poetry' of secular ritual arguably never reaches the intensity evident in much specifically religious ritual.

IT IS NOT ONLY critics and sceptics, but many religious people too, who perpetuate stereotypes of religious practice. For instance, the idea of prayer as literally a talking to God or an asking God for something, whether this be on one's own behalf or that of others, is a notion that sceptics and critics share with many religious people themselves. Indeed, some critics who should know better are inclined to insist that this is the only thing 'prayer' means, so that any other use of the term must be a derivative or metaphorical one. Consider, for example, the following pronouncement by the philosopher Daniel Dennett:

> For some people, prayer is not literally *talking to God* but, rather, a 'symbolic' activity, a way of talking *to oneself* about one's deepest concerns, expressed metaphorically. It is rather like beginning a diary entry with 'Dear Diary'. If what they call God is really not an agent in their eyes, a being that can *answer* prayers, *approve* and *disapprove*, *receive* sacrifices, and *mete out* punishment or forgiveness, then, although they may call this Being God, and stand in awe of *it* (not *Him*), their creed, whatever it is, is not really a religion according to my definition.[14]

Much prayer and worship in religion undoubtedly invokes or petitions God or the gods, as well as other beings such as saints, bodhisattvas or the dead. In this respect the actions of religious people are no different from the requests made, attention sought or signals given in other spheres of human life. By the same token, the processes involved in religious invocation and petition are likely to range from the simple to the complex, just as they do elsewhere. Why would prayer, if it were a genuine form of communication with divine or supernatural beings, be any less complex than some of the this-worldly forms of communication people take for granted (for example radio, the postal service and the Internet)? If prayer is indeed heard, or responded to in some way, why should it not involve a whole network of intelligences, rather than simply God by himself? In medieval Christianity, for example, it was saints and angels who were both recipients and agents within the network of supernatural communications. Similar kinds of cosmology exist in many other traditions – for example, in the Hindu and Buddhist traditions and in shamanic religion.[15] In the present world, if one writes to a national leader or to the head of a large corporation, is it not likely that the reply (if there is one) will come from some person lower in the hierarchy? Thoughtful children doubtful about Santa Claus find that the whole story makes much more sense once the elves are also taken into account.

In any case, prayer means so much more than petitionary prayer – the term also covers practices that are better characterized as communion than communication, as in many traditions of meditation and contemplation. Prayer of this kind is not necessarily an asking, but rather an exploration of consciousness, an ascent to higher worlds or an opening of oneself to the grace or power of a higher being – what the mystic Simone Weil called a 'waiting on God'. None of these senses of prayer are dreamt of in Dennett's philosophy. The only alternative he allows to his caricature of petitionary prayer as 'talking to God' is the metaphorical sense of prayer as a therapeutic talking to oneself.[16]

Critics like Dennett share with all too many religious people the idea that religious practices, whether ritual or non-ritual, are subordinate to religious ideas – that religious practices are performed as 'applications' of particular beliefs, doctrines, laws or precepts. In particular, they are represented as being about obediently conforming to the requirements of a religion, thereby avoiding negative consequences such as being sent to hell, or about securing (or at least seeking) some positive advantage or benefit that is otherwise unobtainable. In any other sphere, this interpretation of human activity would be considered at best a one-sided and at worst a cynical view of life. It is equivalent to saying that people eat and drink purely to avoid dying of hunger and thirst, or to have sex for the sole purpose of procreation, or read books, listen to music, visit museums and art galleries or go for walks in the country only because they believe that these activities will impress others or somehow help them get ahead in the world.

In reality people eat and drink because it is enjoyable to do so, particularly in the company of others. They have sex at least as much for the enjoyment of it as for its procreative consequences. And they engage in all sorts of cultural and recreational activities for the mental, physical and social pleasure these give. Of course it may sometimes also be to their personal advantage – financial or social, for example – to pursue some of these activities, and sometimes this motive may take the lead; but the idea that such considerations constitute the main motive for such activities is absurd. The relevant question, then, is this: why should the actions, activities and behaviour of religious people, or of people in so far as they are religious, be any different from the actions, activities and behaviour of secular people, or of people in so far as they are secular? Why should their practices be any more or less instrumental? Why should they not get the same range of mental and physical enjoyment or fulfilment from their religious practices as they do from their more secular ones?

If these questions sound odd it is because of an assumption that the religious life must somehow function differently from, if not actually in opposition to, the secular life. This is why, for example, some religious people are uncomfortable when the ecstasies of the mystics are compared to the ecstasies of the lover, and why the critic or sceptic will seize upon such parallels as evidence that religion has its source and explanation in all too human factors. Both responses are a product of a culture in which an artificial distinction between the sacred and the secular has come to be taken for granted. On top of this, both responses reveal a kind of cultural parochialism. Neither the Platonists, nor the Catholic mystics, nor the saints of Sufi Islam, devotional Hinduism or Tantric Buddhism find it in the slightest degree inappropriate that these parallels should exist. For them it would be strange if they did not exist. For them, human sexuality is itself an image of the possibility of a profound, ecstatic union with a divine Being.

Many religious traditions suffer from the self-inflicted wound of having turned religious practices into duties and obligations. But humankind – *Homo sapiens* – is also *Homo ludens*. Joy, pleasure and play can have as much of a role in religious life as they do in any other sphere of human activity. Many rituals and ceremonies are often formal and solemn events, but formality and solemnity are not the same as glumness or earnestness. Other rituals and ceremonies are or should be as joyful as their subject requires. There is no reason why participants in religious rituals cannot enjoy, or feel relaxed about, their rituals while also taking them seriously. The same goes for those who engage in the kind of practices I have defined as methods or techniques rather than rituals or ceremonies. These methods and techniques are, as these terms imply, a means to an end, be it the transformation of consciousness, the realization of immanent divinity, or some form of communion or communication with the dead. But, like running to win a race, the means and the ends are not ultimately distinct. Also, like training oneself for a race, religious practice can be mentally and physically arduous. But the advantage and the pleasure of pursuing these techniques lie in the means as much as in the ends, and in the end the means become the end. In the Buddhist tradition, for example, meditation is presented not just as a lengthy and demanding path to a desired goal, but as a manifestation of the goal itself.[17] The Buddha continued to practise meditation after he had, through meditation, attained enlightenment. He cultivated meditative states not simply in order to attain enlightenment but as the very expression of his enlightenment. In religion, as in sport, the means and the end can become one.

At the start of this chapter, I criticized the assumption, often made, that practice in religion is typically subordinate to theory or experience. Yet it is often practices that not only express or illuminate ideas and experiences but initiate and change them. Mary Douglas explains this as the 'framing' function of ritual. Ritual, she says,

> focuses attention by framing; it enlivens the memory and links the present with the relevant past. In all this it aids perception. Or rather, it changes perception ... So it is not enough to say that ritual helps us to experience more vividly what we would have experienced anyway ... If it were just a kind of dramatic map or diagram of what is known it would always follow experience. But in fact ritual does not play this secondary role. It can come first in formulating experience. It can permit knowledge of what would otherwise not be known at all. It does not merely externalise experience, bringing it out into the light of day, but it modifies experience in so expressing it.[18]

Incidentally, what Douglas says here chimes in well with the strategy of analysing religions as multi-dimensional systems.

FOUR

RELIGION AS THEORY

I t is sometimes asserted that what religious people do is more revealing of the nature of religion than what they say: actions, supposedly, speak louder than words. It is certainly the case that for the majority of adherents religion is a practical matter rather than an intellectual one, something lived out rather than thought out. This view challenges those who would discuss and evaluate religion chiefly in terms of its ideas and principles. In a multi-dimensional analysis of religion, however, the simple opposition between words and actions cannot be sustained. Actions cannot be separated from words. It is true that actions sometimes come first, and explanations and justifications later, if at all. But most of the things people do are done deliberately, done for a reason, even when they are done habitually; actions are not easily divorced from their corresponding explanations and justifications. Or to put it another way, words – whether spoken or written – can themselves be seen as forms of action, as part of human behaviour.

In any case, religion is undeniably an intellectual as well as a practical matter. Idea and theory are no less important in religion than they are in art, science, politics, law or education, and it is at the intellectual as well as practical level that religions connect with these and the many other spheres of human life. Moreover, it is usually by reference to beliefs that religious people affirm or explain their religious commitment, while those who say that they are not, or no longer, religious will typically justify their position in intellectual terms. Nor is it difficult to see why the intellectual elements of religion loom so large both in the study of religion and in popular understandings (or misunderstandings) of religion. For ideas are in an obvious sense the most accessible and most communicable elements of religion. Nowadays people can have the texts of this or that religion in their hands or on their screens as quickly as any other kind of intellectual material. And religion in the head generally requires less effort or commitment than religion in the flesh.

It is hardly surprising, then, that it is the intellectual content of religion that gets to dominate definitions and interpretations of religion, and even the life of religions themselves. Again, since words and ideas tend to assume a life of their own, the doctrines and theoretical formulations of religion easily become detached from their experiential and practical settings to form ever-expanding but largely self-contained intellectual (and ideological) systems. It is all the more important, therefore, that we should try to understand how theory in religion relates to the other dimensions of religion.

What is identified as the intellectual or theoretical dimension of religion covers far more than theological, metaphysical or philosophical doctrines. It also embraces religious laws and ethical precepts, the rules and explications of ritual, symbolism and iconography, and the narrative expression of religious ideas and practices through myth, legend and parable. Moreover, this dimension of religion generates such a profusion of oral, literary and iconographic forms that we must inevitably draw some basic distinctions in order to make sense of it all. We will do well, for example, to differentiate history from myth, myth from legend, legend from history, mythology from theology, theology from metaphysics, metaphysics from philosophy, philosophy from psychology and so on, while at the same time recognizing that there are no hard and fast distinctions here. What should also be recognized is that, in many if not most cases, the texts and oral traditions within which these genres appear are of a hybrid nature, comprising different combinations or successions of genres as the case may be.

This inevitably creates ample opportunities for misreading or misinterpreting the nature and intent of any given text.

As a comprehensive term for the second dimension of religion, 'theoretical' seems preferable both to 'intellectual' and to 'doctrinal'. In particular it usefully complements the term 'practical', which identifies the third dimension. The terms 'intellectual' and 'doctrinal' easily reinforce the popular idea that religion is all about believing in this or that intellectual proposition. The word 'doctrine' is harmless enough in itself and simply means 'teaching', but it does fall somewhat under the shadow of the cognate terms 'dogma' and 'doctrinaire', with their overtones of orthodoxy, conformity and intolerance. The word 'teaching' itself has a better image, as well as the advantage of being no less applicable to practical skills than to intellectual knowledge. To talk about teaching is also to talk about the presence or influence of a teacher, and this connects theory with practice. An art teacher or a music teacher, for example, will be mainly concerned with developing a student's practical skills. If a music student is learning not only to play an instrument but music theory, this is likely to be for some practical purpose, such as musical composition. In contrast, learning *about* music is a more exclusively intellectual pursuit. In sum, we might say that in religion, as in any other context, theory may relate as much to doing as to thinking.

It might be objected that to use the word 'theory' in the context of religion is to risk equating religious ideas with scientific ones, and this in turn might seem to play into the hands of those who like to see religious and scientific ideas as in conflict or competition. Yet the use of 'theory' for religious ideas is eminently suitable provided we hold fast to the fullest meaning of the term, which is what scientists, and rationalist critics of religion, often fail to do. The word 'theory' comes from the Greek *theoria*, meaning a view or vision of how things are (or could be). It does not narrowly mean 'explanation', still less exhaustive or exclusive explanation. In this respect it resembles the Sanskrit term *darshana*, used by Hindu philosophers to describe a viewpoint or perspective on reality. The term implies a clear distinction between the truth or reality itself and one's perception or interpretation of it. This in turn suggests that there are or may be other viewpoints too – which is not incompatible with maintaining that one particular viewpoint may be superior to others in some respect. Theory as perception or viewpoint not only constitutes a kind of experience, but enables a corresponding practice, and so fits well with the analysis of religion in terms of distinct but interconnecting dimensions.

Despite the importance of viewing religious ideas in relation to both experience and practice, it must also be acknowledged that – in religion as elsewhere – argument, debate, speculation and sheer intellectual curiosity are fundamental traits of human beings seeking to make sense of the world into which they have, to use Heidegger's expression, been 'thrown'.[1] The proliferation and elaboration of religious ideas is not always a sign of runaway intellectualism or sterile system building; it can also be a manifestation of the curiosity and intellectual exuberance that goes with a love of learning for its own sake. Knowledge need not always have some practical purpose or outcome, or perhaps one might better say that it is in itself a kind of practice requiring no further justification. In religion as in other spheres, intellectual curiosity is justifiable as an end in itself, and knowledge can be cultivated for the sheer joy of knowing. The detailed doctrinal exegeses of religious scholars are comparable in many respects to the theoretical interpretations developed by literary critics, the commentaries produced by political correspondents, or the detailed forecasts and analyses given by sports enthusiasts. Much of such commentary and discussion, being largely speculative or hypothetical, is superfluous in practical terms, functioning rather to express interest, commitment and community among those for whom religion, literature, politics or sport are vital concerns.

GIVEN THE IMPORTANCE of myth and symbol in religion, I shall in this chapter focus mainly on these two modes of theoretical expression. It is important to emphasize, however, that neither myth nor symbol are to be found exclusively in religious contexts;

they also occur in secular contexts and have secular meanings or functions. Nevertheless, it is possible to argue that myths and symbols, no matter where they occur, appeal to that larger sense of order, transcendental or teleological as the case may be, such as finds its richest forms of expression within the religious traditions.

The term 'myth' (*mythos*) in Greek tradition originally meant any kind of story or narrative, but especially one concerning the gods. Because of scepticism about the gods, or about certain representations of them, the term also came to be used in a disparaging sense, to refer to a fanciful story not historically or factually true; and from this tradition of use came the modern sense of myth as any kind of story (or event, or explanation) erroneously considered true, or once thought true but long discredited. This has now become the popular meaning of the word. As such, the term is a gift to sceptics and critics of religion, since any narrative declaring itself to be, or classified by others as being, a 'myth' can *ipso facto* be dismissed as fanciful or untrue.

In the serious study of religion, however, the words 'myth' and 'mythology' continue to be used as neutral generic terms for those narratives, typically featuring divine beings, which reveal the origins and ends of human life, explain the origins of some religious practice, or dramatize the message of religious founders through the story of their lives.[2] These narratives are not to be understood literally, or in an exclusively literal sense, even when they include historical events. Thus the narrative of Christ's death and resurrection is part of Christian mythology,[3] in just the same way as the story of Krishna is part of Hindu mythology and that of Demeter and Persephone part of ancient Greek mythology. A myth, as a 'sacred story', is one that in various ways epitomizes, celebrates or justifies a particular worldview.

Such narratives also have their secular equivalents, so that the word 'myth' can be used, more broadly, to refer to any paradigmatic narrative which helps give shape to people's lives. For example, many nations celebrate foundation stories and other narratives, which can be described as national myths to the extent that they provide a rationale and rallying point for national self-confidence and self-understanding. There can be scientific myths too. The theory of evolution, for instance, is not just a theory in the narrower sense of explaining the origin of species. It is also a theory in the richer, mythological sense, in so far as it affirms human solidarity with the rest of the natural world or envisages a future in which evolutionary processes, guided by human beings themselves, give rise to new forms of humanity. It seems to be the case that the narrative impulse, or appeal of narrative, that under-lies myth is as fundamental to our understanding of the world as, for example, are the ethical sense or the demand for justice. Might one even say that, in almost any sphere of discourse, a 'narrative understanding' of life tends towards a religious understanding?

In any case, to describe a narrative as 'mythic' does not imply its falsity but rather acknowledges its paradigmatic function within a particular culture. Nowadays, in a world generally characterized by what one writer has called 'amythia',[4] even plays and novels can have a mythic function, albeit at a more individual level. Certainly it is no good dismissing myth as fiction when it is acknowledged that fiction itself can be a powerful vehicle of truth.[5] Indeed, the manifest influence of fiction in people's lives offers modern people a good way of understanding the power of myth in more traditional societies.

The truths, or purposes, of myth are trans-historical, even when they involve history. In the Old Testament, for example, the history of the Jews is also their mythology. Historical events can themselves be transformed into myths, or presented in ways that make them exemplary of trans-historical truths. One can see, however, why many Christians are uneasy with the term 'Christian mythology', as they are not uneasy with the terms 'Greek mythol-ogy' or 'Hindu mythology'. This cannot be attributed simply to the instinctive partisan conviction that 'our sacred stories are true, while yours are not.' Nor is it explained by the fact that myths are typically about gods rather than about God. It must also have something to do with the fact that in Christianity, as in Judaism and Islam, sacred narratives actually depend on historical events.

This does not mean that the Christian story is historical as opposed to being mythic; what it means, rather, is that the logically prior truth of the myth is embodied in or illuminated by historical events, unlike those myths that refer to 'events' outside or before history. If Christ be not raised, then our faith is in vain, declares St Paul. But is this resurrection nothing more than an extraordinary historical event? Had Christ's life been minutely recorded using the sophisticated audio and video technology of modern times, it would have provided neither believers themselves with any proof of the 'truth' of Christianity, nor critics or sceptics with ammunition against its truth. As Johann Scheffler (1624–1677), the German mystic commonly known as 'Angelus Silesius', puts it in his famous poem,

> Christ could be born a thousand times in Galilee –
> but all in vain until He is born in me.[6]

The significance of myth can be further explained by contrasting myth with legend. The boundary between myth and legend is a real but a fuzzy one. Historical persons, places and events rather than divine or supernatural ones provide the raw materials that popular memory and the literary imagination convert into legend, or into its lesser cousin, the folktale.[7] Consider, for example, the legendary transformations of figures as varied as St Nicholas, King Arthur, Robin Hood, Elvis Presley and John F. Kennedy. Whereas myths are generally but not necessarily religious in nature, legends are generally but not necessarily secular in nature, and this is true even when they feature religious figures or supernatural events. Thus, in addition to the canonical mythology of Christ, there are also many legends about Christ – for instance, the story that as a boy he came to England with his uncle, Joseph of Arimathea.[8] This story does not have the exemplary purpose or paradigmatic content of myth. On the other hand, one would classify as legends rather than as myths those stories that recount the exemplary lives and deeds of saints (hagiographies). Many of these have a strong historical basis, but the facts are dramatized and elaborated to enhance the status of the saints, much as they are when people recount anecdotes about the lives of ordinary people. Whereas myths typically present a cosmic perspective on reality – one that places human beings, their world and their history within an overall teleological perspective – legends remain earthbound even when they include magical or supernatural elements. The persons and events of legend may be 'larger than life', but they are never far removed from the small-scale interests and aspirations of ordinary people. What is true of legends is also true, albeit to a lesser extent, of folktales. Fairy stories, by contrast, are more closely related to myth.[9]

To confuse one type of oral or literary form with another, or to apply to all of them the same interpretative criteria, is clearly to risk misunderstanding the diverse types and purposes of religious writings. But no less hazardous than conflating categories is the tendency to create artificial distinctions or to exaggerate real ones. One distinction worth attending to here is the one sometimes drawn between mythos and logos. This distinction, like others related to it,[10] has been used by critics of religion, religious apologists and neutral commentators alike. Whereas 'myth', 'mythic' and 'mythology' usefully identify a certain oral or (now mainly) literary genre, we are in much more dubious territory if we think of the 'mythic' as representing a specific kind of mentality, mode of language or (worst of all) phase in the evolution of the human mind. The 'mythic' mode of thought (in these dubious senses) is seen either as antithetical or as complementary to 'logical' or 'rational' thought.

Mythos, it is argued, represents a non-scientific or pre-scientific apprehension of reality, and as such is the language of poetry, the imagination and religion, whereas logos is the language of reason and analysis and hence the natural language of science. Rationalist critics of religion may see mythos and logos – terms rooted in ancient Greek culture – as two permanent tendencies of the human mind, or they may see the relationship between them as an evolutionary one, with logos succeeding or supplanting mythos; but in either case they judge mythos by logos. Religious apologists, on the other hand, are likely to see mythos and logos as complementary, and to criticize rationalists for failing to see that mythos yields valuable insights inaccessible to logos. According to one writer on religion, part of the religious crisis of modern times is the loss of a proper sense of myth. In the past, people had a different outlook:

> In particular, they evolved two ways of thinking, speaking, and acquiring knowledge, which scholars have called *mythos* and *logos*. Both were essential; they were regarded as complementary ways of arriving at truth, and each had its special area of competence. Myth was regarded as primary; it was concerned with what was thought to be timeless and constant in our existence. Myth looked back to the origins of life, to the foundations of culture, and to the deepest levels of the human mind. Myth was not concerned with practical matters, but with meaning ...
>
> *Logos* was equally important. *Logos* was the rational, pragmatic, and scientific thought that enabled men and women to function well in the world. We may have lost the sense of *mythos* in the West today, but we are very familiar with *logos*, which is the basis of our society. Unlike myth, *logos* must relate exactly to facts and correspond to external realities if it is to be effective. It must work efficiently in the mundane world. We use this logical, discursive reasoning when we have to make things happen, get something done, or persuade other people to adopt a particular course of action.[11]

This idea of a sharp distinction between mythos and logos, however, is flawed both in its formulation and in its application. To begin with, the distinction as used by Plato and other ancient writers does not conform to the neat antithesis formulated by modern writers. Mythos and logos are not generally represented as mutually exclusive modes of speech, or as two successive stages of thought; if anything, mythos represents a special mode of logos.[12] The modern use of the distinction is yet another example of how religious apologists unwittingly conspire with critics of religion to segregate religion from the rest of human life (and especially from the scientific sphere). The trouble is that many apologists seem to think that differentiating between mythos and logos in this way will protect religion from invalid criticism: since mythos is the natural language of religion, it is wrong to judge it by or assimilate it to logos, the language of science. Religious critics may be prepared to concede this, but in return they will expect religious apologists to restrict their religious discourse to mythos and steer clear of logos.

But not only is the antithesis between mythos and logos untrue to religion and to science alike. More fundamentally, it is untrue to the nature of language itself, and in particular to religious language. Religious texts can be as rational as any scientific text, while science itself often uses mythical language on its own account. More specifically, mythological texts embody the same range of linguistic forms as do any other texts, just as poetry, whether secular or religious, uses the full range of such forms rather than some exclusively 'poetic' mode of speech. One is entitled to point out logical errors and inconsistencies in poetry just as one is in religious, scientific and every other kind of text. Religion cannot escape rational inquiry or criticism by hiding from logos behind mythos. Naturally one will find myth, metaphor and other figurative forms richly represented in religious texts, but one will also find them in scientific and in many other kinds of writing. So, if a first mistake is to think of the 'mythic' as a separate and specifically religious type of discourse (rather than merely a genre prominent in religion), and a second mistake to think of the distinction between religion and science primarily in terms of the distinction between mythos and logos, a third mistake is to fail to see that logos itself embraces everything in language, and not just the analytical or rational bits, as it were. If mystery and transcendence are disclosed through language, they are disclosed not in any particular form or use of it, but in the nature of language itself.[13] In the beginning, we might say, is the logos.

IF MYTH IN RELIGION is subject to misunderstanding, this is no less true of symbol. Talk about the 'symbolic' can get out of hand just as easily as talk about the 'mythic'. Myth and symbol are of course closely related, symbols being part of the language of myth. A symbol is a particular kind of sign – verbal or visual, literary or iconographic – which, unlike other kinds, embodies or 'participates in' what it indicates or expresses.[14] Symbols differ on the one hand from 'natural' signs, which indicate one thing through its causal connections with another (as smoke indicates fire), and on the other hand from 'conventional' signs, which indicate some one thing by customary or arbitrary convention (as do the letters on this page).

Unlike natural and conventional signs, symbols do not merely indicate something. Rather, they make it present or instantiate it in some form.[15] They embody, exemplify or illuminate ideas or realities rather than merely point to them.[16] They show rather than tell, we might say. And what they show is not necessarily a single or a simple entity, idea or meaning, as it is by definition in the case of natural and conventional signs. Many symbols integrate, within a single image or design, a whole complex of interconnected meanings, part of their appeal lying in their very multivalence, in the fact that they seem open to extensive if not endless interpretation.

As in the case of 'myth', some have attributed to symbols a mainly if not exclusively religious meaning, or they have identified a 'symbolic' mode of thinking that supposedly functions as the primary or natural language of religion, and in particular of myth and ritual. Like myths, however, symbols are important in many spheres of life, although it is not unreasonable to suggest that symbols, like myths, find their richest forms of expression in religious interpretations of the world. The use of symbols is as natural and pervasive in human culture as the use of myth. Symbols, like myths, are human constructions, even if it is true, as some would argue, that there are universal symbols, symbols that appear to share the same meaning across different cultures. But the existence of similar or identical symbols across disparate cultures, where it is not evidence of the 'migration' of symbols, may reveal nothing more surprising than the universality of the human mind, particularly when looking beyond what is ephemerally present. Our appetite for symbols – that is, our appetite both for discerning and for creating symbols – is undoubtedly part of the human desire to find meaning in a universe otherwise thought chaotic or purposeless, which it is not unreasonable to interpret as a broadly religious stance.

In any case, a similarity of symbolic image or design does not imply a similarity of symbolism. In secular contexts, for example, the image of a lion was widely used as a symbol both of courage and of kingship, while in Christianity different features of the lion led to this animal being used as a symbol both of Christ and of Satan. To take another example, the symbolic device usually known as the swastika has existed in cultures throughout the world for at least two millennia, and seems to have functioned variously as a solar, fertility and funerary symbol. In popular Hinduism it is widely used as a good-luck sign, but for many people in the West, where the swastika in different forms was also widely used, this symbol is now indelibly associated with the Nazi regime, which adopted it as a symbol of Aryan supremacy.

This raises an important question about symbols, especially in the context of religion. Are there at least some symbols that have an inherent power or meaning, as distinct from one established through custom in some particular cultural tradition? In the case of religious symbolism, this becomes the question whether (some) symbols can be regarded as autonomous revelations of religious truth or reality rather than as ideas or images bearing this or that meaning through custom or convention. The risk here is that we simply end up conflating the already challenging idea of a religious symbol with the still more difficult idea of a religious revelation, which would do nothing positive for our understanding of symbols. It is true, nevertheless, that some religious symbols do seem to have originated within certain kinds of theophany or religious experience. One may think, for example, of the 'burning bush' witnessed by Moses on Mount Sinai.[17]

By contrast, other equally important symbols are consciously constructed from natural phenomena. Consider the lotus, for example, which is widely used in Eastern religions, particularly in Buddhism, to symbolize the unfolding process of enlightenment. This is a 'natural' symbol, and yet once established in a tradition it subsequently appears not just in exegetical literature but also as a 'living' element within various kinds of visionary experience. It is difficult, therefore, to maintain any clear distinction between natural and revealed symbols, which is to a large extent a false dichotomy. On a wider level, moreover, the whole of the natural world can be seen, by a religiously sensitive person, as a manifestation of a transcendent order of reality.

Symbolism is only one means of expressing or engaging with religious ideas. But it is a means that easily gets out of hand, leading to an inflation and devaluation of symbolism. Encouraging people to see 'symbolic' meanings everywhere weakens rather than reinforces the power of symbols. It is a bit like a psychoanalyst who obsessively finds sexuality hidden in every word, thought and deed, being left with nothing much to say when the real thing appears. There have been periods in the history of many religions when the scholastic mind has sought to turn the symbols of their tradition into some sort of system, where every symbol must be fitted into a consistent symbolic whole. In an over-symbolized world, nothing is allowed to be itself, but is always a symbol of something else, of some deeper meaning hidden from view. The response to symbols in this kind of world is that of decoding or translating their meaning rather than letting the symbol itself communicate. This leads eventually to a devaluation or trivialization not only of individual symbols but of the whole idea of a symbol. Descriptions of something as either 'merely symbolic' or 'highly symbolic' give the game away here. A healthy symbolism is virtually the opposite of all this: a symbol is an object, image or design that embodies, reveals, illuminates or extends a truth or meaning rather than one that hides or disguises it. In ancient Egyptian religion, for instance, the sun's disc in the sky was itself a symbol, as manifestation or revelation, of the sun god Re.

SOME RELIGIOUS apologists have sought to escape from the searching if not hostile questions of sceptics and critics by insisting that religious ideas, since they are chiefly expressed in mythic and symbolic terms, are not to be judged by the criteria that apply in the empirical worlds of science or common sense. Such a strategy is profoundly mistaken. To begin with, myths and symbols are not unique to religion. Nor are the ideas or truths they embody incompatible with philosophical or metaphysical ideas. There is only one human world, and it is a world in which religion, science, art and other concerns all have access to myth and symbol, and whose theories and pronouncements are all subject to the same criteria of truth and value. Second, it is a mistake to think of myths and symbols as either true or false in the narrowly propositional sense in which other theoretical expressions are true or false. Myths and symbols are true or false in the equally important sense of being or not being true to life. Rather than thinking of them as true, we should rather think of them, as we do of poems or paintings for example, as being illuminating, inspiring, enabling, energizing and so forth. Certain myths and symbols may, of course, have qualities the opposite of these. Once we take myths and symbols literally, they cease to be myths and symbols.

Critics of religion who accept everything that has been said here about myth and symbol are still perfectly entitled to ask this question: to what end, and in relation to what realities, are these myths and symbols formulated and preserved within a religious tradition? What is their basis or purpose? Exactly the same questions can be raised about religious laws or precepts, which likewise are neither true nor false in any propositional sense. What such questions imply is that the various non-propositional modes of religious theory – myths, symbols, laws, precepts and so on – must ultimately make sense in terms of some claims, however modest or provisional, about what might very broadly be called 'the nature of things' or 'the way things are'. The same must be said about a whole range of non-propositional statements, observations and recommendations that people of all sorts, including secular humanists, make about morality, art, science, politics, education and other human interests.

Any serious account of any kind of values or activities ultimately rests on presuppositions, or eventually leads to conclusions, concerning the nature of human beings and the universe in which they live. And if a person engaged in or interested in the arts, for instance, were to explain or justify this interest simply in terms of the pleasure and fulfilment it provides, why should it not be enough for a religious person to justify their interest in similarly modest terms? Thus a religious apologist might say of the doctrines of a religion, along with its myths, symbols, laws and precepts, that these have no basis or purpose other than that of enhancing the lives of its adherents and perhaps also of strengthening the bonds of society at large. One will have heard politicians justifying the pursuit of politics in very similar terms. These are hardly modest justifications, but they nevertheless fall short of the kind of ultimate justification that many critics are inclined to demand in the case of religion. But why should any further justification be necessary if it is not necessary in the case of those who recommend or pursue interests in any other sphere? Religious and secular values and activities are all in the same boat when it comes to explanation and justification.

It is not hard to see that myths, symbols, precepts, parables and the other media of religious theory ultimately depend upon a theory of human nature (an anthropology) and a view about the nature of the universe (a cosmology). Such a view need not be teleological in the 'horizontal' sense of envisaging the realization of some ultimate purpose or of some final event or future condition, whether in this world or in another. Teleologies of this latter kind have certainly been developed in some religious traditions, notably in the great monotheistic traditions of the West. But other religious cosmologies have been teleological in the 'vertical' rather than 'horizontal' sense, namely by promoting the conformity of human attitudes and practices with the way the universe already works. Many so-called tribal religions have cosmologies of this kind, as have, for example, the Taoist, Confucian and Buddhist traditions of Chinese culture.

Once it is accepted that a religious worldview, however it is expressed in myth, symbol, precept and so on, implies or incorporates a range of propositions, hypotheses and opinions about the way things are or will be, or would or should be, then to that extent this religion opens itself to the same kind of investigation and evaluation to which theories in any other human sphere are open, whether these be scientific, economic, legal, political, aesthetic or historical theories. Being open to scrutiny in this way, however, does not mean that such investigation and evaluation will come easily. It may well be that only persons specially qualified, or only particular kinds of method, are capable of illuminating, let alone verifying, religious claims. Indeed, in pursuing an evaluation of a religious theory, the sceptic or critic might need to become in effect a member of the religion in question in order to pursue such investigation to its natural conclusion. After all, in many areas of scientific enquiry, for example, the difficulty of the subject matter is such that one must in effect become a scientist oneself to make proper sense of it, just as citizens seriously engaged in fighting for some local cause will sometimes find themselves in effect becoming politicians or lawyers. There are fields such as law, economics, quantum theory, literary theory and philosophy, to name but a few, where the complexity or subtlety of the subject matter means that, for people who have not immersed themselves in it, the subject remains inaccessible, as well as subject to various kinds of oversimplification or misrepresentation. Why should religious truths or realities be any easier to understand by those who are unfamiliar with the appropriate vocabulary or uninitiated in the relevant practices?

Two further moves, however, are made by those who want to insist that religious theory (or at least their own theory) is not open to the kind of rational scrutiny to which theories in other fields are. These are, on the one hand, the claim that their subtlety or complexity make religious truths or realities *in practice* inaccessible to rational communication and investigation, and on the other hand the stronger claim that these theories and practices are *by definition* incommunicable to those who have no direct knowledge of them. In its most extreme form, this latter claim is that the highest truths or realities of religion are incomprehensible even to those who *do* encounter them directly. Whether these truths or realities are impossible to communicate rationally, or merely very difficult to communicate, the argument is that any attempt at rational explanation is liable to misrepresent them, exposing them to the familiar kinds of ignorant and unsympathetic criticism at the hands of critics and sceptics. It may be conceded that some indirect communication of these truths or realities is effected through myth and symbol, and yet myths and symbols, as narrative and representational media, are themselves open to misunderstanding. Perhaps the most constructive alternative to any kind of direct communication is to lead others towards and along the path whereby these incommunicable truths or realities might be directly encountered, be this through asceticism, ritual, worship, prayer, meditation or selfless service to others.

The only remaining strategy is for the prophet, visionary or mystic to keep silence, while following a mode of life in harmony with what has been apprehended. This, it might be said, is close to being the theological equivalent of pleading the Fifth Amendment.[18] The strategy of a consistent silence in the face of a truth or reality at (or beyond) the limit of ordinary human understanding was, in effect, the strategy initially decided upon by the Buddha immediately after his enlightenment experience, according to the mythological narrative of the Buddha's life. 'This Dhamma [truth or doctrine] that I have attained', thought the Buddha, 'is deep, hard to see, hard to realize, peaceful, refined, beyond the scope of conjecture, subtle, to-be-experienced by the wise.' It would be very hard for a generation delighting in and excited by attachments of all kinds to grasp what he himself had now understood concerning 'the resolution of all fabrications, the relinquishment of all acquisitions, the ending of craving; dispassion; cessation; Unbinding [nirvana]. And if I were to teach the Dhamma and if others would not understand me, that would be tiresome for me, troublesome for me.'[19] The story continues with an urgent visit from the god Brahmā, who pleads with the Buddha not to withhold his teaching from the world, since there are some with 'little dust in their eyes' who *would* be able to understand and benefit from it. And so the Buddha decides, after all, to become the 'teacher of gods and men', at which point the Buddhist religion commences.

What is important about this story, which also illustrates well the power of myth, is that the difficulties the Buddha foresees in teaching his Dhamma to others are contingent in nature. There is no difficulty in principle about communicating the Dhamma to others, just as there is no inherent difficulty in understanding it in the first place, as the Buddha himself had demonstrated by his own efforts. It is important to emphasize, moreover, that rational explanation is at least as important in Buddhism as any kind of mythic or symbolic communication. The Dhamma is fully open to intellectual discussion and empirical examination. In fact the Buddha describes his doctrine as *ehipassiko*, which might be translated idiomatically as 'check it out for yourself.'

The stronger argument about the impossibility of communicating or even grasping religious truths or realities, let alone making them the subject of rational inquiry, depends upon drawing a sharp distinction between what lies within and what lies outside the order of nature. This is the familiar distinction between the natural and the supernatural.[20] So-called 'supernatural' truths or realities lie beyond the limit of the ordinary, empirical world; they are 'wholly other'.[21] Inherently inaccessible to rational investigation, we can know about these supernatural truths or realities only through revelation, such as is vouchsafed to favoured prophets, visionaries and mystics. In specifically theistic terminology, this is the distinction between natural and revealed theology. Natural theology is the body of religious truths human beings can discover for themselves, and revealed theology the body of religious truths that discovers itself to us. In the case of natural theology, a limited knowledge of religious truths is there waiting to be discovered through reason and observation, just as other things are: electrons, microbes, prime numbers, evolution and so on. Revealed theology, by contrast, is the direct message of God or the gods to human beings, inevitably at some particular time and place. Such knowledge is not dependent on ordinary forms of knowing, and beyond a certain point not open to rational criticism or inquiry. Paradoxically, therefore, whereas the truths of natural theology are potentially accessible to all human beings, revealed truths are, initially at least, confined within a particular historical context. And yet it is these 'revealed' truths that people often want to proclaim or to turn into universal truths, which can only happen if they are 'developed' and 'interpreted'.

Returning to the distinction between the natural and the supernatural, one must note several difficulties with the idea of the supernatural as a realm of reality above and beyond the natural world of mind and senses. To begin with, as a distinction created within the so-called 'natural' order, it is a distinction that will tend to give priority, and authority, to the natural realm. It is somewhat like making a distinction between married and unmarried people, which tends to imply that the married state is normative. Again, and in so far as the natural is a reflection, expression or creation of the supernatural, artificially detaching the natural from the supernatural can only lead to a diminished view of whatever it is that is defined as the natural. For the natural world is more than it appears to be; the natural is itself supernatural. Once the distinction between natural and supernatural becomes absolute, as tends to happen with any distinction, the natural soon becomes the self-contained entity it is in fact considered to be in much modern thinking.

Finally, the separation of supernatural from natural hardly does the supernatural any favours, if one may put it thus. For those individuals privileged enough to receive an allegedly supernatural revelation are not themselves supernatural beings; they belong in this world and not the supernatural one, which is why what they have received is generally described as 'revelation'. Moreover, whatever attempts are made to communicate or interpret this revelation, perhaps in mythic or symbolic terms, will also be located in the natural rather than the supernatural world. The very act of apprehending, let alone interpreting, so-called supernatural revelations will, by definition, occur within the natural world. This is all the more so in the case of secondary interpretations of the revelation made by those religious thinkers who turn the revelation into a body of doctrine, law and ritual. Given that any expression, interpretation or codification of a revelation takes place within the ordinary world, and is to this extent subject to ordinary criteria of communication and understanding, the question arises as to how one is to differentiate between naturally acquired and supernaturally revealed religious knowledge, since both forms are known only through their expression in natural rather than supernatural terms. This entire dilemma is an artefact of the false and unnecessary dichotomy set up between the natural and the supernatural realms.

Not only is the sharp distinction between a revealed and a natural theology a gross oversimplification, if not misrepresentation, of human knowledge of the transcendent. It is also a distinction that its proponents inevitably find hard to maintain. It is worth noting, certainly, that doctrines defined as, or justified by, supernatural revelation are far more concrete and specific than the rather more general or abstract forms of knowledge traditionally identified with purely natural theology. This will be officially explained as reflecting the detailed content of a divine message as received by a particular prophet or group of people. A critic, on the other hand, will suggest that these detailed doctrines, even if they did originate in a supernatural revelation of some kind, are as they stand very much the product of human reasoning and partisan interests, usually within the highly institutionalized context of a particular religion. In this case, the supernaturally revealed religious truths would appear to be no less 'natural' than the truths revealed through what is generally regarded as revelation's 'poor relation' – that is, through natural theology. In fact, most apologists for the idea of revealed theology acknowledge that even supernaturally revealed truths require interpretation, which does not always sit comfortably with the claim that such revelation is inaccessible to rational discussion or evaluation. Why not, instead, regard all theological or religious knowledge as 'natural', both in the sense that it is in principle accessible to all people and in the sense that it is invariably shaped by the circumstances of its origin?

The idea that there exists a divine or supernatural realm, totally separate from the earthly realm and known only through some special revelation, is not in fact 'natural' to religion, but is, rather, an artefact largely created by Western theology and philosophy. Since so many assumptions about the nature of religion are based one way or another upon Western models of religion, it is hardly surprising that many people assume the distinction between the natural and the supernatural to be the very basis of all religion. The highly questionable division of reality into the 'natural' and the 'supernatural' emerged partly from a theology that sought to emphasize the gulf between the human and the divine and partly from a scientific outlook that made the immediate world of mind and senses the standard by which reality as a whole was to be judged, so that the so-called 'supernatural' realm became pro-gressively more remote and abstract and, consequently, ever easier to ignore or deny altogether. The exile of divinity is unwittingly captured, as in a snapshot, in Browning's evocation of Spring at the end of one of the songs from his verse drama *Pippa Passes*:

> The lark's on the wing;
> The snail's on the thorn;
> God's in his heaven –
> All's right with the world![22]

What this effectively implies is that God's up there (perhaps) but we're down here, in the real world, whereas in other (and earlier Western) cosmology God's presence within the world (his immanence) is no less important than his containment of it (his transcendence). It is strange to think that our largely secular view of reality is, in part at least, based on some unfortunate turns in medieval theology and philosophy. As it is, the separation of divinity from the rest of reality, within a virtually self-contained realm of being, goes hand in hand with the segregation of religion as a whole from the rest of culture and society.

FIVE

IN EXPERIENCES WE TRUST?

'You talk to God, you're religious; God talks to you, you're psychotic,' states the eponymous physician in the TV series *House, MD.*[1] The sentiment here would be endorsed by many religious sceptics and critics. Religion is acceptable, and even beneficial, if it is just a matter of persons having certain kinds of subjective feelings and beliefs, and living by them without the interference of others. But when religion seems to be asserting its own unpredictable authority over an individual, and potentially over others too, it becomes a disease demanding containment if not cure. What is undeniable, however, is that taking religions seriously – taking them on their own terms – means accepting the primacy of various kinds of profound and often extraordinary experiences that lie at the heart of these religions.

Indeed, it is not difficult to make the case that the ultimate explanation or at least justification of religion stands or falls with the status of certain kinds of profound or revelatory experience. Thus if any one of the four 'dimensions' of religion is to be regarded as primary, it would have to be the dimension of experience. This does not imply, however, that those who emphasize 'spirituality' at the expense of religion would be correct in thinking that religious experience by itself is, ideally, all that is required for the leading of a spiritually fulfilling life. Even the most profound enlightenments or revelations seem to depend, without this in any way undermining their authenticity, on their association with doctrines, practices and institutions in order for sympathetic individuals or communities fully to benefit from them. None of the experiences recorded by the early Christians, for example, would have made much sense, or even have been possible, without the Jewish mono-theism and prophetism that formed their background. Nor would the enlightenment of the Buddha, which he proclaimed to be the highest and most authoritative form of human experience, have been possible without the ideas and techniques he had developed over the many years leading up to this event. Experiences may constitute the primary dimension of religion, but their activation and interpretation require a theoretical, practical and institutional context.

Before defining more precisely what is meant by 'religious experience', something needs to be said about the idea of experi-ence as such. The inherent ambiguity of the word 'experience' can be brought out by distinguishing between an experience as some-thing 'experienced' (passively, as it were) and an experience as an 'experiencing' (an act or activity one initiates and to some extent controls). In both cases, experience embraces a whole spectrum of possible sensations, ideas, intuitions, impulses and intentions. For the same reason, experience is something continuous; one lives one's whole waking life, and at least some of one's sleeping life, experiencing the world through the senses or through one's own ideas, memory and imagination. We tend to talk about 'having' an experience of some kind, rather than simply experiencing, only when something particular and in many cases unexpected occurs within the continuum of our ongoing awareness.

Everyone is experiencing and experienced, in the active and passive senses just described, simply by virtue of being sentient creatures with intelligence and memory. When we describe someone as 'experienced', however, we are normally referring to something more specific. When we talk of someone being an 'experienced' swimmer, farmer, sailor or diplomat, for example, we probably mean both that such individuals have had many years pursuing these occupations and also that, in pursuing them, they have acquired and demonstrated particular kinds of skill. In this latter sense, we might instead say that an individual is a 'skilled' swimmer, sailor, farmer or diplomat. If we were to ask such individuals to recount some of their swimming, sailing, farming or diplomatic experiences, however, it would probably be assumed that we were interested not in the routine thoughts, sensations, activities or techniques associated with the occupation in question but rather in some particular incident or episode in which the swimming, sailing, farming or diplomacy was tested or exhibited in some especially vivid or dramatic way. In other words, we want to hear about some particular *episode* that stands out from the routine continuum of experience.

These usages apply to religious no less than to any other kind or context of experience. Religious experience in the more routine sense is about the way one apprehends the world in the context of this or that belief or practice, but religious experience can also be about 'having' ('cultivating', 'enjoying' or 'receiving') certain kinds of special experience. The meaningful experiences of most religious people are by and large quite ordinary and even predictable – for instance, the sense of unity created by communal worship, the enthusiasm of charismatic worship, the enfolding peace of a religious building, the sense of trust or assurance in difficult circumstances, and so on. But the kinds of experiences that most writers have in mind for the term 'religious experience' are those more profound, intense, dramatic or unexpected episodes of experience, and because these stand out from the ordinary continuum of life there is a tendency to consider them more or less independently of the doctrines and practices in the context of which many of them arise. There are some who believe that such experiences can be 'creamed off' from the rest of religion and, liberated from the doctrinal and institutional encrustations of centuries, made the basis of a new vision of reality, or simply enjoyed for their own sake. What encourages this attitude is the fact that many extraordinary experiences of a religious or 'spiritual' kind do occur spontaneously to individuals who, even if they profess a religion, are not engaged in any kind of specialist religious discipline. Some religious experiences come unsought, others in association with some method of prayer or meditation; some occur in specifically religious contexts, others in circumstances that appear to have nothing to do with religion.

What nevertheless justifies the outsider's interest in the more intense episodes of religious experience is the special attention they receive within the religions themselves. This is true above all in those experiences one might call 'foundational': the enlightenment of the Buddha, the identity of self with Brahman realized by Hindu saints, the visions of the Old Testament prophets, St Paul's conversion experience, the revelation of the Qur'ān to the Prophet Muhammad, and so on. It is right therefore to recognize the importance of what I shall call 'extraordinary' religious experience, provided we bear in mind that for most religious people their religious experience is 'ordinary' rather than 'extraordinary'. Equally important is the recognition that not all 'extraordinary' experience is religious, or recognized as religious, in any narrowly doctrinal or institutional sense. Moreover, just as not all religious experience is 'extraordinary', so not all 'extraordinary' experience is religious, at least in any direct or obvious sense. There are, for example, some extraordinary experiences that one is more inclined to categorize as 'psychic', others one would classify as 'aesthetic', and so on. Whether or not an experience is best categorized as religious will depend not only on its inherent qualities but on the intentions and responses of the subject of the experience.

William James, to whose work so many studies of religious experience look back, held the view that by concentrating on the more 'extreme' forms of religious experience one is more likely to get the measure of the subject.[2] Like many authors since, James was especially interested in the range of experiences known as 'mystical', since these are not only emotionally the most intense but cognitively the most intriguing.[3] They include, among other states, what are reported as visions of another world; awareness of one's unity with nature; profound states of lucid and unified consciousness; insights into the meaning of existence; and states of union or oneness with a personal God or transpersonal Absolute. Mystical states of consciousness are sometimes linked with experiences of the kind generally classified as 'psychic', which include telepathy, clairvoyance, precognition and the like – experiences which, although also themselves extraordinary, generally have a this-worldly rather than an otherworldly focus.

SOME OF THE CHARACTERISTICS typical of mystical states, or at least of descriptions of mystical states, are illustrated in the following passage from the account of an ecstatic illumination given by a nineteenth-century Canadian doctor, R. M. Bucke, an account well known largely through its being cited by William James. After finding himself enveloped in a flame-coloured cloud, there came upon him

> a sense of exultation, of immense joyousness accompanied or immediately followed by an intellectual illumination impossible to describe. Among other things, I did not merely come to believe, but I saw, that the universe is not composed of dead matter, but is, on the contrary, a living Presence; I became conscious in myself of eternal life. It was not a conviction that I would have eternal life, but a consciousness that I possessed eternal life then; I saw that all men are immortal; that the cosmic order is such that without any peradventure all things work together for the good of each and all; that the foundation principle of the world, of all the worlds, is what we call love, and that the happiness of each and all is in the long run absolutely certain.[4]

Those mystics who have been prepared to speak or write about their experiences will often comment on the extreme difficulty of adequately describing them, which seems to go beyond the general difficulty (not to mention the reluctance) that people feel in trying to communicate profound personal experiences.[5] And yet the writings of some of the mystics are profuse and detailed, almost as if they are working overtime to communicate to others something of the importance and profundity of what they have apprehended. In hindsight, these experiences are frequently described as having paradoxical features, or at least (which is not necessarily the same thing) as only being describable in paradoxical terms. This often relates to the fact that the temporary disappearance of self or ego characteristic of many such experiences is simultaneously felt to be an enlargement rather than a diminution of the subject's perception and understanding.

Bucke himself says that his 'illumination' (by which he does not necessarily mean the entire experience) was 'impossible to describe'. In one sense, mystics can only make, or try to make, rational sense of their experiences, such as might be communicable to others, at one remove from the experience itself – at which point any descriptions they attempt are also likely to include elements of interpretation. This in turn means that those who learn about such experiences indirectly, from the mouths or the writings of the mystics, are at two removes from the experience, and hence not necessarily in a position to differentiate with any confidence between experience and interpretation. Mystics themselves may not even be able to differentiate clearly between experience and interpretation, not least because interpretation can begin within the experience itself. Indeed it may be doubted whether a clear-cut differentiation between experience and interpretation is possible in any type of experience, religious or other. But in any case, whatever interpretation mystics do make of an experience, whether during the experience or immediately after it, must surely be accepted as an integral part of it. Not to recognize this is to risk removing the experiencer from the experience, and to treat the latter as a set of 'experiential' data detached from the personal history of any particular experiencing subject.

Even so, we can hardly deny the validity of drawing some sort of distinction between an experience in itself and its (immediate or subsequent) interpretation (or interpretations). We can and commonly do judge interpretations both of our own and of others' experiences to be false, tendentious or inadequate. And people not infrequently revise their initial interpretations of an experience. It would certainly be a mistake to regard the interpretations individuals give of their own experiences, even of their most personal experiences, as necessarily sacrosanct and hence immune to correction or modification by others. At the same time, it is important to remember, interpretations of other peoples' experiences are based not on the original experience itself but on whatever descriptions-cum-interpretations the subjects of these experiences have given of them. But this does not, in itself, invalidate the activity of third-order interpretation. The interpretation of any kind of experiencing in this world is a social as well as personal activity, mediated by the shared language of a culture. There is no reason to suppose that any of these considerations should not also apply as much to a religious experience as to any other type of human experience.

The sometimes minimal and sometimes detailed accounts of their experiences given by mystics and others, and the fact that the more detailed accounts tend to include elaborate interpretations of their causes and significance, particularly in the writings of mystics who are philosophically or theologically sophisticated, has encouraged a range of strategies for further interpretation by third parties. These strategies lie between two extremes of interpretation.

On the one hand is the strategy of stripping away what is deemed to be the interpretation imposed upon an experience in order to reveal what is assumed to be the 'pure' or 'essential' experience beneath it, rather as an art restorer might hope to bring the full glory of the original painting back to life after removing the centuries of grime and clumsy restoration work that have obscured it. This 'essentialist' approach to understanding mystical experience may be based on prior assumptions about the universally similar nature of mystical experience across religions and cultures. In any case, essentialists are ready to apply a 'one size fits all' interpretation of their own, sometimes borrowed from traditions whose interpretations are regarded as nearer the mark than those of other traditions. Thus essentialists are like art restorers who, having removed the work of earlier varnishers, are now ready to decide what new coat of varnish should be applied. Critics of this approach will of course say that such restorers have, in reality, ruined the masterpiece by removing much of the painter's original work.

At the other extreme is the strategy of understanding the whole of an experience as a construction arising, in a given set of circumstances, out of a mystic's personal beliefs, feelings and psychology, the norms and presuppositions of their culture, and the official doctrines and practices of their own (or their 'nearest') religious tradition. These experiences have no 'core' or 'essence' to be differentiated from any interpretation. They are, in a sense, nothing but interpretation. Even to think of them as particular, self-contained experiences is misleading. They are part and parcel of a person's ongoing and concurrently interpreted life experience. This 'constructivist' approach is a form of reductionism or scepticism in relation to the claims usually made by religious people on the basis of their own and others' extraordinary religious experiences. If essentialism oversimplifies the distinction between experience and interpretation, then constructivism seeks to abolish it, and with it the basis on which we refine our awareness and interpretation of the world through our experiencing of it and our 'experiences' within it. Strictly and consistently applied, constructivism would hoover up all claims to have experienced truths or realities independent of the subject's own psychology, whether in this world or in some 'higher' world. It challenges the whole idea of the empirical confirmation of theories or propositions through sensory (or for that matter extra-sensory) perceptions. But of course constructivism is not and could not be strictly or consistently applied. It is applied only to 'interior' experiences whose claim to reveal objective truths or realities is doubted, or rejected, from the start. We are back with Dr House here. Religious experiences are in the same category as dreams or hallucinations. The presumption is that these experiences are merely psychological states, unusual and compelling perhaps, but with no foothold in any reality beyond the subject's own mind.

Between the extremes of essentialism and constructivism, however, is a more challenging possibility: that in and through intense religious experience a person may interact or unite with – or at least glimpse or witness – levels of truth or reality as solid, as important and as complex as the truths and realities that define our ordinary lives; but that any subsequent understanding of these experiences will inevitably be delimited by the subject's own biography, psychology, religion and culture. If the content or implications of these experiences encourage scepticism, and even a certain kind of hostility, then the insistent and persisting conviction as to the reality and importance of their experiences on the part of the demonstrably sane subjects of these experiences should at least give pause to sceptics and critics.

Yet the conviction that mystics and other subjects of extraordinary experiences have of the authenticity and objectivity of their experiences by no means implies that they will describe or interpret it with the kind of clear-cut confidence evident in the case of Bucke's illuminative ecstasy. They may have difficulty, both during and following an experience, in knowing the precise significance of what is nevertheless a very real and powerful experience. As a very simple example of this, consider the childhood experience recalled by the American writer Mary Austin:

> I must have been between five and six when this experience happened to me. It was a summer morning, and the child I was had walked down through the orchard alone and come out on the brow of a sloping hill where there was grass and a wind blowing and one tall tree reaching into infinite immensities of blueness. Quite suddenly, after a moment of quietness there, earth and sky and tree and wind-blown grass and the child in the midst of them came alive together with a pulsing light of consciousness. There was a wild foxglove at the child's feet and a bee dozing about it, and to this day I can recall the swift inclusive awareness of each for the whole – I in them and they in me and all of us enclosed in a warm lucent bubble of livingness. I remember the child looking everywhere for the source of this happy wonder, and at last she questioned

– 'God?' – because it was the only awesome word she knew.
Deep inside, like the murmurous swinging of a bell, she
heard the answer, 'God, God . . .'

How long this ineffable moment lasted I never knew.
It broke like a bubble at the sudden singing of a bird, and
the wind blew and the world was the same as ever – only
never *quite* the same. The experience so initiated has been
the one abiding reality of my life, unalterable except in
the abounding fullness and frequency of its occurrence.[6]

In responding to and trying to understand her extraordinary
experience, and being ignorant (or innocent) of theology and
metaphysics, the child reached for an 'awesome' word that seemed
to fit her experience, even in the course of the experience itself.
In doing so she was not, either as child or as recollecting adult,
simply forcing her experience into a ready-made interpretation,
let alone doctrine, nor was she claiming in a simple-minded way
that God was speaking to her, as television's Dr House, like many
real-life doctors, imagines that such experiences are to be understood. Rather than subordinating her experience to the idea of
God, what the child is doing is subordinating the idea of 'God',
or the word 'God', to the authority of her experience. How, other
than in this kind of way, could the word or idea 'God', or any other
kind of theological or metaphysical term or idea, ever grow in the
first place? Indeed, one of the tendencies to which religion perpetually falls prey is that of stifling the dialogue between language
and experience, so that the rich varieties of religious experience,
necessarily individualized by the particular psychology and circu-
stances of the subjects of these experiences, are forced into the
procrustean bed of this or that theological or metaphysical scheme.

HOW ARE INTENSE and 'extraordinary' religious experiences to
be evaluated in relation to the claims made about religion by
its apologists? Must not such experiences be regarded as critically important evidence for the validity or authority of at least

some religious doctrines? If it were a case of a particular scientific theory being supported by one group of scientists and rejected or disputed by another, would not both parties seek to settle the matter by recourse to the available natural and experimental evidence? Of course, the sparsity or ambiguity of the evidence might be a main reason why the two groups of scientists continue to disagree about the theory, but at least they could agree on the vital importance of any available evidence. The other factor would be the fruitfulness of the theory in allowing new and valid predictions to be made. But this too constitutes an appeal to experience, albeit to future rather than present experience. Certainly to accept a theory for which there was no evidence on the grounds that the theory was long-established, elegantly constructed or a widely respected source of authority would hardly do. Whatever differences there may be between science and religion, does not religion, like science, embody theories about the nature of reality and depend crucially upon originating or supporting evidence of some kind? And does it not also rely upon the idea of the fruitfulness of its doctrines, practices and experiences? Surely the most vital empirical and experimental evidence in religion must come from those extraordinary ways of 'experiencing' the world and those intensely 'experienced' episodes that interrupt the normal flow of life that make up the varieties of religious experience.

It is the unilaterally subjective nature of these extraordinary experiences, as well as the seemingly irrational or fantastic nature of their contents, that suggest to religious sceptics that these experiences can be evidence of nothing more than the beliefs and imaginations (and in some cases delusions) of those who report them. All individual experiences are subjective, of course, in the sense of being 'located' in, or shaped by, a particular human consciousness that is inaccessible (other than telepathically, perhaps) to the consciousness of any other individual. But some experience, or experiencing, is intersubjective, by which is meant that two or more individuals can through their mutual reactions and communications know for sure that they in effect share the same set of experiences, that they are perceiving and reacting to the same objectively real external realities. In the simple case of two people playing a card game, for example, the playing of the game depends upon the fact that the two players are simultaneously having both intersubjective perceptions ('the Jack of Hearts has just been played') and purely subjective ones ('I think I'll play the Ace of Hearts'). Now although one can find examples of intersubjective religious experience, the vast majority seem to be 'solitary' experiences of one kind or another, which therefore invite the obvious sceptical criticism that they are in effect purely subjective – that is, they do not depend on (and therefore cannot be evidence of) contact with, or knowledge of, any other being, world or level of reality. What is too often forgotten is the persisting insistence by the perfectly rational subjects of these experiences that what they have experienced was not only real, but in some way more real than the real things that create the contents of ordinary experience. Mystics are as aware as anybody else of the possibility of having experiences of an illusionary, hallucinatory or delusionary kind, and so their denial that their experiences were of any such kind must be taken as seriously as any other element in their descriptions or interpretations.

But if we are to accept the veridicality of a religious experience we must do this on the basis of the same principle by which we accept the veridicality of any other kind of human experience: namely, what one philosopher has called the 'Principle of Credulity'.[7] The principle has been summarized thus: 'When subjects have an experience which they take to be of x, it is rational to conclude that they really do experience x unless we have some positive reasons for thinking their experiences are delusive.'[8] If, in the absence of positive reasons for thinking otherwise, we must accept that people really do have the kind of experiences they say they have had, this does not mean that we will necessarily concur with their interpretation of their experience; but if we do not concur, then we are obliged either to offer some more satisfactory alternative interpretation of it or else to maintain a genuine agnosticism about its status. We cannot say, for example, 'I've no idea what you saw in that supposedly haunted house, but one thing's for sure: it could not have been a ghost!' What we cannot do in regard to an experience that a subject insists was real and important is dismiss it as unreal or unimportant. But if we want to insist that it must have been an illusionary or delusionary experience, we are obliged to specify what kind of illusionary or delusionary experience it is. We cannot simply say: it must have been an illusionary or delusionary experience. We must justify such a judgement. Failing this, we must defer to the estimates or explanations given by the subjects of these experiences themselves.[9] When people are heard urgently shouting 'Fire!', the first presumption must be to take these people at their word and rush to help or at least call the fire brigade. (Nor, at this stage, does anyone need a theory about the source of the fire.)

None of this implies that one ought to accept religious experiences uncritically or at face value; the interpretation of these experiences is, in the best sense of the word, a matter of negotiation. Each new experience we have is, in effect, tested against experiences that we, and other persons we know or know about, have had previously. In religion as in many other contexts, one's confidence in understanding what one has experienced depends not just on one's own instincts and past experience, but on the cumulative experience and collective wisdom of an entire tradition. Most religious traditions have developed methods for sifting the more important or reliable elements of an experience from the less important or less reliable (but often more striking) psychic elements. Many mystics and spiritual counsellors are generally wary of the distracting sensory phenomena that can supervene in the context of contemplative practice – phenomena which do not encourage the growth of virtue, compassion or wisdom. The anonymous author of the medieval *Cloud of Unknowing*, for example, warns how in the case of vain and ignorant individuals 'the devil can deceive their ears with quaint sounds, their eyes with quaint lights and shinings, their noses with wonderful smells – and they are all false!'[10] The sixteenth-century Spanish mystic Teresa of Avila comments on the relatively unreliable nature of what she classifies as 'physical' and 'imaginary'

visions, as distinct from the more profound 'intellectual' visions
– she herself having experienced all three kinds. In some cases
these lower kinds of vision will be purely subjective and leave no
lasting impression:

> Some persons . . . find that their imagination is so weak,
> or their understanding is so nimble, or for some other
> reason their imagination becomes so absorbed, that they
> think they can actually see everything that is in their mind.
> If they had ever seen a true vision they would realize their
> error beyond the possibility of doubt. Little by little they
> build up the picture which they see with their imagination,
> but this produces no effect upon them and they remain
> cold – much more so than they are after seeing a sacred
> image. No attention, of course, should be paid to such a
> thing, which will be forgotten much more quickly than a
> dream.[11]

Of course, every phenomenon, psychic or religious, must mean
something, and in the right hands, as it were, every phenomenon
may have its own usefulness. In the Buddhist contemplative path,
attainment of the higher levels of supernormal concentration
brings with it a range of psychic abilities – telepathy, clairvoyance, out-of-body experience and so on. Given the wrong kind
of attention, these abilities can distract one from the path to
enlightenment, but they can also be useful not just as signs that
one has reached a certain level of mental strength and clarity
but also as further subject matter for meditative insight. In the
Tibetan Book of the Dead, differently coloured lights perceived
mark different stages in the process of dying and rebirth. In any
complete cosmology, every phenomenon, however minor, must
have some explanation within the whole, and it may or may not
be the one attributed to it by this or that spiritual text or author.
In some traditions, the sweeter and potentially more distracting
phenomena encountered in contemplation may be attributed
to the agency of evil spirits, whereas in others they may rather

be understood as manifestations or representations of personal weaknesses a subject needs to overcome.

Given the profound and sometimes ineffable character of the varieties of religious experience, and the variety of their interpretations also, even within the same tradition, it is perhaps not surprising that religious apologists are not always eager to appeal to such experiences in support of the doctrines and practices of their tradition. On the face of it, these experiences would seem to provide just the kind of evidence one needs to counter the objections from sceptics and critics that religion has no empirical basis or is not susceptible to experimental confirmation. From the seventeenth century onwards, however, religious realities have been progressively relegated to a 'supernatural' realm beyond the empirical, whereas in earlier times, as in other cultures still, the sacred and the saintly were thought to be more immediately accessible. Modern religious apologists may suppose that they will be taken more seriously if they defend religious doctrines through rational argument on the basis of sacred texts and of general facts about the world rather than by reference to the truths or realities disclosed in contemplative, mystical and other varieties of extraordinary experience. A religion defined mainly by scriptural authority and rational argument undoubtedly presents a cleaner and more manageable image than one defined by a variety of sometimes unruly religious experiences. Yet any appeal either to the authority of sacred texts or to general facts about the world must itself ultimately rest on the primary authority of experience, in which case the more extraordinary experiences surely merit our special attention if they reveal, as they seem to do to their subjects and to others who have examined them, evidence of truths or realities not otherwise accessible.

It is acknowledged, of course, that at the heart and origin of a tradition are the exemplary religious experiences of founders and leaders. But these 'foundational' experiences, as I described them earlier, are differentiated and segregated from any of the experiences to which ordinary adherents might aspire. They tend to be treated as unique and unrepeatable, even where they also function as exemplary experiences for the followers of the tradition. In the Buddhist tradition, for instance, many individuals are said to have attained enlightenment through following the Buddha's teaching, and yet the Buddha's own enlightenment experience is credited with special qualities unknown to any of his enlightened followers. Thus the only extraordinary experiences known to many religious apologists are those that are safely enshrined in the mythology and ritual of a tradition, their interpretation controlled by a scholarly elite.

Another factor behind the reluctance of religious apologists to engage with religious experience is the sense that certain kinds of experience, or at least too much attention paid to such experience, are thought liable to rock the boat of religious orthodoxy. Since certain types of religious experiences have indeed been associated with radicalism and reform, long-established religious institutions are understandably wary of intense or extraordinary experiences. It is almost as if they would prefer their adherents to make do (in this life at least) with the more predictable, 'ordinary' experiences. Intense religious experiences are set aside for an elite body of saints and mystics, and even these have been given a hard time because of the things they have said about, or on the basis of, these experiences. This is more likely to happen in monotheistic traditions, where any extraordinary experiences are potentially in conflict with the originating revelations of the tradition. It would be unthinkable to have some latter-day Moses, fresh from a close encounter with the Deity, wanting to add (or subtract) commandments to (or from) the long-established Decalogue.

PERHAPS THE MOST substantial reason for not giving too much attention to extraordinary religious experience is the danger of what might be defined as 'experientialism', or of what has been called 'spiritual materialism'.[12] This occurs where someone seeks out or cherishes such experiences for their own sake rather than for what these experiences seem to promise or demand of one.

The term 'experientialism' also describes the tendency, no doubt manifest in this very chapter, for the living experiences of others to be turned into chunks of data for the scrutiny of those who may have no knowledge of, or relation to, the living source of this experience. We saw, in an earlier chapter, how a similar thing happens when the personal activity of 'believing' gets abstracted into impersonal 'beliefs', which then become available for anyone to adopt, second-hand, as their own beliefs.

There is no doubt that 'experientialism' is a real danger not only in the life of religion but in the popular and academic representation of religions. But the danger should not be allowed to obscure what is necessary and genuine in the evaluation of the variety of extraordinary religious experiences. For one thing, mystics themselves have written about their experiences mainly for the benefit of others, and in so doing have assumed that their experiences, as well as the practices and way of life associated with them, will be of both intellectual and practical assistance to serious readers. One might think here of a parallel between mystics and poets (which is in many cases, of course, more than just a parallel): poets too write for others, and face the same problem of ineffability when trying to convey their feelings and insights; but they also believe that their poems can communicate to others something of value from their own experiences. It would be grotesque to describe poems, even when extracted from or anthologized, as being little more than the mummifications of living experience. Why should the accounts of extraordinary religious experiences be any less successful in their power to inform and exhort others? And should they not be valued, even at second hand, for their capacity to do this?

Should we therefore trust in religious experience as the bedrock of religious meaning? Certainly the truth of religion depends on the truth or reality of the beings, worlds and metaphysical insights of which founders, mystics and others claim to have had personal knowledge. For religious apologists themselves to ignore or dismiss these challenging and sometimes disruptive experiences, as no doubt Dostoevsky's Grand Inquisitor would have done, is to risk removing the ground from beneath religion. For sceptics to ignore them is to renege on their own persistent demands for empirical evidence, if not proof, of the claims of religion.

What must not be forgotten, however, is that these extraordinary religious experiences, whatever the degree of their supernormal or divine 'content', are by definition human experiences – not experiences of the kind that might elsewhere be enjoyed by gods, angels, spirits or other intelligent beings. They are, so to speak, this-worldly otherworldly experiences. This being so, we have to treat these experiences critically but with the utmost respect – and with respect also for the sane and mature subjects who report and live by them, insisting that in or through them they have been in contact with another world or seen the present world in a new light. In short, it is not the experiences in themselves that are important, nor the theories and doctrines to which they give rise, but the transformations that they bring about in the lives of those who are their subjects, and through them in the lives of others.[13]

SIX

HERE BE AUTHORITIES AND INSTITUTIONS

R eligion, according to one dictionary definition, is 'an organized system of beliefs, ceremonies, and rules used to worship a god or a group of gods'.[1] Where it is not the doctrines or the practices, or indeed the behaviour of the adherents themselves, that alienate people from religion, it will be the fact that these elements come as part of an institutional 'package', an organized entity managed by authorities. It is hardly surprising that religious as well as non-religious people are often quick to express a strong dislike of 'organized' or 'institutional' religion. These epithets also form part of the rhetoric deployed to differentiate between cold-blooded 'religion' and warm-hearted 'spirituality'. Indeed, in almost any context, words such as 'institution' and 'organization', and for that matter 'authority', tend to have unappealing if not forbidding connotations, despite being in themselves completely neutral.[2]

Religion everywhere is communal in nature; its ideas, practices and experiences necessarily depend upon the presence of others and upon relationships with others. There can be no such thing as a private or completely personal religion. Only a solipsist could sustain such an idea – and only a solipsist would want to! Humans are inherently social beings, beings whose lives and identities are created by, and creative of, many kinds of interpersonal relationship. One's identity, thoughts and actions cannot escape being social in nature, even if one were to live alone on a desert island.

Nor can one escape being in some way part of all the main institutions of one's society. For example, everyone's identity is in part defined by the institution of marriage; everyone will have some kind of relationship with this institution. This is clear enough when we fill out forms asking us to identify ourselves as either 'married' or 'unmarried'. Even if one wanted to do so, one cannot escape social institutions. Even in not being religious, or in not being a member of any religious group, one continues to have some kind of relationship with religion and the institutions of religion.

We may well regard ideas, practices and experiences as forming the living substance of religion and consider its organized and institutional aspects as secondary and potentially deadening accretions. Yet there is no avoiding the inevitability of the social and institutional dimension. The essentially social nature of humankind means that religions too will be social entities. As social entities, religions require organization in order to survive and develop, and hence are likely to develop broader institutional features. The same is true of football clubs, political parties, educational establishments and social media networks, for example. People could no more be members of a non-organized religion than they could be members of a non-organized political party or football club – though they might well be members of a badly organized or a disorganized one. What is important is how well or badly these social entities are organized, to what ends their organization is directed, and how their members relate to this or that aspect of their inevitable organization.

Those religious sects and movements that have tried to abolish, simplify or avoid established organizational structures have often ended up with new structures no less oppressive. Simplicity of organization can mean that one person, text or practice becomes dominant at the expense of others. New or reformist sects that reject established religious institutions as compromised if not corrupt will often have simple but strongly authoritarian structures in which powerful charismatic leaders control everything that their followers do and even believe. At least in the more complex religious institutions, a plurality of texts, doctrines and practices helps to keep the institution open and tolerant. Also, the inefficiency of complex institutions can be a powerful, albeit unintended, safeguard of its individual members' freedom and initiative.

The growth and development of religions depend not only on a variety of external factors (which offer both opportunities and challenges) but on the inner dynamic of the ideas, practices and experiences that form their basis: 'From the unusual religious experiences of unusual people the founded religions emerge, translating and transforming the insights of founders into institutional structures. Thus there arise the formed and formulated entities of belief-systems, systems of ritual and liturgy, and organization.'[3] There is, nevertheless, something of a gap between the necessary organization of a religion and the emergence within it of what might be called full-blown institutional features. The latter include such developments as the formation of ruling elites and hierarchies, the enforcement of orthodoxy and orthopraxy, and cooperation with other organizations or institutions, especially political ones. It is features such as these that many people have in mind when they object to 'organized religion'. Among the more negative features associated with religions as institutions are their authoritarianism, isolationism, exclusivism and resistance to reform. Where the emergence of such features is held to be inevitable, the objection is merely an annex to the objection to religion as such. Where they are not held to be inevitable, the objection will be part of a criticism of a religion for having lost its way or compromised its message.

The tendency of relatively simple social entities to develop more complex institutional features is easy enough to comprehend. For example, a charity will remain a simple organization so long as its activities are confined to the collection and distribution of money for the particular cause in question. Over time, however, such an organization may become so successful as to require professionally qualified staff to plan strategy, manage funds and coordinate activities, the use of offices if not entire buildings to house its operations, and the cultivation of relationships with government bodies at home and overseas. At this point, the charity will have become a complex organization. In time, its own history, along with its carefully managed public 'image', will itself become a part of its institutional profile. The more complex the charity becomes, the greater the chances of its incurring criticism for some aspect of its organization and management. Some criticisms will relate to corrigible flaws within the institution, but others may relate to aspects of its management intrinsic to the kind of institution it has now become. For example, the criticism that it is spending too much on salaries for its top staff is likely to be countered by the reasonable claim that it is only by paying high salaries that the charity is able to recruit and retain the best people for the job. It is hardly surprising that high-profile institutions, including religious ones, also employ staff expert in managing public relations.

One of the main charges brought against religious organizations is their readiness to protect their own institutional identity even at the expense of the truths and values on which they were founded.[4] The tendency of all large institutions to protect the status quo at any cost is nicely illustrated by a joke about Yuri Gagarin, the first man to go into space. At a big gathering held in his honour, the then president of the Soviet Union, Nikita Khrushchev, takes him aside to ask 'Did you see God up there?' 'I have some bad news, comrade,' replies Gagarin, 'I'm afraid that I did indeed see God, surrounded by many angels.' 'As I feared,' says Khrushchev, 'but let's keep this a secret, shall we? It would ruin everything.' A few months later, Gagarin is on a world tour and meets the pope at the Vatican. At a private meeting, the pope asks him, 'Did you see God up there?' 'I'm afraid not, Your Holiness; there was nothing but empty space.' 'As I feared,' answered the pope, 'but let's keep this a secret, shall we? It would ruin everything'. This joke is a distant cousin of the story of the Grand Inquisitor told in Dostoevsky's novel *The Brothers Karamazov*. Christ reappears on earth one day, only to be hauled before the Spanish Inquisition and told that his kind and his message will only create trouble for humanity and in particular for the Church.

A second criticism frequently made of religious institutions is that such institutions become excessively worldly. This worldliness takes various forms. One is the emergence of a class of career-minded professionals for whom the institution provides a comfortable way of life with good prospects of promotion. Another is the cultivation of close links with political or secular power, a feature which in some religions is there from the start and hence not describable as some kind of aberration. Where there is a deliberate strategy of combining religious with secular power, the result is some kind of 'state religion' (such as an 'established Church'). Where the religious ideas and values of a nation are embedded within the secular rituals and ceremonies of a state, the result is the phenomenon that sociologists call 'civil religion'.[5] These and other kinds of 'worldliness' in religious institutions are not in themselves morally suspect and indeed are often defended as highly compatible with the ideals and principles of the religion in question. In many cases, however, critics have no hesitation in applying stronger terms than worldliness, and may, for instance, talk about the corrupt and corrupting nature of such institutional developments. The Gagarin joke satirizes the mendacity, collusion and cover-up for which religious institutions have sometimes been criticized.

A third feature of organized religion is, perhaps, the one most commonly and most easily criticized. This is where the behaviour, attitudes and even experiences of religious adherents become predictable and standardized.[6] What in other institutions might be welcomed as a sign of health and stability is, in religious institutions, readily seen as a symptom of failure. There is, inevitably, considerable ambivalence about routine in the conduct of human affairs. People often complain about having to follow 'the same old routine', and yet sometimes welcome a return to a familiar pattern of life. Again, while routines may in general be good for a complex institution, they may not always be good for those who work in them. A bank may be doing well because its routines are being followed closely, but its employees may become bored or disaffected as a result. Organized religion is commonly criticized for the routinization of what, it is assumed, should stay fresh and spontaneous. This expectation betrays a somewhat romantic notion of religion, and a failure to realize that many worthwhile activities (learning a new language or practising a musical instrument, for example) require routine and repetition. Routine and repetition are, indeed, integral to some of the most serious religious practices, for example liturgical practice and the monastic life. Like the terms 'organization' and 'institution', the term 'routine' is strictly neutral.

It is important to emphasize that the institutional tendencies of a religion – including those of self-protection, worldliness and routinization described above – do not necessarily betray its founding principles or damage the interests of its adherents. This can be illustrated by another joke, which to some extent balances the one about Gagarin. It concerns a pious Irish widower (inevitably named Paddy) who when clumsily buttering his toast in the morning often drops it on the unswept kitchen floor, where it invariably lands butter-side down. One day, however, it lands butter-side up, and Paddy goes straight to the local priest to report what to him is a minor miracle, and one his religion might confirm for him. The priest is sceptical, but under Paddy's insistence reluctantly agrees to consult the bishop in the nearby town. The bishop, more sceptical than the priest yet fully apprised of Paddy's refusal to take no for an answer, reluctantly agrees to visit Dublin to consult one of the Jesuit fathers there. In due course the Jesuit comes back to the bishop, who in turn reports the learned verdict to the priest: 'Tell Paddy that he buttered his toast on the wrong side.' The politics of handling claims about miracles has, of course, been a real enough element in the complex life of the Roman Catholic Church. In the case of Paddy's 'miracle', the ecclesiastical system is able simultaneously to show Paddy that his claim was being taken seriously while protecting the institution itself from damage.[7]

The common factor in these two jokes is the power of the authorities running an institution. In the first, both leaders are prepared to overrule the authority of Gagarin's experience for the sake of their institution's (and, not least, their own) survival. Had Gagarin given different answers, no doubt each leader would gratefully have made Gagarin's experience public. Gagarin, acting more like a trickster figure than an astronaut, clearly enjoys upsetting the apple cart. He could, after all, have given a pleasing answer to both leaders.[8] The status quo of the institutions in question is safely maintained at the cost of a lie. In the second joke, Paddy subordinates the authority of his personal experience to the institutionalized superiority of his local priest, just as the priest defers to the authority of the bishop, and the bishop to that of the Jesuit fathers. Joking aside, these stories can be seen as parables about the sources and forms of authority in religion.

WHAT FIRST SPRINGS to mind when we see or hear the word 'authority' is a human figure of some kind. In any religion, the immediate human authorities will be those responsible for leading worship, defining and communicating doctrine, exercising pastoral care and administering other aspects of the life of the community. In religion, as in other areas of human life, we are more than happy to let the 'relevant authorities' deal with the problems involved in running an institution. We are also more than ready to hold these same authorities responsible for the mistakes or failures of an institution. The fact is that, in religion as in many other spheres of human life, people are often ambivalent about leadership and authority. People criticize their leaders and chafe against rules and regulations. But people also like to be led. So much of the history of religions has been a history of people being led to do or say or believe what they would not have done or said or believed in other circumstances. Again and again, and especially when times are challenging, you will hear people saying that what is needed is a 'strong leader'. They do not usually have long to wait.

But the individuals followed as authorities are elected, appointed or recognized as such on the basis of some prior authority. They are not themselves the sources of the authority they exercise. Charismatic leaders and founders of religions, and figures such as mystics, saints and prophets, typically impute their authority to a divine or transcendental source. Only if such a person were accorded divine or semi-divine status might one say that they were themselves the source of their authority. Even those religious leaders who assume positions of authority through dynastic succession, political influence or military victory will invoke some further authority to explain or justify the power they exercise over others. Thus it might be argued (by them or on their behalf) that it is the will of God or the gods, or the decree of fate, that they should be in authority, or that the real authority lies not in themselves but in the divinely instituted office they administer.[9] The Prophet Muhammad's authority over the early Islamic community was in large part secured through military victory over his opponents, but his victories were themselves seen as divine confirmation of his prior authority as charismatic prophet to the Arab peoples. Some of the later caliphs claimed authority on the basis of their descent from the Prophet; some of them assumed power by removing rivals. Nor is it unknown in the history of religions for wealthy individuals to purchase positions of religious authority. Even these might seek to justify their position on the basis of their suitability, or destiny, as mediators of a higher authority. Human authorities are necessary within any organization or institution, but even the best of them need to be accountable for what they do, say or know. Their authority is always on loan from another source.

One source of authority to which both leaders and followers of a tradition frequently defer will be a 'sacred text' – taking this term to refer to whatever body of written or oral material records the unique and sometimes extraordinary events upon which the religion is founded, preserves the teachings and experiences of the founder or founders, or enshrines a body of laws and precepts by which a community of followers is expected to live. To defer to such texts as 'authoritative', however, is only to beg further questions. It is clear, to begin with, that these texts cannot authorize or interpret themselves; revealed truths could never be like geometrical proofs, for example. From the moment a sacred text appears, differences and disputes arise about its status and interpretation. Most such texts are acknowledged to have been composed, over a long period and often in variant forms, by human authors, albeit (it will often be said) under some kind of heavenly guidance or inspiration. In some cases, a sacred text is said to have been miraculously produced or to have been sent direct from heaven. This is said, for example, about the Qur'ān, about the Book of Mormon, and about certain Buddhist sutras. But even in these cases, it is not the sacred texts themselves but what they record, enjoin or recommend that is authoritative – and this could have been preserved in a purely oral form.

The idea of an unmediated or unconstructed text (or oral tradition) is a contradiction in terms. A sacred text, like any other text, is composed or inscribed in one or more human languages, and this would be true even of a text that was somehow delivered straight from God or the gods. To be recognized as sacred, and to be interpreted as meaning this or that, is all part of the constructed nature of a text. To regard a sacred text as a human construction, just like any other text, and just like every other aspect of religion, is not to belittle it in any way, or to say that it will be any less true than, for example, Darwin's *Origin of Species* or Marx's *Capital*. Both of these are also human constructions, and both are widely regarded as authoritative in their respective fields. So the appeal to 'sacred texts' simply returns us to the original question by another route: on what authority does the authority of the texts regarded as authoritative depend?

What makes sacred texts the sources, or mediators, of authority is the authority of the persons, events, ideas and experiences represented within them. And what makes these texts 'living' texts, texts that continue to speak to people long after the era in which they were composed, is that the kinds of person, event, idea and experience represented within these texts connect somehow with the lives of the religious adherents they address. Being a member of a religion, however sincere a member, does not in itself guarantee any connection with a sacred text other than the merely circular one of regarding it as sacred. A sacred text whose content does not connect with the lives of a community will in effect be as empty as a text that has no meaningful content in the first place. There is a telling satire on the latter possibility in Walter Miller's futuristic novel *A Canticle for Leibowitz* (1960), a narrative that spans several centuries of human history following a devastating global nuclear war. It focuses on the activities of the Albertian Order of St Leibowitz, whose most precious relics include 'sacred texts', which are in fact a collection of shopping lists and other household trivia recovered from a twentieth-century bomb shelter.

The appeal to sacred texts as authoritative, then, dramatizes rather than settles the question about the ultimate source of religious authority. These texts are records of the transforming encounter between human beings and what presents itself as a divine or transcendental reality – but equally of a dialogue among human beings themselves on the nature of this encounter. Along with the commentarial literature that grows up around them, sacred texts are at once the products and the sources of the religious tradition that depends upon them.

ONE MIGHT WANT to say that the highest authority in religion, and hence the one to which all other authorities must directly or indirectly refer, must surely be something like 'religious truth', 'ultimate reality' or a 'Supreme Being'. But this will be so only to the extent that these grand metaphysical titles, and the ideas associated with them, make sense in human terms and connect in some way with what is accessible to human experience. It is no good protesting that reason and experience count for little or nothing in the face of the supernatural and even supra-rational realities of religion. Either the ultimate realities that are the source and goal of religious practice are beyond the range of human experience (thereby negating all religious effort or inquiry) or else they must be accessible to it in some way. How could we make sense of a religious ultimate other than through reason and experience, however much guided by human authorities and sacred texts? Or to put it another way, human experience turns out to be the main *authority* in religion for the simple reason that human beings and their world are the main *subject* of religion. What convinced that most patient and faithful of human beings, the biblical Job, of his place in the scheme of things was a profound experience, one that brought all words to a stop.

An emphasis on the authority of human experience should encourage us to reinvent the ways in which we approach sacred texts – or to recover ways in which such texts were used before they became fossilized into fixed and unquestionable bodies of truth. Sacred texts, both today and in the past, have been regarded as the standard against which people's lives should be judged. These texts have told people what to do and even what to think. People have been encouraged by authority figures in their religion to conform their lives to these sacred texts. It is as if a human life should be lived like a commentary on these texts. Nowadays, with our greater awareness of the oneness of humanity, together with the recognition that there are many different religions, each with an equal claim to truth, as well as many different traditions within each religion, this approach to sacred texts has diminishing purchase on us. If we are not to reject them altogether, we must invent, or reinvent, another and more creative approach to them. We can do this by thinking of human lives as the 'primary texts' and of the sacred texts as commentaries on these lives. Rich in wisdom both intellectual and practical, sacred texts will have value only if they help us to interpret our own experience in this world.

But if we treat human experience as the primary source of authority, will this not encourage people to pick and choose among the ideas, texts, precepts and practices of world religions, constructing forms of religion that simply pander to their own illusions and prejudices? Would not such a criterion undermine the integrity of each religion, and even abolish the distinction between one religion and another? The first thing to be said here is that religions not only change with, but actually originate in, human experience. Buddhism, Christianity and Islam – to name but three of the world's major religions – were initiated by the extraordinary experiences of their founders and earliest followers, while at the same time calling into question the authority and identity of the traditions out of which they emerged. The same process happens within established religions, where denominations arise and change in relation to other denominations. If the value or integrity of a religious institution were to be defined merely in terms of its ability to resist change, to remain insulated from other traditions, then lamenting either its decline or its transformation will amount to little more than a form of nostalgia.

A second and more important point is that all human experience demands interpretation, religious experience no less than any other kind of experience. Its interpretation does not take place in a vacuum, but in relation to the ideas and experiences of others, and within the context of a particular culture. And this point brings us to the all-important idea of tradition. 'Tradition' is a term with fewer negative associations than 'institution', 'organization' or 'authority', although the epithet 'traditional' does tend to connote what is old-fashioned or conservative. Interestingly enough, however, when people talk about the 'weight' of tradition, they are as likely to be talking about something serious and substantial as they are something merely heavy or burdensome. Unfortunately, just as people like to be led by strong religious or political leaders, or to hand their intellectual or spiritual life over to self-appointed gurus of one kind or another, so they may seek security in affirming or relying upon something identified as 'traditional' for no better reason than that it seems the right thing to do to go on believing or practising what, in their view, has always been believed or practised.[10]

In religion as in other spheres, however, tradition properly understood is about the judicious application of ideas and methods, inherited from the past, which are worth attending to not because they are old but because they are intellectually fruitful or practically beneficial. When we talk about a 'scientific tradition', for example, we do not intend to talk about some unchanging or unchangeable body of truths or methods, but a body of ever-changing ideas and practices that continues to fulfil the ideals and requirements of science. There is no reason why the idea of tradition in religion should be any different in principle from the idea of tradition in science or in any other field. Tradition in religion is not about hanging on to ancient ideas or practices for their own sake, or for the sake of escape or comfort, but rather is about testing one's ideas and experiences against the best of the past, paying special attention to those who have the most respected places in the tradition. And if it is tradition that enables human experience to be the primary authority in religion, then the leadership and organization of a religion can be judged by the success with which they act as the guardians of tradition. Tradition should be understood as a rich resource and a support network created by the ideas and experiences of others. This is why it makes sense for the adherents of a religion to test their ideas and experiences against those of others, not for the sake of maintaining institutional conformity (as a Grand Inquisitor might wish) but because individual ideas and experiences can only make sense in relation to the ideas and experiences of others.

To illustrate the priority of experience in religion and how it relates to tradition and authority, let us consider the example of Buddhism. When asked who should succeed him as leader after he had gone, the Buddha replied that he would leave behind no authority other than the Dhamma, the body of teaching he had made known over many years. This Dhamma (in the form of the Buddhist canonical texts) would be preserved and disseminated by the Sangha, the monastic organization the Buddha had founded. Buddhists ever since have acknowledged the Buddha, the Dhamma and the Sangha as the three 'refuges', which are, in effect, three interconnected sources of authority. The ultimate authority, however, is the experience of enlightenment itself. It is this which qualifies the Buddha ('Enlightened One') as teacher, just as it is the Dhamma which mediates the Buddha's insights and methods to his followers. But the fact that these individuals have the potential to realize their own enlightenment makes them and their experiences also authorities of a sort. The Buddha's teachings are described as *ehipassiko*, 'what you can come and see'; they represent something to be tried and tested rather than simply taken on trust.[11] Religious followers are (or should be) the ultimate authorities in roughly the same way as patients are the real authorities when it comes to medical treatment or customers in the case of commercial transactions.

The Buddha at the end of his life continued to emphasize both the authority of Buddhist doctrine (*dhamma*), as confirmed in his own personal experience, but also to acknowledge the personal authority and responsibility of his followers in making this Dhamma their own. 'So . . . each of you should make himself his island, make himself and no one else his refuge; each of you must make the Dhamma his island, the Dhamma and no other his refuge.'[12] Inevitably, as in the history of any other religion, internal and external factors alike have conspired to complicate the organization and institutionalization of Buddhist ideas and practices. By no means have all these developments been conducive to the proper maintenance of the Buddha's message. The Buddhist tradition, however, has rich intellectual and practical resources wherewith adherents can test their ideas and experiences, as well as standards for judging what is or is not proper to the religion. Similar standards and resources exist in all religions.

The emphasis on the authority of experience is not an emphasis on the authority of *my* experience as distinct from *your* experience, for example, but an emphasis on the collective experience of those within a tradition. It is the constraint of tradition, including respect for the ideas and judgements of those whose authority is based on the most profound experiences within a tradition, which minimizes the risk of the followers of a tradition succumbing to wayward or 'heretical' interpretations of a religion. Objections to affirming the authority of human experience will come, if not from those promoting their own particular experience as authoritative, then from those who regard a religion, or some particular institution within it, as authoritative beyond question or criticism. One great religious teacher is recorded as reminding people that 'The Sabbath was made for man, not man for the Sabbath.'[13] What is true of the Sabbath is true of everything else in religion too.

SUSPICION OF, or merely distaste for, organized religion and religious institutions is understandable and all too often justified. But the cultivation of such suspicion and distaste is often just another excuse for avoiding the challenge religions pose to our aimless or anxious lives. Religions, being social entities, are inevitably subject to organization, with all the advantages and disadvantages that follow. It is, however, the responsibility of the adherents of religious institutions to hold to account those who have been entrusted to lead them, and to play their own part in maintaining them as living traditions.

In a religiously plural world, moreover, the traditions of any one religion have become increasingly open to those of other religions or of no religion who may find its ideas instructive or its practices of value. Some people may fear that the mutual openness of traditions will lead to the merging of one religion with another or to the muddying of the distinctions between them – a fear of what is known as syncretism. And yet syncretism, or syncretistic borrowing, has been a constant feature of religious history. One might even say that religion is syncretistic by nature, and that syncretistic borrowing is to be seen as an enrichment rather than a degradation of a tradition. It is, if nothing else, testimony to the authority of human experience.

SEVEN

NO GOOD BEING
RELIGIOUS

A common assumption about religion, made by religious and non-religious people alike, is that religion is centrally concerned with 'being good'. This is why critics of religion insistently point out that one does not have to be religious in order to be good. More than this, however, they claim that religion has done, and continues to do, more harm than good in people's lives. It is certainly true that religion has, directly or indirectly, caused much harm and suffering throughout history, just as it is also true that much good has come out of religion and/or been done in the name of religion. But the attempt to judge religion through a calculation of its good or bad effects – even if such a calculation were possible – is a fool's errand. Would one attempt to make similar kinds of judgement about science, art, politics, sport or education? All it would show is that human beings, and the institutions they create, are flawed and often corrupt – all part of the 'crooked timber of humanity'.[1] In any case, who says that religion is all about 'being good' or 'doing good'? These are assumptions that need to be questioned.

That there are and always have been close links between religion and morality is not in dispute. A prominent general feature of religions is a moral code of some kind. What need to be questioned are both the assumption that morality depends on religion and the contrary assumption that religion depends on morality. But first we need to differentiate moral precepts from the other kinds of prescription and proscription that have played such an important role in religion. Let us begin with a parable from the Buddhist tradition.

Two monks, whom I shall represent here as a revered elder monk accompanied by a zealous young novice, are on a journey together. At one point in their journey they come to a ford across a river. Standing on the bank, hesitating to cross because of the swiftly flowing current, is a beautiful young woman. Without a second thought, the elder monk lifts her up and carries her across the river. The novice is astonished, and outraged, by the behaviour of the elder, and continues the journey in silence, inwardly seething. After several miles, however, he can contain himself no longer, bursting out with the accusation that the elder monk has blatantly flouted the rule against monks looking at, let alone touching, a woman. The elder monk stops, turns to the younger one and says, perhaps with something of a twinkle in his eye: 'I set that young woman down as soon as we had crossed the river. You, it seems, are still carrying her.'[2]

Implicit in this story is a distinction important not only in Buddhism but in other religions too. It is the distinction between moral precepts on the one hand and the various institutional, legal and ritual regulations governing the life of a religious community on the other. Clearly the monastic regulations of Buddhism are governed by the more generic Buddhist moral principles by which all Buddhists are called to live. But the monastic regulations are not, in themselves, ethical precepts or principles, even if their ultimate purpose is to promote the same ends. The immediate purpose of the monastic code is to maintain order and well-being within the community. The elder monk, unlikely to have been disturbed by the young woman's charms, acts from a sense of care and compassion such as we might suppose to have become instinctive in a wise and experienced elder. Technically, he does indeed infringe the monastic regulations, but he does so knowingly in order to promote the welfare of a fellow human being. The main loser in the story is not the elder, and certainly not the young woman, but the novice, whose anger and resentment add up to what, in Buddhist terms, is an 'unskilled' state of mind. The religious mentality represented by the novice is one that is liable not merely to put obedience to regulations above ordinary social virtues, but also to turn moral precepts themselves into a rigid set of regulations.

The regulations governing religious communities deal with matters as varied as diet, personal hygiene, marriage and sexual relations, burial and mourning, ritual procedures, monastic discipline, and so on. Religious and non-religious people alike often fail to discriminate between these institutional regulations and the moral or ethical precepts of a religion. Partly this is because these things naturally tend to get lumped together, under the more general rubric of religious duties and obligations, as things it is either right or wrong to do (or to refrain from doing). After all, the general moral precept about caring for others and, for instance, the law of zakat (the fifth pillar of Islam, which obliges Muslims to give one-fortieth of their income to the poor) are clearly oriented towards the same end, although in Islamic terms the latter is a legal requirement rather than a moral imperative. But the failure to discriminate between moral precepts on the one hand and laws, prescriptions and customs on the other also arises from the fact that ethical codes themselves incorporate, or have not completely detached themselves from, laws, rules and customs that have nothing directly to do with morality in the modern sense of the word. That is, they have nothing directly to do with 'principles concerning the distinction between right and wrong or good and bad behaviour' (OED). Indeed, in many cases what is prescribed by legal code or established custom will be judged immoral by more universal ethical standards. Examples might include the slavery that was integral to the social structure of ancient Greece and Rome, amputation of hands as a punishment for theft in some Islamic societies, and enforced clitoridectomy as a pre-condition of marriage in some African cultures.

The word 'morality' derives from the Latin *moralis*, from the word *mos* (plural *mores*), meaning custom (or customs), which suggests that morality in the modern sense – what we might call simple or common morality – is a refinement, or universalization, of more culturally specific rules and customs. The alternative word 'ethics' comes from the Greek ἔθος or ἦθος, as of course does the English word 'ethos'. Both 'morality' and 'ethics' connote an entire mode of civilized living rather than just a code specifying certain forms of behaviour as socially acceptable or unacceptable, or as 'good' or 'bad'. But ethics typically implies a theory of human behaviour such as would make ethical principles universally applicable, whereas morality can suggest a potentially narrower and more culturally specific set of duties or obligations, closely associated with the idea of reward and punishment. Thus someone identified as a teacher of morality would be expected to be inculcating correct behaviour of some sort, whereas someone identified as a teacher of ethics would be expected rather to be teaching the principles of right behaviour in a more universalist way. An 'ethics committee' within some project or institution is unlikely to be described as a 'morality (or morals) committee'. On the other hand, it sounds reasonable to describe those religious officials who enforce aspects of Sharia Law in Saudi Arabia as policing morality, but would sound odd to describe them as policing ethics.

In religious contexts, moral precepts and practices are linked with ideas about the nature and destiny of human beings. In monotheistic religions especially they will also be seen as integral elements of a divine revelation enshrined in sacred texts and oral traditions. These connections are exemplified by the well-known but much misunderstood concept of sin. There are uses of the English word 'sin' that follow the sense of the Hebrew *hata* (ḥeṭ')[3] and the Greek *hamartia* (ἁμαρτία) in referring primarily to a failure, fault or error of judgement. In the Greek Christian tradition, sin is described as a failure to hit the mark, as an archer or spear thrower might fail to do. Beyond this basic etymology, however, these terms also describe acts of transgression against the commands embodied in a divinely revealed law. In the Hindu tradition, for example, we find such commands in the *Laws of Manu*. In the Jewish tradition we find them in the Decalogue and, much more comprehensively, in the 613 commandments of the Torah as a whole.

Eclipsing the idea of sin as an act (or failure to act) of some kind is the more radical idea of sinfulness as a permanent human condition or inheritance. This is evident in a very simple way in the Jewish tradition, where human behaviour is said to manifest two contrary impulses, the impulse to good and the impulse to evil.[4] Beyond psychology, however, sin is also 'ontologized' into something existing over and above the contingent acts or tendencies of an individual.[5] The relevant development here is the shift from sin understood as a particular act, whose negative consequences might be removed ad hoc, and sin understood as the very condition of human existence. This more fundamental condition of sinfulness cannot be removed merely through a ritual act of atonement or purification. To be a sinner is not just a matter of having committed this or that particular sin but rather is a matter of being in a persisting state of sinfulness. We are all of us sinners, as certain kinds of preacher like to remind people.

This idea of sin as a condition finds its most extreme form in the Christian doctrine of 'original sin', the idea that human beings are diminished by a primordial sin that affects all subsequent generations in potentially every aspect of their lives. Sinful acts, and the urge to act sinfully, are evidence of a permanent flaw. It is to this flaw that Augustine refers when describing the perverse pleasure he and his friends derived from the relatively trivial misdemeanour of stealing pears – not for the sake of the pears themselves but for the thrill of stealing them.[6] The good news is that this condition can be corrected, and humankind restored to its original glory, or advanced to a new state of oneness with the divine. The largely Western (and largely misunderstood) idea of original sin has some correspondence with Eastern ideas about karma – the burden of negative tendencies which individuals inherit from the previous lives that have led to or created their present life. Other religious traditions are more optimistic about human nature, not seeing in it some primordial or permanent flaw, but rather an ignorance or immaturity that religious practice serves gradually to remove.

The understanding of religious morality as obedience or disobedience to a set of divine commandments dominates popular ideas about religion and is also what many religious people themselves affirm. But religious morality can be understood in many other ways, and in fact offers as fruitful a means of entering into a deeper understanding of religion as do the mythology, art or ritual of a religion. Nowadays, moreover, the focus of serious religious thinking about morality is on understanding what the various forms of moral and immoral behaviour can tell us about the nature of the relationship between human beings and whatever is sought and valued as the ultimate reality.

THAT THERE IS – or should be – an intimate connection between the goal or purpose of a religion and the morality of its adherents seems to many people, both religious and non-religious, to be so obvious as to be hardly worth stating. But the role of morality in religion is not always what people suppose it is, or think it should be. It is important, therefore, to set out some of the ways in which the connections between religion and morality have been understood.

To begin with, and because basic moral precepts tend to be markedly similar across cultural and religious boundaries, morality seems to be an obvious element of continuity between religions that may be incompatible in so many other respects. If religions agree about anything, surely it is the importance of maintaining personal and social morality. This much can easily be agreed. But this is far from saying that moral and social codes are necessarily the most important constituents of a religious view or way of life. Some would say that what one believes about ultimate reality, or what one does in the way of ritual practice, matters equally if not more. Even so, many would still agree that anything that links otherwise divergent systems of belief and practice will have especial value for dialogue and cooperation across religious boundaries.

It is, moreover, a view commonly held by religious as well as non-religious people that morality is not merely the common denominator between different religions, but somehow the very essence of religion. In a story recorded in the Babylonian Talmud (*Shabbat* 31a), a gentile approaches Rabbi Hillel with the proposition that he will convert to Judaism if the rabbi can teach him the whole of the Torah while standing on one leg. Rabbi Shammai, to whom he had earlier made the same request, had immediately rebuffed him. Rabbi Hillel, however, obliges, stating: 'That which is hateful to you, do not do to your neighbour. This is the whole of the Torah. The rest is commentary. Go off and study.'[7] Hillel is here giving a negative version of what is generally known as the 'golden rule', namely the principle that one should behave towards others as you would have them behave towards you. This golden rule is sometimes said to be the common element of all moral systems, including religious systems.[8]

If the leading or essential element of religion is its moral teaching, and if this moral element can exist independently of religion, then it is clearly open to sceptics and critics to conclude that religion itself is at best merely a support for moral living – and at worst a redundant weight around its neck. This view is the easier to maintain the more closely a religious morality comes to a purely secular morality, since in effect there is no longer anything specifically religious about it (as there is, for example, when moral commands are part and parcel of a divinely revealed law).

But if the 'religion is morality' hypothesis works to undermine the status of religion, the reverse hypothesis, that 'morality is religion', would reinstate religion as the goal or perfection of morality. Such seems to have been the view held by Matthew Arnold, for example, who responds thus to the question whether or not there is a difference between morality and religion:

> There is a difference; a difference of degree. Religion, if we follow the intention of human thought and human language in the use of the word, is ethics heightened, enkindled, lit up by feeling; the passage from morality to religion is made when to morality is applied emotion. And the true meaning of religion is thus, not simply *morality*, but *morality touched by emotion*. And this new

elevation and inspiration of morality is well marked by the word 'righteousness'.[9]

It was the philosopher Immanuel Kant who produced the most sophisticated theory about the intimate relationship between morality and religion, although the nature and validity of his arguments are much debated. Kant, according to one interpretation, regards God less as the transcendent Being of traditional theology than as the Idealization of a rationally based morality whose goal is the harmonious perfection of human virtue and happiness – this being the *summum bonum* of any true morality. According to another interpretation, however, the very possibility of human morality and hope of its fulfilment depend upon the immortality of the soul and the existence of God as supreme moral agent. The laws of morality, asserts Kant, lead to

> the recognition of all duties as divine commands, not as
> sanctions, that is to say, arbitrary ordinances of a foreign
> will and contingent in themselves, but as essential laws
> of every free will in itself, which, nevertheless, must be
> regarded as commands of the Supreme Being, because
> it is only from a morally perfect (holy and good) and at
> the same time all-powerful will, and consequently only
> through harmony with this will, that we can hope to
> attain the summum bonum which the moral law makes
> it our duty to take as the object of our endeavours.[10]

For Kant, belief in God is part and parcel of belief in the possibility of attaining the highest good, which is the aim of the moral life. With God as his 'theoretical postulate', Kant's primary emphasis is on the absolute reality and authority of the moral law as revealed by human reason. But it does not seem to matter whether God is regarded as the name for the author of this law or for the moral law itself.

The idea most closely associated with theism, and in particular with monotheism, is that morality is obedience to the will of a

Supreme Being, usually as codified in a set of divine commandments, such as the Decalogue's 'Thou shalt not kill' or 'Thou shall not bear false witness.' This is an instrumentalist view of religious faith and practice where moral behaviour is religiously motivated and religiously regulated, with the further implication that without the rewards and punishments of religion, people would tend to behave immorally, sinfulness being seen as the normal (though not necessarily natural) human condition. To get to heaven one has to do good or be good – otherwise one might, or will, incur divine wrath and punishment. Even in those theologies which insist that sinful human beings are saved from damnation by the grace of God – despite their sins and regardless of their good works – there remains the assumption that such human beings are at least deserving of damnation!

To the arguments of those who ground morality in religion in this way, sceptics and critics have obvious objections. You do not need to be religious in order to live a moral life; and in any case, what sort of morality is it that is based on fear of punishment or desire for reward? Moreover, does it not ring hollow to identify as the arbiter of morality a God who not only allows evil acts to go unpunished (in this life at least) but who has created a world in which so many natural disasters overwhelm the innocent? Indeed, the ubiquity of evil and suffering, whether of human or of natural origin, constitutes for many sceptics a powerful argument against the existence of God, or at least the existence of the kind of God whom people consider worthy of worship and obedience (one who is omniscient, omnipotent, just, merciful and so on).

In the face of human and natural evil, and the innocent suffering these cause, the ethical monotheist is presented with the following dilemma: why does God, defined as a being at once benevolent and omnipotent, not punish or prevent all the manifest evil in the world? Neither of the two alternative answers to this question seems satisfactory: God is either benevolent but not omnipotent, or else omnipotent but not benevolent. Christian theologians and philosophers have for centuries agonized over this so-called problem of evil, the attempt to work out a convincing theodicy ('justification of God') being one of the most prolific yet least constructive of all theological activities. To a large extent, however, the insolubility of theodicy is a self-inflicted problem, one created by a persistent refusal to abandon notions of God as an allegedly wise and powerful individual being who is somehow active on the world stage. Unfortunately, it is this conception of God, rather than the God of the mystics, that has for too long been imprinted on the minds of believers and sceptics alike.

For most monotheists, the 'divine command' theory of religious morality presupposes a Deity who is the author of the moral law and the judge of those to whom these laws are revealed. But the distinction between God and a revealed moral law guarantees the persistence of the classic theological conundrum: is an action or intention good because God commands it or does God command it because it is good? If the first condition applies, then theists may be obliged to do things which their own conscience or instinct rejects. If the second applies, then it has to be acknowledged that God is to be judged by a standard other than and perhaps higher than himself. This dilemma is first presented in a systematic way in Plato's *Euthyphro*, where in response to Euthyphro's confident definition of holiness as anything the gods love, and sin anything that the gods hate, Socrates points out that since the gods notoriously disagree among themselves about what is right and wrong, it would seem to follow that it is not from the gods that we derive our judgements as to what is good or bad but from standards other than the gods – standards to which the gods themselves must appeal. And yet, observes Socrates, even if all the gods were to agree that something was holy, the fundamental question remains: do the gods love what's holy because it's holy, or is it holy simply because the gods love it?[11]

One way of solving this dilemma – one that is perhaps easier for monotheists than polytheists – is through abolishing the distinction between the divine and the good on which this dilemma depends. In this way, an instrumentalist view of the relationship between religion and morality could be replaced by a demonstrative view of this relationship. Rather than thinking of God or the gods as loving the good, and as judging conformity with the good, why not simply identify God (or the gods) *as* the good or the holy? Rather than defining God through a mass of overblown metaphysical compliments (omnipotent, omniscient, all-merciful, and so on) which require Him, if He is to be allowed to exist in the first place, to be the solution to every imperfection on earth, why not think of God as the source or ground of what we already recognize as the good?

If morality has a divine or transcendental source, our moral sense is to this extent an argument for the reality of God, if not for the ultimately divine nature of human beings themselves. A corollary of this idea is that morality brings one closer to this ultimate just as immorality distances or alienates one from it. 'Blessed are the pure in heart; for they shall see God.' This demonstrative view of morality differs fundamentally from the instrumentalist view. On the demonstrative view it makes no sense to have an ulterior motive for one's behaviour, or to see morality as a (perhaps unwelcome) means to a desired end. Nor is it a case of moral behaviour 'being its own reward' (rather a smug attitude at the best of times). Instead, 'good' or 'virtuous' behaviour is recognized as already and in itself a manifestation of the divine 'goodness' at the heart of things. This would be a radical version of what in the Western monotheistic tradition is known as the moral argument for the existence of God – the argument that a moral conscience and a recognition of the objective authority of the moral law bespeak the existence of a divine Being who is the author of this law and the source of our moral consciousness.

Similar arguments have been deployed in other traditions, not necessarily to prove the existence of a divine Being, but rather to explain the innate wisdom and compassion of human beings, which is already more than many secularists are willing to allow. The Confucian philosopher Meng-tzu (*c.* 371–289 BCE)[12] famously used the example of a child about to fall into a well to argue that all people 'have hearts sensitive to the suffering of others':

Suppose a man were, all of a sudden, to see a young child on the verge of falling into a well. He would certainly be moved to compassion, not because he wanted to get in the good graces of the parents, nor yet because he wished to win the praise of his fellow villagers or friends, nor yet because he disliked the cry of the child. From this it can be seen that whoever is devoid of the heart of compassion is not human, whoever is devoid of the heart of shame is not human, whoever is devoid of the heart of courtesy and modesty is not human, and whoever is devoid of the heart of right and wrong is not human.[13]

According to Meng-Tzu, this compassion is implanted in us by *Tiān* (heaven), along with the other human virtues, these virtues being nourished into full growth through such means as ritual and education. What is debated among scholars, however, is whether *Tiān* in Confucian thought is (in Western terms) closer in meaning to heaven (or God)[14] or to Nature (in a sense similar to Nature as understood by Spinoza or the Stoics, for example).[15] Either way, what Meng-tzu is suggesting is that human virtues reflect or reveal transcendental principles of some kind.

IF ONE OBSTACLE to understanding the relationship between religion and morality is confusion about the nature of religion, then another must be uncertainty about the nature of the good as the goal of morality. The nature of the good, like the nature of truth or beauty, is obviously an immense topic that cannot be tackled here. But it is at least worth considering one alternative to the popular understanding of religious morality, outlined above, in terms of obedience to a set of rules or commandments, with all the ideas about guilt, shame and punishment this brings in its train.

Consider, for instance, how two of the most famous parables of the New Testament have been used to promote a narrowly moralistic view of religion. These are the parables of the 'Good

Samaritan' (Luke 10:25–37) and of the 'Prodigal Son' (Luke 15:11–32), neither of which unfortunate titles belong to the original stories.[16] In the first of these parables, told in response to the question 'Who is my neighbour?', we hear the story of an unidentified traveller who, after being stripped, beaten and left half-dead by robbers, is avoided first by a priest and then by a Levite before finally being helped by a member of the Samaritan people (a people generally despised by the Jews of that time). What the Samaritan does for the traveller is of course good, but what motivated the Samaritan was not 'good behaviour' or 'moral duty', in the sense intended whenever this parable is cited as a moral template for good behaviour, but rather an immediate sense of compassion, or fellow feeling, for another human individual. The behaviour of the Samaritan is contrasted with the behaviour of the priest and Levite, but it is important to see that neither of these latter individuals was in fact acting badly. In their religious code, contact with a dead or dying person was recognized as potentially polluting, and so their behaviour was at least prudent (and prudence is an important virtue in some systems). Indeed, nowhere in the parable are the terms 'good' or 'bad' used. What the word 'good' in the imposed title 'Good Samaritan' connotes for many people is the idea of the Samaritan's choosing to do good (where he might have chosen otherwise), as if he were obeying some moral law or rule – as in 'It is my duty to help wounded strangers.' On the contrary, like the Buddhist elder in that earlier parable, he is acting directly from the heart, and would no doubt be doing so even if this were to mean breaking some moral or ritual commandment. As for the question that provokes the parable, 'Who is my neighbour?', this in itself betrays a partisan morality, since it divides people into the two categories of 'neighbour' and 'non-neighbour'. One might as well ask, for example, 'Which persons can I abuse and which should I not abuse?'

The parable of the so-called 'Prodigal Son' was in the earliest Christian centuries identified by commentators as the parable of the 'Two Sons', but might just as well be called the parable of the 'Loving Father' or of the 'Self-righteous and Unforgiving

Brother'.[17] The father and the two sons have equally important roles in the story. When the younger son asks his father for his share of the family estate, such as he would normally have inherited at his father's death, neither his father nor his elder brother seem to have raised any objection to the request – although such a request would, by the standards of the day, normally be considered an act of filial impiety.[18] Desirous of making his own way in the world, he quickly takes himself off to a distant country. As things turn out, however, this younger son soon squanders his entire inheritance on wild living, and ends up earning a mere subsistence by feeding pigs. He is then described as 'coming to himself' again, and plucks up the courage to return home, determining to ask his father for forgiveness and for a menial job on the estate. But his father, seeing his returning son in the distance, eagerly rushes out to embrace him, brushing aside the son's request for forgiveness and employment. Instead he fusses lovingly over his son, and immediately arranges a lavish 'welcome home' party.

The elder son, coming home from working in the fields to find the celebration in full swing, protests to his father that he should not be wasting yet more resources on this worthless son when it is he, the elder son, who has always been the hardworking and dutiful one. His attitude here closely resembles that of the novice in the earlier Buddhist parable. Many people who hear or read this parable have more than a little sympathy with the elder son, and in fact siding with his point of view would be the rational response in a world in which moral rectitude counted more than love, compassion and forgiveness. This parable has indeed commonly been used to wag a moralistic finger at those who might, like the younger son, be tempted to waste their substance and fall into an immoral way of life. But the story does not celebrate or recommend moral rectitude any more than it dwells – unlike some of its later commentators – on the younger son's prodigality or supposed sinful behaviour when in that far-off country. Far more important to the story is the moment of the younger son's 'coming to himself', which implies that he has somehow got lost but has now found himself again. This move is what is behind the idea of 'repentance'. The original Greek term is *metanoia*, which means a turning around or turning back of the mind, a movement from self-ignorance to a state of self-knowledge. This understanding of repentance as insight, however, tends to get obscured by what might be called the 'secondary' phenomena associated with it – guilt, confession and contrition. And this plays into the hands of those who see morality chiefly as a rule-based conformity monitored externally by the threat of punishment and internally by feelings of guilt and remorse.

The trouble with religion is that the more institutionalized it becomes the more likely both its leaders and its adherents are to identify morality with obedience to commandments or mere conformity with precepts. But the ultimate purpose of morality in religion is to see things as they really are and in this way to open the mind to the divine or the transcendent. If the ultimate purpose of morality is forgotten in the pursuit of the rules or precepts that are designed to support and further this purpose, then we turn morality, and its precepts, into idols. This is what the young novice was doing in the Buddhist parable recounted earlier.

According to one prominent crusader against religion, 'Many religious people find it hard to imagine how, without religion, one can be good, or would even want to be good.'[19] This statement – which, sadly, may come close to how religious people themselves often see the matter – reveals a mindset that is as mistaken about the good as it is about religion. Religion is not about being good, or respectable, as many people seem to think – including those atheist parents who are ready to bend or flout all the rules in their eagerness to send their children to what are called 'faith schools'. Although it is notoriously difficult to generalize about religion, it is fair to say that religion is, in its most mature expressions, about becoming whole. This is the same as saying that religion is about becoming hale, or healthy, as we can see from the generic word often used to describe the end of purpose of religion – namely, salvation. The word 'salvation' derives from the Latin *salvus*, meaning safe or unharmed, and is related to cognate words for health and wholeness.[20] The goodness sought or expressed in the highest forms of religious morality, therefore, is best thought of as the goodness of being whole or healthy.[21] The word 'holy', which has itself come to be understood in a moralistic way, also has the root meaning of whole in the sense of healthy.[22] And the precepts of such a religious morality will be designed not to enforce conformity to rules and regulations that serve the interests of particular institutions or social systems, but rather to quicken and nourish those virtues and powers that enable individuals to reach the fulfilment of their existence, whether in this world or the next.

It is no good being religious if religion is understood simply to mean conforming, willingly or reluctantly as the case may be, to some moral code or set of commandments. If the rules or precepts of a religion do not lead to human flourishing, then whatever other ends they may happen to serve they do not serve, or manifest, the highest purposes of religion. Morality is central to religion only to the extent that it is about goodness in the sense of wholeness. This goodness is not like the goodness of a child being well behaved at meal times or finishing up all its food. Rather, it is like the goodness of good food itself.

EIGHT

IDOLATRIES ANCIENT AND
MODERN

'Idolatry' is an old-fashioned word for practices and mentalities
that will never be out of fashion. As a term of opprobrium,
describing something negative by definition, it is in the same
category as 'murder' or 'foolishness', for example. To name these
things is in the same breath to condemn them. But we need to be
clear how and why idolatry has been regarded as the religious sin
par excellence. In doing so, however, we shall also see that idolatry
is the Achilles heel of religion as such, revealing a weakness in the
whole idea of religion, so that religion easily comes to be seen as a
form of idolatry. What is more, idolatry has no need of religion in
order to flourish, even if religion offers some of the richest soil in
which it does so. Finally, if religion itself can be, or can become, a
form of idolatry, and if idolatry is endemic to all forms of human
culture, then perhaps one should also be looking for whatever is
good in, or about, the idolatrous tendency.

'Idolatry' comes from the Greek εἰδωλολατρεία,[1] which
combines a word for image (εἴδωλον) with a word for worship
(λατρεία). The word εἴδωλον (*eídōlon*), like the other Greek word
for image, εἴκων (ikon or icon), is in itself a neutral term, describing a copy, image or representation, natural or artificial, of some
physical reality. But already in Greek philosophy the word acquires
a negative connotation, describing what is considered a false or
misleading imitation of reality. The English word 'idol' (like its
equivalents in other languages) is chiefly reserved for a wrongly

worshipped religious image, typically a three-dimensional image of some kind and hence also an object. The term is also used more loosely to describe any person or thing that receives admiration or adulation out of all proportion to its actual worth. By contrast, the word 'icon' tends to be used as a positive term for an image of any kind, and in specifically religious contexts refers mainly to two-dimensional sacred images.

The term 'idolatry' is ambiguous in so far as it is used to refer both to the worship of a physical image (or object) as a god, and to the wrongful worship of God or a god *by means of* an image (or object).[2] The problem in respect of the first meaning, as the philosopher Voltaire pointed out long before any systematic study of religions, is that idolatry thus defined can hardly be said to exist, for it is a simple ethnographic fact that people worship gods and spirits, not images or objects. Even the most unsophisticated worshippers are aware of the difference between a lifeless physical image and the supernatural or spiritual being this image is intended to represent.[3]

What we do find throughout the history of religions, however, are alleged examples of idolatry in the second sense: forms of worship that make use of images or objects representing or symbolizing God or a god. Such images are typically two-dimensional or three-dimensional ones deliberately made for this purpose, but the term 'idolatry' would also apply to the worship of objects of purely natural origin, such as stones or trees. Again, while many devotional images and symbols are figural, whether anthropomorphic or zoomorphic in form, others are non-figural – abstract or 'aniconic', meaning that they do not reproduce, or aim to reproduce, some real or imagined likeness of another being. Moreover, cult images of either kind, figural or non-figural, will embody various forms of symbolism: symbolism which represents ideas about divine persons or realities rather than these persons or realities themselves.

If the trouble with idolatry in the first sense is that there are few if any genuine examples of it, then the trouble with idolatry in the second sense is that there are far too many examples – so many, in fact, as to limit the usefulness, or at least the force, of the term. It is difficult to find, or even imagine, a religion – mono-theistic, polytheistic or non-theistic – in which there are no sacred or revered physical images or symbols. Moreover, many of those who censure idolatry in others are party to the same kind of prac-tices themselves. The only way one can censure someone else for doing something one does oneself is to say that the other person is doing it in the wrong way. This is a possible but a perilous criticism to make, however. A Roman Catholic who affirms the real presence of Christ in the host (the eucharistic bread) but criticizes a Hindu for affirming the presence of, say, the God Shiva in a devotional image of Shiva is treading on ice so thin that it might as well be water. It might of course be said that the objection here is not to the idea of a divine presence in an image or object but rather to the supposed reality of Shiva in the first place, but in this case the objection has nothing specifically to do with the use of images. The objection amounts to nothing more, and nothing less, than saying that one's own God or gods are real, whereas the God or gods of others are false (either because they are non-existent or because they are not really gods). The use of the term 'idolatry' in this looser sense becomes a synonym for false belief or for unbelief. As proclaimed in the hymn 'From Greenland's Icy Mountains',

> In vain with lavish kindness
>   The gifts of God are strown;
> The heathen, in his blindness,
>   Bows down to wood and stone.

Although largely redundant in the two senses defined above, the word 'idolatry' has also acquired a broader, metaphorical usage which, as we shall see, has as important a bearing on religion as do its more specifically theological uses. This is its use to refer to any kind of extreme attachment or devotion to an idea, thing or person, normally (but not invariably) with the implication that such attachment or devotion is excessive if not dangerous. When we say of someone, for example, that she 'worships the ground he walks on', or that he 'idolizes' his football team, we are no doubt ourselves exaggerating the exaggerations to which we refer; but we are nevertheless referring to a very real human tendency to attribute an importance or value to things and persons that they simply cannot bear, and more importantly we are implying that such adulation can be damaging not only to those who engage in it but often to the objects of such adulation too.

Religion no less than any other kind of human activity offers fertile ground for all sorts of idolatries in this metaphorical sense, with perhaps religion itself, or some particular religion or denomination, emerging as the ultimate idol. As for the many forms of what can be called secular idolatry – in sport, entertainment, the arts, politics and so on – these may either be regarded as evidence that the religious impulse is as likely to express itself outside as within explicitly religious contexts, or else as evidence of the all too human character of religious worship itself. To explore these questions in greater depth, we need to begin by examining some of the classic sources of ideas about idolatry in religion.

IT IS VARIOUS TEXTS from the Old Testament that provide the baseline for discussions of idolatry in Western religion. In the books of Exodus and Deuteronomy are set out the Ten Commandments that Moses, the leader of the Israelites, brought down from his meeting with Yahweh on Mount Horeb. The second of these is the prohibition against idolatry:

> You shall not make for yourself a carved image, or any
> likeness of anything that is in heaven above, or that is on
> the earth beneath, or that is in the water under the earth.
> You shall not bow down to them or serve them; for I the
> Lord your God am a jealous God . . . (Exodus 20:4–5).

Later on in the book of Exodus, we find the famous episode about the worship of the Golden Calf, which ironically enough occurs while Moses himself is away on Mount Horeb receiving the Ten Commandments:

> When the people saw that Moses delayed to come down from the mountain, the people gathered themselves together to Aaron and said to him, 'Up, make us gods who shall go before us. As for this Moses, the man who brought us up out of the land of Egypt, we do not know what has become of him.' So Aaron said to them, 'Take off the rings of gold that are in the ears of your wives, your sons, and your daughters, and bring them to me . . . And he received the gold from their hand and fashioned it with a graving tool and made a golden calf. And they said, 'These are your gods, O Israel, who brought you up out of the land of Egypt!' When Aaron saw this, he built an altar before it. And Aaron made a proclamation and said, 'Tomorrow shall be a feast to the Lord.' And they rose up early the next day and offered burnt offerings and brought peace offerings. And the people sat down to eat and drink and rose up to play (Exodus 32:1–6).

This story of the golden calf was destined to become the classic literary account of the sin of idolatry. As the story unfolds we also get what comes to be seen as the classic account of the response to idolatry – namely, iconoclasm, the breaking of images. For as Moses comes down from Mount Horeb, bearing the tablets of the Law he has received from Yahweh, he hears the sound of music and celebration. Seeing the golden calf and the celebration around it he angrily smashes the tablets of the Law on the ground, burns and grinds to powder the golden calf, and mixing this with water makes the people drink it. He then orders the Levites to put to death all the instigators of the worship of the golden calf, three thousand men in all. To cap it all, Yahweh sends down his own punishment upon the Israelites in the form of a deadly plague.

It would be naive to think of Aaron and the Israelites simply as a group of wicked idolaters deliberately flouting the prohibitions against the use of images in worship. Nor would they have decided on a whim or at random upon the form of a golden calf or young bull for their cult image. The calf is likely to have been modelled on the winged bull, symbol of Apis, a manifestation of the creator god Ptah, with whose cult the Israelites would have been familiar during their long exile in Egypt. Bulls were commonly used as symbols in the ancient world. With Moses possibly gone for ever, and with no suitable image or symbol to act as focus for their worship and celebration, the Israelites seem to have intended the calf as a *masecha*, or intermediate representation, of Yahweh, the god who had led them out of Egypt. Aaron does, after all, explicitly identify the calf with Yahweh. It is all too easy to read back into ancient history (as the texts recounting these events themselves do) the strictly aniconic monotheistic theology of later times. Not only was the Ark of the Covenant to become a visual (and mobile) physical symbol of God's presence; it also shared with the golden calf a similar iconography, since it bore two golden images of winged cherubim. Nor is this the last we hear of the golden calf. In the First Book of Kings, we read how King Jeroboam, in order to consolidate his rule, creates two golden calves, which are again understood as cult images of the god who brought the Israelites out of Egypt.

Judaism, and later on Islam, both succeed in keeping their forms of worship largely free of figurative forms. Moreover, both religions not only eschew the use of images in worship but tend to avoid images in any context. According to several of the *hadith* – the traditions that preserve sayings or deeds attributed to the Prophet Muhammad – God on the Day of Resurrection will command those responsible for creating images of living forms to breathe life into their creations and on their being unable to do so will consign them to eternal punishment.[4] God alone is creator and any attempt to imitate his creative work is blasphemous.[5] The idea of idolatry, then, broadens to include not simply the error of worshipping images of false gods, or indeed false images of the true God, but the activity of making images at all – images that might or might not then incite one to worship created things in place of their creator.

The rationale for this more comprehensive avoidance of images is already adumbrated in the biblical texts, not least in the second commandment quoted earlier. Here the prohibition not to make images of any living thing seems to be prescribed prior to and independently of the prohibition not to make such images into cult images. According to the Hebrew Book of Wisdom (13:10),

> But wretched are they, and in dead things are their hopes,
>   who termed gods things made by human hands:
> Gold and silver, the product of art, and images of beasts,
> or useless stone, the work of an ancient hand.[6]

The human proclivity to fashion, and be fascinated by, images of living things is seen as a danger in its own right, whether it is the cause or the expression of idolatry. Iconophilia provokes the reaction of iconophobia. Thus the objection to the cult of images can be set within the context of a wider and more fundamental objection to the creation of and fascination with images, and indeed art of other kinds. We find it outside as well as within religious contexts, for example in Plato's more purely philosophical objection to images as the weakest representations of reality.

What we must next explore, however, is how the supposedly false worship of God or the gods identified as idolatry relates to the nature and logic of worship as such. Before the word was exclusively appropriated by religion, the 'worship' of something or someone meant no more and no less than attributing to them respect or value, such 'worthship' (the older form of the word) being acknowledged through words or actions of some kind. As we can see from the few surviving non-religious uses of the term, worship does not in itself imply the divinity of the thing or person worshipped. His worship the mayor is not mistaken for a divine being, nor is a man's spouse when in the Anglican service of matrimony he says to her: 'With my body I thee worship.'

But the word 'worship' has now come to be restricted to the worship of a divine being – yet another example of the segregation of religion from the rest of life.[7] If we were to revert to the broader meaning of the word, then it would be perfectly acceptable to talk not only about the worship of divine beings, but about the worship of angels, saints, images, times, places, people and events. As it happens, of course, alternative generic terms are available for this purpose, the most obvious ones being 'veneration' and 'devotion'.

The early Christians were well aware of the Mosaic injunctions against images in worship, and yet were now dealing with rather different conceptions of God. The issue of idolatry came to a head in the Eastern Church, in what is generally known as the iconoclastic controversy. For more than a century, the iconodules (venerators of two-dimensional images) were in debate and conflict with the iconoclasts (destroyers of images). In seeking to rebut the charge of idolatry brought by the iconoclasts, the iconodules insisted that Christians no longer needed to follow the Mosaic injunctions against the use of images in prayer and worship. For whereas in the past it was blasphemous to portray or attempt to portray the divine Being in or as an image, now it was permitted (and even encouraged) to depict such images since God had revealed Himself in the human form of Christ. To venerate such images was now a proper means of affirming the truth of the Incarnation. As for images of the saints, who were not divine but created beings, these sanctified individuals could themselves be revered as images of Christ. The iconodules differentiated between two kinds of veneration: on the one hand the adoration or worship due to God alone (*latreia*), and on the other hand the honour or devotion directed towards the saints (*proskynesis, duleia*).[8] It seems counter-intuitive, however, to suggest that those venerating different kinds of image are engaged in two different kinds of activity. Veneration is veneration, and will differ only in respect of the level of concentration or intensity of emotion involved. It is difficult to credit the idea that there can be two distinct kinds of veneration, so that persons who venerate first an icon of Christ and then an icon of a saint, for example, are doing two different things despite their actions and emotions being broadly similar.

In seeking to justify not merely the depiction of Christ and the saints but the devotional use of these depictions in the form of humanly manufactured icons, the iconodules also invoked another distinction implicit within the 'logic' of the veneration of icons. For in venerating an icon of Christ or a saint, one was not venerating the image itself, but rather, in or through the image, its original or 'prototype'. One might say the same about someone who gazes at a photograph of a loved one: technically the photograph is the object of their attention, but emotionally and epistemologically it is the actual person depicted who is the focus. (Only if it could be shown that someone valued the photograph more than the person whose photograph it was might the charge of idolatry apply.) This distinction between image and prototype is in itself an obvious one, and indeed is the basis for the scepticism of Voltaire and others that anyone knowingly mistakes inanimate objects or images for the gods themselves. Once again, however, this sophisticated defence of the veneration of images by the iconodules is as unsustainable as it is unnecessary. Why not simply accept that in the act of worship, the image is worshipped *as* the prototype, and that the intellectual discrimination of its dual 'objects' does not apply? It would obviously be crass to tell a person grieving over a photograph of a lost loved one not to make so much fuss over a mere photograph. But it would be no less insensitive to say such a thing if the person were lamenting the loss of the photograph itself.

The more intense the act of veneration, the less awareness there is likely to be of two separate objects of this veneration – its ulterior object in the (invisible) god or saint represented and its proximate object in the (visible) representation of this god or saint. The god or saint and the representation of the god or saint are, in and for the moment of veneration, one and the same, just as Hamlet and the actor playing Hamlet are one and the same during the performance of Shakespeare's play.[9] This unity of representation and represented is understood, and experienced, in a particularly close way in the Hindu tradition, where consecrated images of the gods are treated both ritually and emotionally as if they were the gods themselves. They are ritually fed, washed, clothed, cooled with fans and so on. To the iconoclastically minded critic, Hindu worship appears to offer particularly rich pickings, and yet the illusions are on the side of the iconoclast rather than on that of the Hindu iconodules, most of whom are perfectly aware (at least outside the devotional moment) of the actual distinction between a god and a god's physical representation – even in those cases where the god is thought to have a real presence in a ritually consecrated physical image. Some Hindu devotional images are purely temporary, modelled out of clay or butter for example, and are disposed of when no longer needed. Even the permanent stone images in temples are replaced when worn out or broken.

This brings us to what is perhaps the strongest argument against the iconoclasts – namely, that mental images are no less harmful than physical images and potentially far more harmful, both in worship and in the understanding of religious truths or realities. As Indologist Alain Daniélou observes,

> The error of the iconoclast is to believe that a mental image is less an idol than a physical one. In fact, the external form of an image is rather a help to the understanding of its relative value. It is among the most violent iconoclastic religious groups that we find the most material, childish, anthropomorphic conceptions of God. To have any meaning, the objection to images should refer not only to those that are material but also to those that are mental.[10]

What this suggests, indeed, is that a physical image or 'idol' may well be preferable to a mental one. For it is surely obvious that an inert physical image or object cannot be identical with what it represents, or symbolizes. Moreover, people are perfectly aware that multiple representations of the same deity exist, a plurality of images of the same deity often being visibly present within the same space. In the case of a mental image, or idea, it is much easier to confuse one's non-dimensional idea of something with this something in itself. The sensory or physical image may itself represent or convey an idea, or ideas, about what it represents, but it does this transitively, clearly referring to something other than or beyond itself. In being obviously distinct from what it represents, such an image may help people accept the relativity of their own ideas about the deity or divine reality in question. With a mental image, on the other hand, it is easier to ignore the gap between thing and idea, and in the unchallenged and dimension-less privacy of one's own head to identify the two.

That our conceptions or 'mental images' of a Supreme Being or ultimate reality are liable to lead us astray if they are not subject to careful scrutiny, including the scrutiny of those wiser or more experienced than ourselves, is a theme as old as religion itself. It is after all the basis of the observation by the ancient Greek writer Xenophanes that if cattle, horses and lions were able to paint pictures, they would represent the gods as cattle, horses and lions, just as humans have represented them in human form. Likewise, the anonymous medieval mystical handbook *The Cloud of Unknowing* mocks those would-be contemplatives who,

> if they read, or hear it read or spoken about, that men should lift up their hearts unto God, at once they are star-gazing as if they wanted to get past the moon, and listening to hear an angel sing out of heaven. In their mental fantasies they penetrate to the planets, and make a hole in the firmament, and look through! They make a God to their liking, and give him rich clothes, and set him on a throne, and it is all much odder than any painting!

A basic question here is whether images – in worship, prayer or contemplation – are working as bridges or as barriers. Do they assist the mind to reach towards divine realities or do they stand in the way of such efforts? Do they illuminate the religious under-standing or distort it? These questions have been the subject of much debate – and conflict – in religious traditions. The leaders of the Western Church, who were sceptical of, if not hostile to, the veneration of icons, were strongly in favour of images as 'visual aids' for the faithful, whether as informative illustrations of the life of Christ and the saints or as a means of encouraging them in their religious lives. When it comes to prayer, especially contemplative or mystical prayer, images are regarded sometimes as obstacles to be removed and sometimes as useful stepping stones from lower to higher conceptions of the religious ultimate. In Plato's *Symposium*, for example, we find an early example of what is to become an important idea within the Neoplatonism that informed so much subsequent Christian thought: the idea that we can ascend gradually from physical beauty through more abstract ideas of spiritual beauty to the form of Beauty itself. Similarly one might ascend, initially through images, to progressively higher concepts of God.

Ultimately, if not initially, contemplatives may seek to purge their consciousness of all images whatsoever in order to realize the ultimate state of oneness with God or the Absolute. The German mystic Meister Eckhart, a near-contemporary of the author of *The Cloud of Unknowing*, is uncompromising in his rejection of all images:

> Isaiah says, 'To whom have you likened Him or what image will you give Him?' [Isaiah 40:18]. Since it is God's nature not to be like anyone, we have to come to the state of being nothing in order to enter into the same nature that He is. So, when I am able to establish myself in Nothing and Nothing in myself, uprooting and casting out what is in me, then I can pass into the naked being of God, which is the naked being of the spirit. All that smacks of likeness must be ousted that I may be transplanted into God and become one with Him: one substance, one being, one nature, and the Son of God. Once this happens there is nothing hidden in God that is not revealed, that is not mine. Then I shall be wise and mighty and all else as He is, and one and the same with Him.[11]

This suggests that, at least for some people, any idea about God or the Absolute will be defective, and that it is only by going beyond image and word altogether that can one expect to come into direct contact with the ultimate reality.

CONSIDERATION of the proclivity to idolatry reaches well beyond questions as to whether, or how, images are to be used in worship, or about the extent to which one's consciousness can or should be cleared of the ideas and images that are for many people what actually constitute religious consciousness. The supposed dangers of idolatry in prayer or worship are as nothing compared with what might be called the generic idolatry of the human mind. The Enlightenment philosopher Immanuel Kant, for whom religion was essentially a support for morality, acknowledged the inevitability, but warned of the dangers, of anthropomorphic representations of God:

> Anthropomorphism, scarcely to be avoided . . . in the theoretical representation of God and His being, but yet harmless enough (so long as it does not influence concepts of duty), is highly dangerous in connection with our practical relation to His will, and even for our morality; for here we create a God for ourselves, and we create Him in the form in which we believe we shall be able most easily to win Him over to our advantage and ourselves escape from the wearisome uninterrupted effort of working upon the innermost part of our moral disposition.[12]

Ironically enough, Kant here seems to be providing his own example of an idolatry of sorts – albeit not a self-serving form of it – in his idea of God as epitome of the moral law or supreme lawgiver.

In fact some of the most insidious forms of idolatry, and not only those with a specifically religious focus, relate to ideas and ideals that appear to be beyond reproach. For instance, according to Simone Weil, one of the most damaging examples of idolatry is patriotism, the blame for which 'pagan virtue' she lays at the door of the ancient Romans: 'The Romans really were an atheistic and idolatrous people; not idolatrous with regard to images made of stone or bronze, but idolatrous with regard to themselves. It is this idolatry of self which they have bequeathed to us in the form of patriotism.'[13] Weil finds the source of this and other kinds of idolatry in the attribution of absolute value to something human, something whose entire reality is confined to this world alone. In her understanding, moreover, 'the real sin of idolatry is always committed on behalf of something similar to the State. It was that sin that the devil wanted Christ to commit when he offered him the kingdoms of this world.'[14] Although idolatry derives ultimately from our thirst for absolute good, we lack both the 'power of supernatural attention' and the necessary patience to develop this, and so we need idols to keep ourselves motivated in the world of shadows in which we live. 'Idolatry is thus a vital necessity in the cave. Even with the best of us it is inevitable that it should set narrow limits for mind and heart.'[15]

> Man always devotes himself to an order. Only, unless there is supernatural illumination, this order has as its centre either himself or some particular being or thing (possibly an abstraction) with which he has identified himself (e.g. Napoleon, for his soldiers, Science, or some political party, etc.).[16]

In addition to patriotism, science and political parties, the abstractions and institutions that all too easily become idols would include ideas such as progress, evolution or freedom of speech, institutions such as marriage, monarchy or religion,[17] and even individual figures such as Shakespeare, Jesus or the Buddha. Undoubtedly the Church, the Bible and God himself have been some of the most powerful objects of idolatry in human history.[18] In themselves all of these things are or can be good things. They are turned into idols not by their intrinsic qualities, but by the ways in which they are appropriated, and painted, by their admirers. Relevant here is Kierkegaard's point about the difference between an admirer and a follower (of Christ, in this particular instance):

> The admirer never makes any true sacrifices. He always plays it safe. Though in words, phrases, songs, he is inexhaustible about how highly he prizes Christ, he renounces nothing, gives up nothing, will not reconstruct his life, will not be what he admires, and will not let his life express what it is he supposedly admires.[19]

Those who venerate physical images of saints and deities are in little danger of confusing these images with their 'prototypes', or of not following or living by the ideas or persons they venerate through these images. It is much easier to take for granted or be uncritical about those larger and more abstract values and institutions, and to turn them into idols unaware.

Thomas Carlyle may well have been near the mark in saying that society was founded on hero-worship. What he seemed unaware of was that his enthusiastic endorsement of this worship was in effect an endorsement of idolatry:

> We all love great men; love, venerate and bow down submissive before great men: nay can we honestly bow down to anything else? Ah, does not every true man feel that he is himself made higher by doing reverence to what is really above him? No nobler or more blessed feeling dwells in man's heart. And to me it is very cheering to consider that no sceptical logic, or general triviality, insincerity and aridity of any Time and its influences can destroy this noble inborn loyalty and worship that is in man.[20]

Taken out of context, this and similar passages in Carlyle's book might reasonably be understood as intentionally ironic. But Carlyle is being perfectly serious.

Hero-worship, or its equivalent, is an obvious form of idolatry within the sphere of religion too. Such potentially idolized heroes will include not only the leaders, saints, mystics and martyrs that make it easier for one to divert one's efforts from costly commitment into detached admiration. It will also include the most sacred and enlightened figures in whose names the religious traditions are founded. This takes us back to the root meaning of 'idolatry' as the worship of a false image of God and to the efforts of the mystics and contemplatives to rise about all images. Pertinent here is Simone Weil's observation that 'the only choice is between worshipping the true God or an idol. Every atheist is an idolater – unless he is worshipping the true God in his impersonal aspect. The majority of the pious are idolaters.' Weil saw that it is ideas about God, rather than particular physical images or visual symbols of God, which function as the most harmful forms of idolatry. For this reason, atheism itself can be valuable as a purification of the idea of God:

> Religion in so far as it is a source of consolation is a hindrance to true faith; and in this sense atheism is a purification. I have to be an atheist with that part of myself which is not made for God. Among those in whom the supernatural part of themselves has not been awakened, the atheists are right and the believers wrong.[21]

One should perhaps add that atheism can itself become an idol, as it seems to do when it is held up as an item of belief, or even faith, worth holding on to against all arguments and evidence to the contrary. One may recall here the suggestion by the character in Tom Stoppard's play *Jumpers*, mentioned in Chapter Two, who suggests that atheism could function as a 'crutch' for those unable to bear the reality of God.

Something equivalent to 'atheism as purification' is to be found in Buddhism too, specifically in the Rinzai Zen tradition, whose founding master, Lin-chi, is reputed to have announced to his disciples: 'If you meet the Buddha on the road, kill him!'

This, and similarly iconoclastic statements, can be interpreted in various ways, but essentially they provide a salutary shock to those accustomed to relying on pre-conceived ideas and images that then stand in the way of one's true liberation from all attachment.[22]

MIGHT NOT THE FEAR of idolatry – whether of its physical or of its more abstract varieties – itself become a kind of idol? In iconoclastic periods of religion, the relentless seeking out and smashing of devotional images seems to suggest as much. Insistent belief in the falsity of what others insistently believe to be true can be as imprisoning as any other kind of belief, and a potential for idolatry too. Simone Weil and others allow that idolatry of any kind derives from the best in human nature and motivation. But it is scant consolation to those who cannot shake off images to be reminded, without apparent remedy, that the road to hell is paved with good intentions. It is important to ask, therefore, whether what gets labelled as 'idolatry' is necessarily to be seen as a fault or failure in the first place. Or, since to identify something as idolatrous is automatically to censure it, it is perhaps better to ask whether the needs and tendencies that all too often lead to idolatry must necessarily lead there. While mystics and others may be able to reach beyond all images and all ideas in their quest for absolute or ultimate realities, is it unreasonable to accept that, for many and perhaps most others, images and ideas will be the only way of connecting with them? And might not those same needs and tendencies be the very ones responsible for the works of art which are the very stuff of human culture? Moreover, perhaps the tendency to venerate physical beauty and other qualities, whether in physical objects or human persons, is itself testimony, in any context, to a human instinct for transcendent realities, however distorted or misdirected this instinct might be. Thus although history might show us that it is possible to take the idolatry out of religion (at least for a time), psychology will show us that it is not possible to take the religion out of idolatry. The idolatrous tendency seems to be an inevitable part of the nature of religions as humanly constructed entities.

The censure of idolatry, consistently applied, can lead us into very deep waters. It can take us from images of false gods to false representations of true gods, and from false representations to the falsity of representation itself. But could such an austere regime survive on its own? Is it not possible that, without the corrective of surrounding images, aniconism could itself become one of the subtlest and most pernicious forms of idolatry? God loves a sinner, it is sometimes said. If so, perhaps he would have a particular love for an idolater. To transcend images presupposes the existence – and persistence – of images; and for many people images may offer a perfectly safe passage to the transcendent. Moreover, the kinds of images usually associated with religious idolatry, if they are idols at all, are certainly not the most egregious kind of idols. The most egregious kind of idolatry is the uncritical worship of or devotion to ideologies or institutions which so limit one's vision that one can no longer see that it is limited. Devotional images and symbols, however much they may caricature sacred realities, at least announce their own relativity. One might of course be superstitious about this or that image, treating it as something sacred (or magical) in its own right, but even superstition could be seen as healthy if it helps keep the mind open to the idea that there is more to this world than what is immediately apparent.

Let us return finally to Mount Horeb, where Moses – hardly a role model for idolaters – encounters Yahweh, the god who forbids all images of created things. But Moses does not encounter God as some abstract or aniconic being. Rather he hears a voice from the burning bush, where God is represented in the anthropoid form of an angel. And yet, despite these vivid perceptions, he does not come away thinking that God himself is a voice, an angel or a burning bush.

NINE

UNIVERSALITY IN PARTICULARITY

I n the modern world, and especially in the modern West, it is no longer possible to speak about one religion without speaking, implicitly at least, about other religions too. This is true not only for those who observe religions as outsiders, but for those who are the adherents of a religion. In speaking about religion one must also be speaking about the plurality of religions, and in speaking about the plurality of religions one must thereby be open to questions about the relationship between religions.

What has been called the encounter between religions is not a new phenomenon. Religions have always been in contact and there has always been interchange between the various religious traditions. But in modern times a greater awareness of the ideas, practices and institutions that define 'other religions' has increasingly affected how religious adherents think about the ideas, practices and institutions of their own religion. This greater awareness of religious pluralism has gone hand in hand with a greater awareness of the pluralism *within* religions. And just as there are religious adherents who seek to heal the differences between the various denominations within their own religion, so are there those who seek to bring the world religions at large closer together.

Each tradition, however much it expands or divides into different denominations, is defined, and limited, by the historical and cultural particularities within which it originated; and each tradition forever looks back to the special events and experiences identified with its origins. But the fact of religious pluralism and the cultural contingencies that characterize each separate tradition provide the basis for much of the scepticism and criticism attending religion in the modern world.

For many observers, but especially for sceptics and critics of religion, the plurality and cultural diversity of world religions suggest that each of them has purely naturalistic origins, reflecting the needs, values and prejudices of particular peoples at particular times. Such observers will not necessarily deny that religions have made positive contributions to human civilization, and sometimes played a vital role within it, but what the historicism and cultural pluralism of religion suggests to many critics and commentators is that the claims of any religious system or institution to be the unique mediator of some transcendental or divinely authorized truth cannot but wither under the spotlight of history, anthropology and psychology.

Is it not more reasonable to find in the historical and cultural contingencies that define the origin of each religion an alternative explanation of its claims to authority? The fact that there is a multiplicity of religions, each of them proclaiming a message seemingly incompatible with those proclaimed by others, surely suggests the much simpler hypothesis that none of them can be accepted as full or final statements of religious truth. In any event, it is undoubtedly the case that the adherents of each religion must face up both to the contingent nature of much that they hold sacrosanct and to the intellectual and other challenges posed by the existence and the claims of the 'other religions'.

In examining the implications of religious pluralism for religious truth (or for the truth claims of particular religions), we shall find that much turns on understanding the nature of the relationship between the particular and the universal in religion. Religions typically make claims of a universal kind, or at least claims that have implications stretching far beyond the immediate concerns of the particular groups or nations with which the religions are most closely associated: claims about a Supreme Being or Absolute

Principle, about the origins of the world, about the nature and destiny of humankind, about the right way to live our human lives, and about the nature of a life beyond death. And yet everywhere religions express these universalities in what might be called concrete particularities. They express the universal in terms of the particular, and through the particular aspire to the universal.

I TURN FIRST to the challenge of religious pluralism. The fact that there are many different religions, each constituted by a different set of ideas and practices, and that the ideas and practices of one religion are incompatible with those of other religions, would seem to present a substantial challenge to those who take religious claims, or the claims of a particular religion, seriously. It is not simply that the particular claims of each religion can be challenged on either logical or empirical grounds. It is also that the very plurality of religious claims renders the claims of all of them suspect. As Christopher Hitchens puts it, 'Since it is obviously inconceivable that all religions can be right, the most reasonable conclusion is that they are all wrong.'[1] This would not of course be said about, say, a plurality of incompatible scientific theories, presumably because the methodology of science would (over time) eliminate the false theories and establish the true one through observation and experimentation. Some religious apologists would argue that a parallel process has indeed gone on in the history of religions, with spiritually or morally superior ideas and practices displacing earlier and inferior ones. In this manner, it might be argued, the religions of the Egyptians, Iranians, Greeks and Romans, among other ancient peoples, were seen off by the superior ethical monotheisms of Judaism, Christianity and Islam. The same might be said about Buddhism and Sikhism, for example, in relation to the earlier religious traditions of India. On the view put forward by Hitchens, however, all religions will one day be like the religions of ancient Babylonia, Egypt, India and so on – cultural relics of the past to be contemplated in museums and studied in libraries but no longer practised in home or temple.

But the plurality of religions cannot in itself be proof of the truth or falsity of any one of them. Either one must have some a priori reason for rejecting *any* kind of religious claim or each claim must be examined separately. Nor would examining religions for truth or falsity merely be a matter of establishing or undermining their theoretical or doctrinal claims. Religions arguably resemble technologies as much as scientific theories, and a technology will not necessarily be accompanied by a satisfactory theory of how or why it works (or does not work), or indeed by any theory at all. When we talk about a religion or religious doctrine being true or false, we should bear in mind that its truth will, at least in part, be an instrumental or pragmatic truth rather than a purely theoretical one. Indeed many religious doctrines are better understood as 'catalysts' for action in the world than as 'claims' or 'propositions' about the world. Again, a religious theory, just like a scientific theory, may be on the right lines despite being erroneous in some respects, or alternatively may be as correct as the prevailing world-view or paradigm allows it to be.

But so long as we appreciate that religious pluralism cannot simply be reduced to doctrinal pluralism, it is useful shorthand to think of the relationship between religions in terms of a relationship between different (compatible or incompatible) doctrines. Logically, there seem to be four main alternatives to the possibility that all religions are false: that one religion alone is true and the others false (or largely false); that one religion embodies the whole truth and other religions only parts of the truth; that no religion is (or could be) fully true – all religions being partly true, incomplete in respect of the full truth; and that religions contain the same essential truth (or truths) manifested in, or perhaps obscured by, diverse cultural forms. These positions can be identified respectively as the exclusivist, inclusivist, relativist and essentialist positions. There are ways of developing each of these positions that are no less intellectually respectable than the position asserted by Hitchens.

The exclusivist and inclusivist positions are similar in being unilateral, meaning that they privilege one tradition above the others. Accordingly, a 'unilateral' position will only be argued from within the one religion claiming to be the true or truest tradition. In theory, all religions could take an exclusivist position, in which case all but one of them (if not all of them) would be mistaken in taking this position. Undoubtedly many religions have asserted an exclusivist approach to 'other religions'. But they have not necessarily done this consistently or in respect of every aspect of religion. Nor, importantly, does exclusivism necessarily mean absolute exclusivism: there are, for instance, many religious exclusivists who have said that although those professing other religions may be in error regarding doctrine they are not thereby excluded from the saving truth of the true religion. Exclusivism in regard to knowledge of a particular truth does not imply exclusivism in regard to access to that truth. What absolute exclusivists say, however, is that those following other religions are *ipso facto* excluded from salvation.[2]

Historically, in fact, few religions have consistently or persistently claimed that every other religion is in complete error. It would be a more reasonable generalization to say that each religion claims to be truer than (or at least as true as) all the others. Thus Christianity claims that Judaism is, or was, provisionally true, true so far as it goes, just as Islam claims that both Judaism and Christianity are imperfect (and partly corrupted) versions of the pure truth now republished in the form of Islam. Muslims denounced Hinduism as polytheism and idolatry, and yet it was partly under the influence of Islam that the new religion of Sikhism came to birth. These points lead us to the second of the four positions.

The exclusivist and inclusivist positions operate almost on the 'bad cop, good cop' principle. The inclusivist position can be seen as a more flexible version of exclusivism, to the extent that it maintains the superiority and unique authority of one tradition over all other religions. But although one religion manifests the full truth, this truth is recognized as also being present in other religions, albeit expressed in partial or imperfect forms. From another point of view, however, inclusivism might be seen as a more arrogant and condescending position than exclusivism. Exclusivism at least allows other religions to be what they say they are, whereas inclusivism reinterprets them as unwitting approximations to the superior religion. No one likes to be told that when they say *x* what they really mean is *y*. There are, however, significant variations within the inclusivist position that mitigate or remove its potentially condescending approach. Thus inclusivist thinkers will often acknowledge that the doctrines and practices of 'other religions' reveal new aspects of religious truth or expose deficits in the 'superior' religion. Either way the inclusivist position is not incompatible with the idea that the true or truest religion has much to learn from 'other religions'.

The relativist and essentialist positions, in contrast to exclusivism and inclusivism, express a multilateral approach to religious truth. For the relativist, no religion can provide anything other than an approximation to a full or final truth; each of them sees through a glass darkly. By the same token, of course, it will be impossible to know how near or how far any particular religion is from expressing the full or final truth; or, more negatively expressed, to know how much in error each religion must be. Whereas exclusivism and inclusivism may see the existence (and especially the persistence) of other religions as a challenge to their own unique authority, relativism takes strength from their existence, just as it also takes strength from the internal pluralism of each religious tradition and indeed from the pluralism evident even within a particular denomination. Many people nowadays would accept that the more profound a truth of any kind, the more difficult it is to wrap it up in a single formulation.

Essentialism concurs with relativism in seeing religious pluralism in a positive light. For essentialist thinkers, all religions proclaim the same fundamental message, but this message is coloured and sometimes compromised by cultural trimmings of one kind or another. It is these trimmings that account for the obvious differences between religions. But how could a single (or ultimate) truth survive in a particular historical or cultural context other than by being expressed in language and customs meaningful within that context? Essentialism is in a way the inversion of relativism. Whereas relativism takes the view that any divine revelation or enlightenment experience would, from the moment of its reception and in the process of its interpretation, become distorted or degraded by the relativities of language and culture, essentialism affirms the certainty of common human insights and experiences and sees the rest of religion as cultural accretion that may variously enhance or degrade the basic religious truth.

The ways in which religious apologists in the various historical religions have actually interpreted 'other religions' in relation to their own religion is, of course, more complex than the neat division into four logically distinct positions might suggest. What is also worth noting is that each of these four positions reflects a tendency present almost by definition in every religion. Thus each religion has, by the very nature of its doctrines and practices, a tendency to make universal claims about human existence and the cosmos, and to regard its own formulations about these as superior to those of others (exclusivism), but also a tendency to seek support for them in the formulations of others (inclusivism). Likewise each religion has a tendency to treat its own formulations as failing to do full justice to the truths they express (relativism), and also a tendency to affirm that certain of its ideas (and practices) are more fundamental than others (essentialism).

Is it possible to make any general judgements about the validity of these different ways of coming to terms with religious pluralism? In the context of an increasingly globalized humanity, it is difficult for the members of one religion to maintain an exclusivist or even an inclusivist stance towards 'other religions'. Even if there were a Supreme Creator God who occasionally but directly intervened in human history with a vital message for humankind, it is difficult to believe that such a God would direct such a message to one group or selected groups only, or make the ability to receive or understand such a message dependent on cultural or geographical circumstances. At least there is logic in the Judaic and Islamic idea that God has intervened repeatedly. It can certainly be no accident that as knowledge of world religions has become more sophisticated, and our sense of the essential unity of mankind more established, exclusivism has given way to inclusivism, and inclusivism to relativism or essentialism.

Like any other relativist position, however, the weakness of the relativist position on religious pluralism is that it seems ultimately to depend on a knowledge of the full truth that the theory itself denies is possible. Who could say that the various religions are like different paths up the same mountain except someone viewing these paths from the top of the mountain – a view which according to the relativist stance is not available? If at least some people (even just a tiny elite) have privileged access to the full religious truth behind the culturally limited forms which for others (perhaps the majority) represent the highest truth available, then the relativist position collapses into a theory about esoteric and exoteric levels of truth (or access to truth).

As for essentialism, this requires a reinterpretation of the real meaning of a religion in terms of some common denominator – which, given the doctrinal variety and complexity of religions, usually turns out to be the moral code of each religion. Apart from this, essentialism is little more than a strategy for minimizing the differences between religion, in the unquestionably laudable interests of harmony and cooperation, by selecting non-controversial common elements. In this case the different religions might well be likened to similar paths up different mountains.

Two things are clear. First, at least where universal claims are being made, each religion implies, or stands in need of, a theory of world religions. That is to say, claims to universal truth, or claims with universal implications, made in one religion are logically bound to take account of claims of a similar nature made elsewhere, be these in religious or non-religious contexts. This may be less obviously true in the case of what might be called 'ethnic religions' – that is, religions whose doctrines and practices are seemingly relevant only to a particular group of persons, rather as the rules and constitution of, say, a sports club have relevance only for its members. In fact, such religions do make statements with universal implications or, once in contact with outsiders (through travel, trade and so on), are forced to confront the cultural limitations of their own traditions. One might say that religions are like nations, some of which have explicit foreign policies, others of which have no such policies, but all of which, by virtue of their knowledge of being one nation among many others, are sooner or later bound to express views about the status of other nations near or far.

Each religion should have, if not a general theory of religious pluralism, at least a theory about how its own beliefs and practices relate to those of other religions. Christianity should have not just a theory about Judaism but also a theory about Buddhism, Islam not just a theory about Christianity but also a theory about Hinduism and Zoroastrianism, Buddhism not just a theory about Hinduism but also a theory about Christianity, and so on. The same should apply within as well as between religions: Roman Catholicism should have a theory of Protestantism, and vice versa, and so on. This brings us to the second point. Whatever theory or theology of religious pluralism is elaborated will, from a strictly logical standpoint, conform to one or another of the four positions outlined above. What is common to all four positions is the attempt to bring the various religions together within a single conspectus. For example, a Buddhist might predict (if an inclusivist) that the nature of the universe is such that all beings will eventually attain enlightenment, or a Christian lament (if an exclusivist) that those outside the Church stand in danger of eternal estrangement from God, or a Muslim (if a relativist) defer to the Quranic verse about God at the end of time revealing to the nations of the world the meaning of the different religions among them.[3]

None of the four positions, however, fully engages with what really separates one religion from another, or one denomination from another within a religion. What separates the religions, and defines their uniqueness, is not simply or even mainly their divergent doctrines or philosophies. Indeed we might say that these doctrines or philosophies if anything serve to unite religions, making comparisons between, and evaluations of, religions relatively straightforward. Taken in abstract isolation, religious doctrines, like moral codes or scientific theories, can be compared on the basis of universally accepted rational criteria. In reality, of course, religious doctrines embrace much more than propositions and prescriptions that can be juxtaposed with the propositions and prescriptions of another religion; in reality they are intertwined with all the experiential, practical and institutional elements that make up religion as actually lived; and it is these elements within each religion, as much as the doctrinal elements, that contribute to the particularity of religions and the differences between them. Religions are not just doctrines. They are also experiences, practices, texts, institutions, people, places, events, objects, times and so on. To understand religion, or any particular instance of religion, there needs to be an understanding of the relationship between its particular and its universal elements.

THE CHRISTIAN DOCTRINE that the eternal creator God was uniquely incarnate as a particular human individual in a particular province of the Roman Empire a little over two thousand years ago has been described as a 'scandal of particularity'.[4] Far from being a source of embarrassment, this 'scandal' is often celebrated as the distinctive mark of Christianity. But one could equally well identify the idea that on the life and death of a single individual should hang the salvation of the whole of humanity as a 'scandal of universality'. What tends to be forgotten, however, is that other religions have their own scandals of particularity: their own equally distinctive claims to uniqueness within the history of world religions; and their own scandals of universality: their own historically particularized claims to a message relevant to all humanity. Judaism claims for its people a special role among the nations of mankind; Islam proclaims itself to be God's final revelation to humanity; Buddhists claim that, of all those who have taught a path to liberation, the Buddha alone discovered the true path, and so on. All of this raises important questions about how the historical and cultural particularities of religions variously define, restrict or empower the ideas they express concerning the nature of the world and of human existence within it.

In religion, just as in other areas of human concern, we find constant interplay between the universal and the particular, or rather between the universalizing and the particularizing tendencies. The mistake is to see these tendencies as antithetical. What from one point of view is a scandal of particularity is from another a scandal of universality. The abstract truths of mythology and religion everywhere become objectified, localized, personified. All religions have to start (or are identified as starting) at a particular time and place, and every religion is indelibly marked by the circumstances of its origins – be these ethnic, geographical, historical, political, linguistic and so on. No human idea, movement or institution begins in a vacuum. For similar reasons the initial focus of a religion will be a local (or relatively local) one. But it is in the nature of social movements energized by new ideas (and this includes religions) to spread outwards from their sources, not only accidentally through human movement and communication but in large part from the desire both of its adherents to share the message with others and of others to share in its perceived benefits. As it spreads, moreover, a religion inevitably broadens its message and adapts its ideas and practices to accommodate new circumstances – circumstances that may differ markedly from those obtaining at the time of its origin. But this process of expansion is matched by a contrary process, for in the course of its expansion a religion will re-localize itself around the particular circumstances of new members and communities. There are, in short, contrary tendencies at work in the historical trajectory of any religion: on the one hand a universalizing tendency and on the other a particularizing or re-particularizing tendency. Thus one of the central features of religious systems, whether we look at them as cultural systems or as intellectual systems, is that in varying degrees or proportions they combine the universal and the particular.

The balance between the universal and particular elements can vary considerably. It is true that some religions might be regarded as more 'tribal' or 'ethnically' grounded than others, with many beliefs and practices relating to the particular interests of a particular people in a particular location, while other religions actually start out with a more outward-looking or universalizing agenda. But this distinction tends to be blurred by the fact that the more a religion spreads outwards from its original source, the more opportunities arise for the creation of culturally and intellectually specific versions of the religion – in the form of movements and denominations, not all of which will see eye to eye about the nature of the tradition of which they are part. Buddhism, for example, began as a missionary religion in the area now known as Nepal. Its rapid spread through many different cultures produced a huge variety of schools and sects, resulting both from new doctrinal and practical developments within Buddhism and from the influence of other traditions. In the Tibetan cultural region Buddhism was profoundly influenced by the indigenous Bon religion, just as in China the Ch'an (later Zen) tradition was profoundly influenced by Taoism. In the Qur'ān, God states, 'We have sent it down as an Arabic Qur'ān that you might understand' (12:2).[5] Arabic remains the sacred language of Islam, because it is the language spoken to the Arabic people by God himself. This both universalizes and sanctifies Arabic within Islam while at the same time setting up a potential fault line between Arabic and non-Arabic Muslims. Again, cultural differentiation within a religion can act both to generate tensions and to accommodate diversity. For example, the division between Sunni and Shia, which reflects conflict within early Islam and continues to breed conflict, has also served to bring very different types of people and of religious sensibility into the Islamic fold.

Christianity, a 'world religion' originating in the Near East, spread into many nations, and in the history of these nations God became as multiply partisan as any of the gods of India, being invoked in support of this group against that group, this cause against that cause, and so on. For example, John Milton was one among many Christian thinkers of great intellectual stature who believed that England had a special place under divine Providence.

According to Milton, God has favoured the English as he had favoured the Israelites:

> Yet that which is above all this, the favour and the love of Heaven, we have great argument to think in a peculiar manner propitious and propending towards us. Why else was this nation chosen before any other, that out of her, as out of Sion, should be proclaimed and sounded forth the first tidings and trumpet of Reformation to all Europe?[6]

In views of this kind we can see the seeds of what, at least in other minds than Milton's, can easily lead to idolatry – an idolatry not only of God, or of the Church, but of the nation. Nor do such statements merely represent the lingering survival of primitive or narrow-minded concepts now abandoned.[7] People will always co-opt the Supreme Being to their own particular agenda, as the philosopher Kant explains in the passage quoted in Chapter Eight. In time of war, the armed forces of opposing nations, and their weapons too, continue to be blessed in God's name. Similar sentiments, and actions, can be found in the religious literature of every Christian nation.

It is, however, in the 'concrete universals' of religion that we find much of the tension, and the paradox, of religion. Thus a local or tribal god may become a universal or supreme god, while a supreme god may be re-domesticated to the needs of a particular culture. Religions must constantly renegotiate the relationship between the universal and the particular in their ideas and practices, whether these concern conceptions of ultimate reality, the use of images and other objects in worship, the sacralization of time and space, and so on. Extremes of universalization can lead both to the kinds of large-scale idolatries discussed in Chapter Eight and to the dissipation of religion into moralism or metaphysics – or, worse, oppressive ideology. Extremes of particularization, on the other hand, can lead to those smaller-scale forms of idolatry or superstitions which occur when a particular idea or practice comes completely adrift from a larger religious vision and way of life. Even superstition, however, can be read in a positive light, in so far as it indicates that one will not have completely closed one's mind to the possibility that there are 'more things in heaven and earth' than are dreamt of in the imagination of secular materialism.

Arguably it is the scandal of universality that will always play second fiddle to the scandal of particularity. For it is inevitable, and indeed appropriate, that religions everywhere should ground their doctrines and practices, even when they relate to universal concerns, in the particularities of daily life – in particular places, in particular things, in particular events and in particular persons. Almost by definition the history of religions is a history of religious particularism, whereas religious universalism tends to be a second-order concern.

APOLOGISTS AND CRITICS alike are accustomed to thinking of religions as complete and final systems of universal truth, and this image of religion, especially when institutionalized, is what alienates so many other people from religion. It is a view of religion that not only inflates the importance of the doctrinal dimension of religion, but encourages the doctrine itself to become overdeveloped. It is this universalist view of religion, moreover, that dominates attitudes to 'other religions', as if each of them is competing for recognition as truest or most complete religion. This is most obviously the case with exclusivist and inclusivist interpretations of other religions, but relativist and essentialist interpretations are far from being immune to this tendency. Relativist interpretations may also depend on the idea of a complete or ideal religion (such as each of the historical religions may aspire to realize), while essentialist interpretations seek to rediscover universal truth at a more humble level, beneath the cultural overgrowth of each tradition.

Rather than thinking of religion in idealistic and universalist terms, it could be more fruitful to think of them in more openly particularist terms: that is, as evolving cultural (and intellectual) systems that help us to find meaning, value and salvation in the irreducible particularities of our lives, and also serve to reveal or particularize for us, where we happen to be, those truths and insights already acknowledged. This will require us to accept that religions do not and cannot 'own' their own truth. We should think of religion and the religions neither as competing projects for the soul of humankind, nor as systems of belief and practice ripe for demythologization and secularization. We should rather think of them as we think of the arts, or of science, or of the natural environment, as part of the common heritage of humankind.

In the biblical book of Genesis we find the well-known story of the building of the Tower of Babel, a story commonly interpreted as an example of God's punishment of his sinful creation. But there is a more positive way of interpreting this story that also serves to illustrate a possible attitude to religious pluralism and the particularism of religion. The story tells us that the people of earth, now gathered together in one place and united by a common language, cooperated in the building of a city, including a tower reaching up to heaven. Fearing that humankind will now get out of hand, God confuses their language, dispersing the people into different groups and disrupting the building of the city. Beyond being simply an aetiological myth explaining the diversity of human language and culture, this story can also be read as a warning against what might happen to a complacent, self-contained society cut off from independent standards or alternative voices. Paradoxically, truth is better preserved in a plurality of views than in some single, supposedly self-sufficient vision.[8]

Despite many attempts to build a Tower of Babel, in the form of monolithic, conformist and often oppressive societies, the general situation of humankind remains untidily and even infuriatingly pluralist. This pluralism, while in some respects obstructing the much needed unity and cooperation of humankind, is at the same time a safeguard against any one voice crowding out all others. As history clearly demonstrates, religion is especially susceptible to becoming monolithically oppressive both towards its own adherents and those of other religions and cultures. The pluralism of religions can itself be regarded as a revelation of the richness and ambiguity of religious truth, while the strengths and weaknesses of one religion can provide valuable correctives for the adherents of another.

Truth may ultimately be one, and yet our experience of reality being so obstinately plural suggests that the transcendent might reveal itself to us in the plural too. One way in which its pluralism would be expressed is in the fact that in responding to what is sacred or transcendent in or beyond the world, human beings have constructed many different religious worldviews, which all have something in common while also being irreducibly different. Nor should one be misled by the language of unity and transcendence so characteristic of theology and metaphysics. The language here is not that of mathematics, logic or even philosophy. In fact religious unities are often, when you look again, also pluralities. The Christian concept of the Trinity is an obvious example. Even in Islam, the strictly defined oneness of God (*tawḥīd*) is balanced by the idea of the ninety-nine names of God. But perhaps the best example of harmony between unity and multiplicity is found in the Chinese idea of *tao*, the principle or 'way' of all things.

> The great Tao flows everywhere,
> to the left and to the right.
> All things depend upon it to exist,
> and it does not abandon them.
> To its accomplishments it lays no claim.
> It loves and nourishes all things,
> but does not lord it over them.[9]

A religious truth or insight, from whatever source it comes, must surely apply to all human beings, just as any scientific, social or moral truth or insight does. This does not mean that 'all religions are one', or are simply 'different paths leading to the same summit'. Rather what it means is that, because all human beings are one, their diverse religious insights and achievements belong to all. Each religion is a resource within a common human heritage.

TEN

THE COSMOLOGICAL
CONNECTION

In a review of Charles Darwin's *Origin of Species*, Thomas Huxley, famous as much for his support of Darwin's theory as for his own work as a biologist, deploys dramatic imagery to describe the retreat of religious orthodoxy in the face of scientific discovery:

> Extinguished theologians lie about the cradle of every science as the strangled snakes beside that of Hercules; and history records that whenever science and orthodoxy have been fairly opposed, the latter has been forced to retire from the lists, bleeding and crushed if not annihilated; scotched, if not slain. But orthodoxy . . . learns not, neither can it forget; and though, at present, bewildered and afraid to move, it is as willing as ever to insist that the first chapter of Genesis contains the beginning and the end of sound science.[1]

Darwin in a letter to Huxley expresses enthusiastic approval of this imagery.[2] Not many years after the publication of Darwin's *Origins* in 1859, two books in particular would do much to reinforce in the public mind the idea that there is an essentially antagonistic relationship between science and religion. These books were John William Draper's *History of the Conflict between Religion and Science* (1875) and Andrew

Dickson White's *A History of the Warfare of Science with Theology in Christendom* (1896).

As these two influential books demonstrate, the long and complex relationship between science and religion (especially in the West) does provide much evidence that seemingly justifies the language of conflict or warfare. Certainly the simple word 'and' in the anodyne phrase 'science and religion' masks a long story of tension and misunderstanding that continues to this day. Although no longer the subject of public controversy that it was in Darwin's time, tensions between science and religion continue to infect many areas of contemporary life. It is not simply that people look to science rather than to religion, or to religion rather than to science, for answers to personal, social and global questions. What they more specifically do is look to science *as opposed to* religion, or to religion *as opposed to* science. For many people, accepting the values of the one seems to mean rejecting the values of the other. Or at least they assume it does. Even those who acknowledge, or want to acknowledge, the value of both seem to accept that doing so must involve some kind of balancing act, or at least some strategy of compartmentalization.

It may of course be protested that today, as in the past, the extent of the conflict between science and religion has been much exaggerated, and that many of the disputes have been due to mutual misunderstanding, institutional rivalry or other factors having little to do with science or religion as such. Even before further analysis, however, one is tempted to say: no smoke without fire. And in any case, whatever the basis of the perception that science and religion are incompatible, at least the perception itself should be taken seriously as an important cultural fact that continues to be part of our history. False ideas are still ideas and can be as powerful as true ideas for damagingly long periods of time.

Various explanations have been given for the conflict, or apparent conflict, between science and religion. Explanations that seek to demonstrate that the conflict is only apparent, or at least due only to misunderstanding, focus on the rivalry between science and religion in some third area of human concern (in politics, law, morality or medicine, for example), or bring forward cases where either science or religion seems to have strayed outside its own domain or 'magisterium'.[3] Explanations that argue that the conflict is real and deep-seated point to cases where both sides lock horns in genuine disagreement about what is true in or about the world. The themes of such disputes include the existence of God, the origins of the universe, the sources of human behaviour, the epistemological status of religious experience, and the possibility of life after death.

ONE OF THE CHIEF reasons for the widespread disenchantment with religion, and for the decline in religious belief and commitment particularly in the West, is the conviction that advances in the natural and social sciences have in various ways undermined key religious claims. Especially since the Enlightenment, the sciences of geology, biology, physics and psychology have demonstrated enormous success in explaining features of the natural world, just as anthropological, historical and textual studies have demolished the privileged status of religious institutions and of the sacred texts to which they appeal for their authority. It is a widely held presumption among those who describe themselves as non-religious that science has now 'disproved' religion. More cautious sceptics might be inclined to use the term 'discredited' rather than 'disproved', maintaining that, although religion cannot be demonstrably disproved, its credibility has nevertheless been catastrophically undermined by the methods and discoveries of modern science. The same people would never think of saying that science has now discredited politics, or art, or sport, however.[4] No amount of evidence of insincere or corrupt politicians, of bogus or incompetent artists, or of cheating or ungracious sports contestants, would ever lead to such a judgement. Why, then, does it come so easily to so many to say that science has disproved or discredited religion?

Clearly, what sceptics generally mean by religion here is religion as a system of metaphysical propositions or theories about the universe. Given the manifest discoveries of science, religion is not just wrong; it is also redundant. Religion has lost out to science, or been replaced by science, in the attempt to understand the world. When it comes down to it, then, to say that modern science has now disproved religion amounts to little more than saying that modern science has disproved the scientific or pseudo-scientific pretensions of religion. It is ironic that science has, for many people who reject religion and even spirituality, now assumed the kind of authority formerly associated with religion.[5]

The idea that science undermines religion – an idea not necessarily expressed or accepted without regret – is not simply a popular idea, but one held by a large number of scientists and secular intellectuals. In fact the opposition between science and religion has in recent times intensified and shifted in emphasis. In the past, scientists were generally reluctant to emphasize the negative implications for religion of their theories and discoveries, while religious thinkers were aware of the need to re-evaluate or reinterpret religious doctrines in the light of scientific discoveries, readily confessing the past errors and excesses of religion and acknowledging the truth and value of current scientific theories. More recently, however, a new breed of explicitly atheist scientists is taking the battle to the enemy – trumpeting the explanatory and salvific power of science and attacking both the irrationality and the negative social and psychological effects of traditional religion. The dicta of the so-called 'new atheists', with their passionate championing of science and equally passionate denunciations of religion, may be more significant here than either the acceptance by religiously minded scientists that faith is beyond the reaches of scientific enquiry or the reassurances of scientifically minded theologians that religion has nothing to fear from science. The 'warfare' clearly is not over. Or if the warfare is illusory, then the illusion is proving very hard to dispel. We might even say that the illusion of warfare is so strong that it might just as well be regarded as real warfare.

But why, in any case, should disagreement, or even conflict, be seen only or mainly in negative terms? Progress within science and religion alike surely depends partly on conflict and disagreement, just as it does in other spheres. Conflict and disagreement are catalysts for, or symptoms of, the ways in which competition between alternative theories is resolved and in which different interest groups settle into their most fruitful or stable relationships. In any case, the incompatibilities between religious and scientific ideas, and the hostilities between scientists and religious leaders, have themselves been much exaggerated.[6] For one thing, many of the individuals in question have had both scientific and religious commitments. To this extent the so-called 'warfare' between science and religion has been a civil war. Again, much of both science and technology was developed within, and defined by, the institutions of religion. The same is true of the relationship between art and religion, politics and religion, morality and religion, and so on. Sometimes it was a case of religion providing the motivation for the development of science and technology, sometimes a case of its providing the necessary resources or opportunities. Two very different examples would be the development of detailed astronomical knowledge in ancient Mesopotamian religion and the experiments on heredity in sweet peas conducted by the Augustinian monk Gregor Mendel. Whatever else they are, religions have over the centuries been the main institutions within which intellectual and cultural life, including the development of scientific ideas, has been advanced.

Even so, what is now almost the established view of the relationship between science and religion is that science and religion are not, or at least no longer, in conflict because they have different subject matters and hence pose different kinds of question about the world: science talks about facts and theories and religion about meaning and values. One way of putting this is to say that science and religion constitute two 'non-overlapping magisteria':

> the magisterium ... of science covers the empirical realm: what is the universe made of (fact) and why does it work this way (theory). The magisterium of religion extends over questions of ultimate meaning and moral value. These

two magisteria do not overlap, nor do they encompass all inquiry ... To cite the old clichés, science gets the age of rocks, and religion the rock of ages; science studies how the heavens go, religion how to go to heaven.[7]

The second of these clichés is a variation on a statement wrongly attributed to the astronomer Galileo Galilei: 'The Bible shows the way to go to heaven, not the way the heavens go.' What Galileo actually said in his 'Letter to the Grand Duchess Christina', was that 'the intention of the Holy Ghost is to teach us how one goes to heaven, not how heaven goes' – a statement he quoted from Cardinal Caesar Baronius.[8] But things cannot be that simple, for Gould's if not Galileo's use of the word 'heaven' is equivocal here. 'Going to heaven' is either just a vague metaphor for living the religious life, or pursuing the path to salvation, or else it is a cosmological and eschatological reference. If it is the latter, then 'heaven' refers to some kind of reality, and is part of what constitutes and explains the universe. In this case, the magisteria of science and religion would, after all, overlap in some way. Religions, whatever else they are, are also cosmologies, and functioned as such long before modern science came on the scene, with its own demythologized cosmology.

In the treaty sometimes forged between science and religion, both parties may agree that while science will deal with knowledge of the physical world, religion will deal with knowledge of the spiritual world. This is all too easily interpreted, by sleight of hand, to mean that religious knowledge is purely subjective, and does not concern itself with or provide knowledge of the real world. If we agree that science is about discovering facts and proving theories about objective reality, we can let religion be about something completely different – faith, feelings or morality, for example. Many religious people themselves have learned to repeat the cliché that it is the role of science to ask the 'how' questions and that of religion to ask the 'why' questions. But nowadays scientists and scientifically minded secularists are often tackling the 'why' questions as well as the 'how' questions – and quite legitimately so, since in any context in which one can ask *how* of something one can also ask *why* of it. Religious thinkers are by the same token entitled to ask the 'how' as well as the 'why' questions. All we need state at the moment is that knowledge (or a coherent claim to knowledge) plays as important a part in religion as it does in science. Such knowledge includes, without being confined to, empirical knowledge of the kind in which science is interested.

Arguably 'science' is as problematic a word as we have seen 'religion' to be. By itself the word simply means 'knowledge'. But there are different kinds of knowledge as well as different organs, objects and conditions of knowledge – in which case we must ask whether the 'science' in modern science refers to any and every kind of knowledge, or to just one kind of knowledge, or one particular way of obtaining knowledge. 'Science' also connotes discernment or intuition about facts, and about the connections between facts, as well as the mere awareness or perception of them. It occurs in compound words such as prescience and conscience. Rather than saying, as many do, that there is religious knowledge as distinct from scientific knowledge, what we should say is that the religious sciences form a continuum with the natural sciences and with any other kind of sciences we might wish to identify.[9] This leaves open the question whether the disciplines and traditions of the religions have access to forms of knowledge which so-called modern science has (for whatever reason) either ignored or found impossible to confirm by its own methods. There may, for example, be various forms of extrasensory knowledge, as well as what might be called mystical ways of knowing, from which science on the whole steers clear. One problem is that the most obvious kind of knowledge – our immediate sensory knowledge of the world – tends to be the model for talking about any other kind of knowledge.

ONE BY-PRODUCT of the conflict, or perceived conflict, between science and religion is the tendency, most in evidence since the

Enlightenment, for those on either side of the divide to seek advantage by stealing the other's aims and methods, or at least what are imagined to be their aims and methods. As Mary Midgley has shown, there has been a tendency in recent centuries for science to present its methods and its theories quasi-religiously, or for some particular theory to masquerade as a salvific truth of some kind. Thus the biological theory of evolution is sometimes presented not just as a defeat of religion but as an alternative worldview by which to live one's life.[10] Religion for its part has sometimes sought to borrow the explanatory power of science to establish this or that religious truth, text, doctrine or miracle.

Perhaps the most notorious example of this occured in 1650 when Archbishop James Ussher claimed, on the basis of ancient calendars and chronologies, to have dated the creation of the world to the early evening of Saturday, 22 October, 4004 BCE. Such a claim not only flies in the face of logic, and of the facts about the age of the earth established by geological science, but just as importantly disregards the nature of the Genesis narrative itself. Ussher's calculation was a blatant example of the misapplication of scientific method to completely inappropriate material.[11] Although the purpose of the six-day creation account in Genesis is mythic, in the sense that it is intended to celebrate the order of the world under God's creative power, the details in this account correspond to the ancient Hebrew 'scientific' cosmology; that is, to what they took the physical world to be. Religious texts of all kinds do often contain factual and even scientific ideas and information, and may sometimes even be valuable resources for modern scientists, but whatever facts or theories are presented are, of course, those accepted by the knowledge and methods of the time. Accordingly, cosmological statements in sacred texts can only be called 'unscientific' when they are at odds with the science of the age in which they were composed, not when they are compared with, or judged by, the scientific knowledge of a subsequent era.[12]

It is instructive to compare Ussher's approach to the creation of the world with that of another scholar bishop, the fourth-century

Augustine of Hippo. In his commentaries on biblical texts, Augustine makes use of ideas about the nature of the universe we now know to be wrong but which, in his capacity as an educated person, he accepted as true (but that, had he suspected them to be wrong, he would as a rational and scientific person have rejected or at least questioned). By contrast, statements made by modern Christian fundamentalists about the world being only a few thousand years old, or about the world being created in seven ordinary days, are not only factually and scientifically wrong but false to the nature of the texts and subject matter in question. What is far more interesting in Augustine's commentary, however, is that what he has to say about dating the creation puts him closer to Albert Einstein than to Archbishop Ussher. For what Augustine points out is that questions about when the world was created cannot be asked, for the simple reason that time is itself part of the creation: 'the world was not created *in* time but *with* time.'

> An event in time happens after one time and before another, after the past and before the future. But at the time of creation there could have been no past, because there was nothing created to provide the change and movement which is the condition of time.
>
> The world was in fact made *with* time, if at the time of its creation change and motion came into existence. This is clearly the situation in the order of the first six or seven days, in which morning and evening are named, until God's creation was finished on the sixth day, and on the seventh day God's rest is emphasized as something conveying a mystical meaning. What kind of days these are is difficult or even impossible for us to imagine, to say nothing of describing them.[13]

Augustine's treatment of the theme of creation here is metaphysical rather than scientific or pseudo-scientific, one that (true or false) is entirely rational and fully compatible with observations about the world that all sensible people accept. The theory that the world is only about 6,000 years old is not a scientifically discredited religious theory but a scientifically discredited scientific one, but in the centuries before the discoveries of modern science concerning the nature and age of the earth and universe, it was perfectly rational for educated religious writers such as Augustine to express their metaphysical arguments in terms of chronologies now known to be completely mistaken.

IF ONE QUESTION concerns how religious authors make use of the scientific knowledge and theories of their day, then the other question – broached earlier – is whether religious traditions are based on, or have access to, forms of knowledge or ways of knowing ignored or denied by modern science. The short answer here is that, in principle, science and religion have access to (or operate with) the same range of knowledge and means of knowing. Thus those Buddhist practitioners who charted in detail the subtly different stages of meditative consciousness in the quest for liberation through enlightenment were operating within the same epistemological universe as those physicists who explored aspects of nuclear fission in order to build thermonuclear bombs. One should not be misled by pleonastic terms such as 'scientific knowledge' or 'scientific fact'. Science means knowledge, whether we are talking about the natural sciences, the social sciences, the religious sciences or any other sciences. There is no such thing as a (specifically) 'scientific fact'; or, to put it otherwise, *all* facts are 'scientific'. But, of course, what people generally mean by a 'scientific fact' or by 'scientific knowledge' is a fact or knowledge established through scientific methods. This should prompt us to consider both the purpose of the scientific method and the status of science as a culturally institutionalized repository of knowledge.

Scientific propositions and theories can never assume the status of absolute truths or final solutions to a given question or set of observations. The process of scientific discovery is never complete and always corrigible. Science must forever seek to test and extend its own discoveries through further hypothesis and experiment. New facts, and new connections between facts, are constantly emerging, which means that scientific theories are always fallible and always provisional. Good science never stands still. The history of science is littered with discarded theories once thought to be beyond revision, as we see, for example, from the successive theories about human origins or the origins of the universe. This history is one in which individuals, groups and even institutions have got hung up on some particular theory, refusing to consider alternatives and even manipulating the facts in order to keep a favoured theory intact. Matters are not altogether different in the case of religion. Although certain foundational doctrines or principles may be non-negotiable, religious doctrine is always open to new interpretations and applications, as the history of religions clearly demonstrates. What happens in both science and religion, however, is that particular formulations and theories become institutionalized, and in the process resistant to challenge and change. In both cases, it can be argued, this tendency is at odds with their fundamental purposes, which are to explore the world and respond to its challenges.

Nevertheless many scientists confidently imagine that scientific knowledge is ever more closely approaching the goal of a complete theory of everything. Such confidence is understandable given science's cornucopia of new discoveries and the innumerable technological applications that follow. Stephen Hawking and other physicists are bold enough to think that modern physics, taking over medieval theology's role as 'queen of the sciences', is now the discipline asking the ultimate questions about who we are and why we are here. Paul Davies enthuses as follows about the success of the scientific method:

> Physics, the queen of sciences, has opened up vistas of human understanding that were unsuspected a few centuries ago. From the inner workings of the atom to the weird surrealism of the black hole, physics has enabled us to comprehend some of nature's darkest secrets and to gain control over many physical systems

in our environment. The tremendous power of scientific reasoning is demonstrated daily in the many marvels of modern technology. It seems reasonable then, to have some confidence in the scientist's world-view also.[14]

History shows us, however, that just at the point when it is confidently expected that we have understood everything, some new discovery or some new theory of existing discoveries can easily upset the apple cart. As another physicist has put it:

> Rather than providing certainty, every major scientific advance has increased our uncertainty, reduced our status as a species and undermined our sense of purpose. Before Nicholas Copernicus we enjoyed a privileged position at the centre of God's Universe. Now we have come to realise that we inhabit a tiny planet orbiting an average star in an unremarkable galaxy, adrift in a vast impersonal cosmos. Until Charles Darwin came up with his ideas on the origin of species, we occupied a niche unique among God's creatures as the focus and crowning glory of his creation. Science tells us, we are an accident of fate. We evolved by chance through natural selection, a process that Darwin described . . . as one of 'the clumsy, wasteful, blundering, low and horribly cruel works of nature.' In our century, the ideas of Bohr and Heisenberg, of Erwin Schrodinger and Paul Dirac, have brought us face to face with the limitations of the most powerful tool [physics] we have yet created for carving out an understanding of ourselves and the cosmos.[15]

While making his point about the uncertainties and limitations of science, however, this author indulges in the very kind of judgements of which science as such is incapable. Science cannot tell us that we are an accident of fate (even if we are), nor that we inhabit an unremarkable galaxy (since our own presence within it makes it far from unremarkable), nor indeed that the cosmos is impersonal and that we are adrift in it. Darwin too should have known better than to describe the 'works' of nature in the somewhat moralizing way that he does. These and other such judgements flatly contradict, while being similar in kind to, what many religious doctrines affirm about the universe and humankind, which makes these judgements metaphysical rather than scientific.

What both these views of science suggest – one in an upbeat and the other in a downbeat way – is the idea of a scientific worldview. Strictly speaking, however, there is no such thing as a scientific worldview. This is because science is in principle a value-free method of acquiring knowledge whose results are always provisional and always corrigible, a method that proceeds through the constant modification and overturning of existing theories. The scientific method cannot in itself interpret its findings in terms of human values or purposes. Indeed, it is the impersonal character of the scientific method that constitutes the distinctive mark of modern science. One can quite legitimately talk about a scientific *approach* to the world, but not in any strict sense about a scientific *worldview*. All religions are worldviews, although not all worldviews are religious. Science, by contrast, neither is, nor has, nor can have a worldview. That science cannot answer questions about meaning or value, including the value of the scientific enterprise itself, is a point made by Max Weber in his essay 'Science as a Vocation' (1919):

> The natural sciences, for instance, physics, chemistry, and astronomy, presuppose as self-evident that it is worthwhile to know the ultimate laws of cosmic events as far as science can construe them. This is the case not only because with such knowledge one can attain technical results but for its own sake, if the quest for such knowledge is to be a 'vocation'. Yet this presupposition can by no means be proved. And still less can it be proved that the existence of the world which these sciences describe is worthwhile, that it has any 'meaning', or that it makes

sense to live in such a world. Science does not ask for the answers to such questions.[16]

The idea that there is or can be such a thing as a scientific worldview comes from not distinguishing carefully between a 'worldview' and a 'cosmology'. A cosmology in the fullest sense is any theory, religious or scientific, about the origins, nature and inhabitants of the universe (including in the case of a religious cosmology various non-human agencies). A 'worldview' (from the German *Weltanschauung*) is something broader than this: an all-inclusive philosophy or interpretation of life, religious or secular, 'in which a picture of reality is combined with a sense of its meaning and value and with principles of action'.[17] A cosmology can be understood as a picture of the way things hang together, which can be constructed and contemplated as if from the outside. In reality, however, we are inside the cosmologies we construct and contemplate. We are part of them. In the case of a religious cosmology, we need to understand our place within it and to discover how it might help us to direct our lives. This is the point at which a cosmology becomes a worldview. Thus while a cosmology might be compared to a picture, a worldview is better compared to a map – a practical device for negotiating one's path through life and perhaps into another world.

Thus a worldview, whether religious or secular, goes beyond a cosmology understood as a picture of how everything fits together, since unlike a cosmology it depends on values, commitments and interpretations of experience that exceed the remit of science. Before the advent of modern science, cosmologies were usually associated with mythology and religion, although there is no necessary connection with these. Following the rise of modern science, the term 'cosmology' was increasingly appropriated by science and is now treated by many people as an exclusively scientific one, meaning either the study, or a particular theory, of the physical universe. What tends to happen, however, is that the properties of a worldview – properties that science itself is unable to supply – get smuggled into some scientific cosmologies.

When people talk about the or a 'scientific worldview', therefore, what they are really referring to is a secular, materialist or humanist worldview, in support of which many of the findings and theories of modern science are commonly invoked. And because humanists, materialists and secularists are liable to think that science favours or supports their worldview, this gets to be described as a, or even *the*, 'scientific' worldview. The most that the phrase 'scientific worldview' could mean would be a worldview that claimed support from scientific knowledge of some kind, or one endorsed by scientists outside their laboratories, as it were.

IF IT IS THE ABSENCE of a 'worldview' that separates science from religion, then what makes the connection between them is the presence in both of them of a cosmology. The universe is what it is, whether we take a scientific, religious, artistic or any other kind of interest in it. And what the universe is, as the name indicates, is everything there is (or has been, or will be).[18] Thus if there are religious truths and realities, these must exist in the same universe in which (or on the basis of which) scientific truths and realities exist. They all take place, and have whatever effects they have, in one and the same universe.

Some religious people may now be content to accept that religion constitutes no more – and no less – than a personally and culturally powerful psychodrama, and that religious ideas, experiences and practices have no objective correlative. Many other religious people, however, persist in wanting to understand religion in terms of some form of objective or realist metaphysics. They may want to affirm, for example, the efficacy of prayer, the survival of the dead or the existence of angels as a class of non-human intelligences, insisting that all of these are as objectively real as any of the phenomena studied by the natural sciences. There are two alternative ways of accommodating the reality of such religious truths or realities, which I shall define as the naturalist and supernaturalist approaches.

The naturalist approach is to accept that religious truths and realities sit cheek by jowl with everything else that is true and real in the universe, which means that they are *in principle* all equally accessible to the same range of scientific and other enquiry. The supernaturalist approach is to argue that religious truths and realities refer to or belong in some separate part of the universe, one that is completely (or at least normally) inaccessible to the kind of inquiry to which ordinary, non-religious truths and realities are subject.

Now both alternatives raise difficulties for their proponents, at least in the eyes of their critics. One possible weakness of the naturalist view – that truths and realities of whatever kind all belong together in one undifferentiated universe – is that it may seem to diminish or downgrade religion. It takes the 'super' out of the supernatural. It turns religion into science, or at least it allows that religion, like everything else, is open to the scrutiny, judgement and correction of science. This naturalistic view is liable to place the subject matter of religion in something of a no-man's land between the materialism and worldliness associated with science and the spirituality and otherworldliness associated with religion. As a result, this subject matter is regarded by theologians as too materialist and by scientists as too 'spiritual'.

The main weakness of the supernaturalist approach, which by its advocates is more likely to be regarded as its greatest strength, is that it creates a sharp division between the natural things in the universe and the supernatural things in it: that in effect it juxtaposes two distinct worlds, a natural one and a supernatural one, within the single universe, in this way protecting the attributes of gods and angels, the power of prayer or ritual and all the other elements distinctive of religion from being reduced to merely natural phenomena. Either way, however, it raises the question as to how human beings, in the midst of the natural world, can acquire any knowledge of or have any contact with the supernatural world. It might be said that it is a supernatural element or dimension within each person (the soul or spirit, for example) that is the locus, organ or real subject of religious knowledge. But this is simply to shift the problem from the macrocosm to the microcosm, only to raise a similar question. How does this super-natural or non-empirical element within each individual make itself known to, or interact with, the non-supernatural, empirical part of that individual? How, to put it crudely, do the supernatural elements in the universe communicate with the natural elements within it? That is, how do the material bits of the universe join up with the spiritual bits? If there is no continuity between the natural and the supernatural world, the latter might as well be purely imaginary – which is of course how it has come to be seen by sceptics and critics.

One answer to all these difficulties is to suggest that the naturalist and supernaturalist views as defined above represent one-sided versions of what is better approached within a hier-archical cosmology that both recognizes the boundary the supernaturalist approach is anxious to preserve, while also acknow-ledging, with the naturalist approach, that given the ultimate unity of knowledge and reality this boundary must be a relative and not an absolute one. The cosmologies of modern science are themselves hierarchical in so far as they picture evolutionary trees, solar systems, progressively smaller particles of matter, and so on. Religious cosmologies likewise picture multiple levels of being, each with their corresponding properties and inhabitants, one of which is of course our own world with ourselves its inhabitants. Multiple levels of being can be pictured macrocosmically, as in Buddhist diagrams of the various heavens and hells above and below the earth, but also microcosmically, as in schematizations of successive levels or phases of human consciousness, for exam-ple. In both cases, the discrete planes of existence or modes of consciousness identified constitute contiguous realities within the same overall reality. Extraordinary experiences, such as reve-lations or mystical states, can be understood as communications between different levels within a single hierarchy.

The cosmologies of modern science, however much they dress themselves up as worldviews, cannot satisfy the yearning for a vision of the universe consonant with human values and human purposes. Some scientists may seek to eliminate troublesome human subjectivity from their understanding of reality, either by ignoring the human subject (as if human subjects had not constructed the cosmology in the first place) or by objectifying the human subject in some way. But this supposed elimination of the human subject is a conjuring trick that simply cannot be made to work. It is like a child rushing into a room to see if it can catch what it looks like when nobody is there. Human subjectivity is both the presupposition of any cosmology and the basis, by definition, of any worldview. It is difficult to see how human consciousness, if understood simply as an accidental by-product of natural processes, could ever be in a position to understand the universe even in the limited way in which scientists do understand it, let alone in a position to find any kind of meaning in it. Consider instead this exciting possibility: that far from being accidental products of blind evolutionary processes, we are part of the fundamental meaning and purpose of the universe.

What marks out religion from other areas of human interest is its recognition that our experiences of the world cannot make sense in their own terms, but only in reference to a wider order of reality.[19] Those worldviews promoted in the name of secular humanism, with or without the support of modern science, are unable to address humanity's deepest questions concerning the nature and destiny of the individual. That human beings are accidental to the universe, and that the universe itself is devoid of meaning or purpose, are ideas no more coherent (or, to the extent that they are coherent, no better founded) than the views represented in or by the religions: that consciousness comes first not last, that humanity is a crucial part of the order and meaning of the universe, and that the human quest for transcendence is as natural a response to the world we experience as any of the more physical needs that define human existence.

ELEVEN

LOSING OUR RELIGION?

The Greek writer Plutarch (*c.* 46–120 CE) recounts a story told by an acquaintance who had been a passenger on a ship travelling from Italy to Greece. Passing by the island of Paxi, the passengers suddenly heard the anguished cry 'Great Pan is dead!' The unknown author of this utterance then shouted out to the pilot, Thamus, to repeat this message when the ship was passing close to a particular place further along the coast. This he duly did, whereupon the passengers heard rising up from there

> a great cry of lamentation, not of one person, but of many, mingled with exclamations of amazement. As many persons were on the vessel, the story was soon spread abroad in Rome, and Thamus was sent for by Tiberius Caesar. Tiberius became so convinced of the truth of the story that he caused an inquiry and investigation to be made about Pan; and the scholars, who were numerous at his court, conjectured that he was the son born of Hermes and Penelope.[1]

There is no other record of this strange story in classical sources, but much was made of it in later literature, with Christian writers in particular seeing it as emblematic of the death of paganism at the coming of Christ, who was born in the reign of Tiberius. The idea of the death of a god was not necessarily either an absurd or a tragic one in the ancient world, as we see from the cults of dying and rising gods associated with fertility and spiritual rebirth. For Jews and Christians, and not many centuries later for Muslims too, the death of the old gods was all part of the good news of the triumph of monotheism. In later Western culture, however, the idea of the death of God came to assume darker meanings.

Perhaps the most famous successor to Plutarch's account of the death of Pan, two thousand years on, is Nietzsche's story of the madman who proclaims, to a crowd of scoffing atheists in the public square, the news that God is dead:

> God is dead. God remains dead. And we have killed him. Yet his shadow still looms. How shall we comfort our-selves, the murderers of all murderers? What was holiest and mightiest of all that the world has yet owned has bled to death under our knives: who will wipe this blood off us? What water is there for us to clean ourselves? What festivals of atonement, what sacred games shall we have to invent? Is not the greatness of this deed too great for us? Must we ourselves not become gods simply to appear worthy of it? There has never been a greater deed; and whoever is born after us – for the sake of this deed he will belong to a higher history than all history hitherto.[2]

This classicizing 'madman' goes on to elaborate the causes and consequences for humankind of the murder of God. Nietzsche's story dramatizes the loss of religious faith and the decline of religious institutions, serving as a parable of how a certain way of thinking about God, and thereby of 'domesticating' his tran-scendence,[3] cuts us off from God and thus, in effect, kills Him.[4]

The original impact of both stories has been gradually blunted by their familiarity and their safe historical distance from us. We need to find a new story of dramatic religious crisis. Let us imagine, therefore, that one day in the not too distant future, perhaps at the end of an international conference of world religious leaders, important public announcements begin to emerge from the representatives of the world's religious traditions. These announcements – issuing from the pope, archbishops and Protestant ministers, from the Dalai Lama and other Buddhist leaders, from the chief rabbis of many nations, from prominent Muslim imams and ayatollahs, and so on – are to the effect that their respective religious institutions have all decided to shut up shop, so to speak, having finally accepted that their doctrines are no longer credible or relevant to modern humanity and that whatever good things are associated with religion will be better managed by secular institutions of various kinds.

This fantasy, of course, flies in the face of everything we know about the resilience and indeed renewal of religion throughout history, not least in the modern West. The nearest thing to its realization has occurred in authoritarian societies whose religion or religions have been proscribed or persecuted, as was the case at various times in the Roman Empire, in Soviet Russia and in communist China. In the long term, however, such prohibitions have served to strengthen rather than weaken the religions in question. But let us nevertheless briefly indulge the fantasy by asking what effect this global 'annunciation' of the end of religion might have on the world's population. Each religious community would undoubtedly respond to the news with a heady mixture of astonishment, disbelief and consternation, and perhaps even anger. But what of the effect upon the wider population, including those who no longer had any religious affiliation or who did not think of themselves as religious at all? Would there be, especially within the more secularized population, feelings of sympathetic relief or, alternatively, a sense of knowing triumph? Or might there instead be a sense of profound unease similar to that expressed by those hearing the news about Pan? And what of the longer-term consequences? Pan and the other gods may be dead, but relatively few, in the last two thousand years, have expressed regret at the decline of paganism.[5] Is it conceivable that the world might very soon become accustomed to the decline and even disappearance of religion, with people first forgetting, and then being born in ignorance of, the fact that religion once held powerful sway throughout the world?

Nietzsche's madman announces the death of God, not the death of religion. No one seems to have noticed God's demise, apart from this prophetic madman. The scoffing atheists he addresses are presumably too busy worshipping their own idols (science, progress and so on), while the philosophers and theologians no doubt believe that God is still alive in the elaborate and self-serving ideas and practices in which they have for centuries been smothering Him. One possibility raised by the third story, where it is the death of religion and not the death of God or the gods that is announced, is that such an announcement would for many interested parties be far more troubling than news of the death of God. For those whose religion has in effect displaced or domesticated God, the loss of religion could bring back all those awkward questions about human existence long ago tidied away and forgotten about. Like Dostoyevsky's Grand Inquisitor, many have seen in religion a powerful social and political tool for making human beings happy by suppressing their freedom.[6] For them, the death of religion would be disastrous.

What makes this story of the death of religion a fantasy, of course, is precisely the ubiquity, variety and persistence of religion. The shock of hearing about a religious institution shutting up shop, let alone about all of them doing so in concert, would have little effect in the long run on people's need or instinct for religion. Religions may come and go, but religion itself is ineliminable. Predictions of the eventual decline of religion, whether sociologically based or ideologically motivated, have been perpetually frustrated by the resilience if not revival of religions in our modern, so-called secular age. Secularization theories that envisage a steady shift from a religious to a secular period in human affairs can only maintain credibility by changing the definitions of religion or of secularization.[7] The disappearance of religion is more unthinkable even than the death of God, one might say. After all, the death and resurrection of deities is a commonplace of religious mythology, and there are, in any case, many non-theistic and trans-theistic religions.[8]

The disappearance of religion is no more thinkable than the disappearance of art, politics, education, science or sport. These interests and activities, and the institutions associated with them, are integral to human culture. A crucial question, therefore, concerns what particular forms religions will maintain, assume or lose in the future – what forms of practice, doctrine or organization will define religion. This leads on to further questions about how successfully these forms communicate the truths and realities of religion, either helping or hindering individuals or communities seeking to relate to these truths and realities. Religion and the religions will surely survive whatever events, discoveries or currents of thought might initially seem capable of undermining them.

WHAT DO WE LOSE when we lose our religion? Losing in any sphere of life can be a negative or a positive experience. We can lose friends, lose money or lose a race. We can also lose excess weight, lose ourselves in a good book or lose our anxieties and illusions. Losing one's religion can also be negative or positive, but in many cases it will be a mixed experience. In many cultures, individuals wishing to lose their religion, whether through conversion to another religion or in order to be free of religion altogether, have found that social pressures and obligations make this difficult if not impossible. Apostasy – the renunciation of one's religion – is in some societies, even today, subject to the death penalty. Quite apart from this, abandoning the traditional religion of one's culture may be accompanied by feelings of regret or even guilt that one could not go on believing, or pretending to believe. Reassurances that one is better off without religion, or without some particular religion, will not necessarily assuage one's anxieties. Others will feel that in abandoning religion, or in simply growing out of a religion chosen *for* them rather than *by* them, a heavy weight has been lifted from them, as they move into a new phase of life.[9]

But the loss or abandonment of religion may entail subtler forms of ambivalence. Those who have 'lost' their religion – whether as a personal event or process or in the sense that they come from a society or generation without religion – will often express regret at the loss, acknowledging the intellectual, ethical, aesthetic or ritual richness of a tradition with which they can no longer identify or to which they have never belonged. In many cases such regret amounts to a kind of religious nostalgia. This must, it seems, be something distinct from the forward-looking nostalgia that religion itself seems to embody – for example, in the idea of a return, whether here on earth or in an afterlife, to some kind of primordial Eden or paradise. But how are we to distinguish between these two kinds of religious nostalgia – between on the one hand nostalgia for the richness, rhythm and reassurance of religion, or of some particular form of religion, and on the other some more direct longing for contact or communion with the sacred?

The first of these is certainly easier to write off as a form of sentimentality, akin to (and sometimes even combined with) nostalgia for one's childhood, or for one's country (and culture) of origin.[10] There is pleasure as well as pain in such nostalgia. Firmly grounded within a non-religious or even anti-religious worldview, such religious nostalgia can be safely exercised without much risk of its coming off the leash. It could be, however, that such nostalgia itself represents a sublimated longing for sacred reality or transcendent experience, collapsing the distinction I have just drawn between nostalgia for (a) religion and (b) for what it represents. Alternatively, nostalgia might have a role in disguising or deflecting one's regret at having lost the religious ideals or practices of one's earlier years, or in being unable to take the necessary steps to recovering them. Sceptics commonly argue that a religious worldview may be a way of avoiding the harsh truths about the world laid bare by the disenchantments of science. And yet religious scepticism could be regarded in a similar way itself. Ambivalent attitudes towards religion and the loss of religion are well illustrated in the poetry of Philip Larkin, who in one poem characterizes religion as a 'vast moth-eaten musical brocade /

Created to pretend we never die',[11] and in another observes that those who, like him, make passing visits to inspect old church interiors will forever be surprising in themselves a 'hunger' to be 'more serious'. His summary estimation of the church he is visiting continues this ambivalence:

> A serious house on serious earth it is
> In whose blent air all our compulsions meet,
> Are recognised, and robed as destinies.[12]

The sense of loss evident in Larkin's poetry – a sense of loss that relates to many things in addition to religion – comes across not as the result of conscious choice, or of unwillingness to connect or reconnect with what has been lost, but rather as something inevitable in the kind of life one now perforce is leading.

This raises the important point that it is not simply that people have consciously or willingly distanced themselves from religion, but also that religion has distanced itself from them. In other words, the loss of religion works from two sides. Consider the analogy of someone who no longer eats fish. This could be through a conscious decision to stop eating the fish of which there is still a plentiful supply, but it could also be because there are no more fish to eat – or because finding what fish are left has become too difficult. People cut themselves off from religion, and this may be in part because religion has in effect cut itself off from them. Yet many of those alienated by religion may still desire religion in some form. For these people, who tend to be doubtful or hesitant about the bolder claims of religion, what count are the experiences, intentions and behaviour that constitute an individual's personal spirituality. The transient historical forms of religion matter little or not at all. Spirituality in this context is not so much religion without God (although it is often this too) as religion without religion: that is, religion without the constraints, both intellectual and practical, of 'organized' or institutionalized religion. It is partly out of this ambivalence about religion that there arises what for many people is the saving distinction between religion and spirituality.

For other people, however, form and content are harder if not impossible to separate in this way. And the closer the identification made between form and content, the more deeply felt will be any loss of (or even alteration to) the form. Thus for those who identify religious truths and realities with particular doctrinal tenets, ritual practices or institutional structures, there is always the possibility of what could be called an 'objective' loss of religion. For such individuals – to revert for a moment to the fantasy story outlined earlier – the declaration by their religious leaders that they had decided to shut up shop would not only be bringing a religious institution to an end, but putting in jeopardy the religious 'safety' (salvation) of its members.

Undue attachment to particular religious forms, be these doctrinal formulations, religious practices or institutional structures, is one of the weaknesses of what in an earlier chapter I defined as the exclusivist and inclusivist positions taken in regard to other religions. By contrast, those who take a relativist or an essentialist view of religions will tend to regard religious forms as having a more contingent relationship to transcendent reality. For them the transcendent is not going anywhere in a hurry. Certainly it will not be nagged into action by being identified with particular forms or formulations. If anything it will be nagging at us, whatever the forms or lack of forms by which we live.

ANY COMPLETE UNDERSTANDING of the 'loss of religion' in our times will need to correlate what this loss means as a personal experience or condition of mind with what it means as an objective, social phenomenon. Personal disillusionment with, or alienation from, religion does not take place in a social or historical vacuum. Not only must we take into account the marginalization of religion as a social entity and the sequestrations of its assets by secular institutions. We must also recognize the failure of religions to meet the intellectual and practical needs of their adherents or would-be adherents. This latter failure has sometimes been due not to a neglect of doctrine or ritual but rather to the over-determination of these things – due, that is, to attempts within a religious tradition to button down too tightly the truths and realities it addresses, or to identify its practices too closely with the ends to which these practices are directed. There is no doubt that for some people religions have failed through the vagueness or evasiveness of their message. For many others, however, the failure of religion has come rather from an excess of certainty or from overconfidence in its practices.

Within the broader perspective of the history of ideas one must also acknowledge changes in the intellectual landscape that have worked to undermine both the claims and the appeal of religion. Sigmund Freud, in the course of analysing the reasons for the widespread resistance to the idea of psychoanalysis, identifies 'two major blows' to which the 'naïve self-love' of human beings has had to submit in recent centuries:

> The first was when they learnt that our earth was not the centre of the universe but only a tiny fragment of a cosmic system of scarcely imaginable vastness. This is associated in our minds with the name of Copernicus, though something similar had already been asserted by Alexandrian science. The second blow fell when biological research destroyed man's supposedly privileged place in creation and proved his descent from the animal kingdom and his ineradicable animal nature. This revaluation has been accomplished in our days by Darwin, Wallace and their predecessors, though not without the most violent contemporary opposition. But human megalomania will have suffered its third and most wounding blow from the psychological research of the present time which seeks to prove to the ego that it is not even master in its own house, but must content itself with scanty information of what is going on unconsciously in its mind. We psychoanalysts were not the first and not the only ones to utter

this call to introspection; but it seems to be our fate to give it its most forcible expression and to support it with empirical material which affects every individual.[13]

Freud's analysis of the human situation might suggest that the balance has long been firmly tipped in favour of religious scepticism, and that this can only have hastened the decline in the appeal or credibility of religion unwittingly wrought by the religions themselves. Others, however, would argue that the scientific discoveries described by Freud have been just as much opportunities for the further flourishing of religion as they have been for the flourishing of any other human interests.

Whereas Freud saw the 'blows' inflicted on human self-importance by science and psychoanalysis as signalling positive ways ahead for human happiness and self-understanding, his contemporary, the sociologist Max Weber (1864–1920), took a more ambivalent view of the situation of modern humanity and its new scientific and technical culture.[14] Taking his cue from the work of poet and aesthetician Friedrich Schiller (1759–1805), Weber argued that it was humanity's inescapable destiny to experience the consequences of what he called the 'disenchantment of the world'.[15] This disenchantment is a by-product of the rationalization and domination of all aspects of human life by modern science and technology. In the case of religion, this was rationalized first through the rise of monotheism and the progressive elimination from the natural world of all magical and supernatural forces, and more recently by the rationalization of monotheism itself, with God no longer materially or ritually embodied in the world but kept apart within his own supernatural sphere. The logical endpoint is the metaphorical 'death of God' announced by Nietzsche's madman.

Whatever analysis we accept of the condition of religion in the modern world, the loss or decline of religion, however brought about, should be seen as both a subjective and an objective phenomenon. It can be understood on the one hand as an anxiety or crisis of the individual confronting questions about what to affirm, celebrate or aspire to in life, and on the other hand as the rationalization, marginalization and, at least conceivably, complete failure of religion as a social institution. The question of what, if anything, might take the place of religion, either personally or institutionally, is also a question about the definition of religion. In particular, it might be asked, are there equally satisfying ways of finding meaning and order in the world apart from religion, or must we recognize that alternative ways of finding meaning and order may themselves be regarded as instances of 'religion'?

The idea that an atheistic or secular society requires its own substitute for religion is still current in many quarters, and has probably been a constant theme in the history of religions. In many ways, the state religion of ancient Rome and the civil religion of the United States can be treated as cases of secular religion, their ideas and practices largely geared to inculcating social and political values. Other forms of secular religion, largely of an intellectual kind, have emerged from within the religious traditions themselves. Their rationale has been that the supernatural or miraculous content of a religion can be removed or demythologized while leaving the ethics, the rituals and many of the doctrines (appropriately reinterpreted) not only intact but rejuvenated. In particular there are several versions of what can be described as secular Christianity. Perhaps the most famous has been the 'death of God' theology, where belief in God is completely abandoned and the focus set instead on the historical Jesus as secular exemplar.[16]

Some of the 'death of God' theologians trace their ideas back to the writings of Dietrich Bonhoeffer, the German pastor and theologian executed by the Nazis in 1945. In one of his letters from prison, Bonhoeffer had stated that 'We are moving towards a completely religionless time; people as they are now simply cannot be religious anymore. Even those who honestly describe themselves as "religious" do not in the least act up to it, and so they presumably mean something quite different by "religious".'[17] His writings helped establish the use of the phrase 'religionless Christianity'. In fact Bonhoeffer's theology, unlike that of the 'death of God' theologians, was not atheistic but rather was a theology of radical silence about God, which connects with the long-established tradition of 'negative theology' in Christian thought. The question Bonhoeffer's writings pose (and not just for Christianity) is how to express religion in and for a supposedly increasingly secular age.

The most elaborate and systematic attempt to create a new and completely secular religion, expressing all four of the 'dimensions' of religion, took place in nineteenth-century France. This was Auguste Comte's 'Religion of Humanity', devised to replace what was judged the failing Christianity of the times. It was intended to provide the morally uplifting and socially unifying function hitherto fulfilled by traditional religion. Suitable buildings were found or designed, and rituals, calendars and a catechism were created. The Supreme Being worshipped in this religion was none other than Humanity itself. Although the influence of this new religion (or at least of its idea) was extensive, its failure to be taken up on the grand scale intended was inevitable, for the obvious reason that it did not provide, or recognize, any genuinely transcendental focus. Humanity simply cannot worship itself, in however idealized a form.

One admirer of Comtean religion, Alain de Botton, has suggested that, rather than simply ditching wholesale the religious systems in which we no longer believe, we should acknowledge the virtues and benefits of religion and sequester the best religious ideas and practices for the secular worldview that for many people has replaced a religious one. Rightly emphasizing that religious institutions have no exclusive rights to many of the ideas and rituals they claim as their own, he urges atheists to put the rich assets of the religion to better secular use:

> Secular society has been unfairly impoverished by the loss of an array of practices and themes which atheists typically find it impossible to live with because they seem too closely associated with, to quote Nietzsche's useful phrase, 'the bad odours of religion'. We have grown frightened of the word *morality*. We bridle at the thought of hearing a

sermon. We flee from the idea that art should be uplifting or have an ethical mission. We don't go on pilgrimages. We can't build temples. We have no mechanisms for expressing gratitude. The notion of reading a self-help book has become absurd to the high-minded. We resist mental exercises. Strangers rarely sing together. We are presented with an unpleasant choice between either committing to peculiar concepts about immaterial deities or letting go entirely of a host of consoling, subtle or just charming rituals for which we struggle to find equivalents in secular society.[18]

This writer is perfectly correct in saying that many of the ideas and practices associated with religion do not belong exclusively to religion. Where he begs the question, however, is in thinking that these ideas cease being religious (in the broader sense he would presumably deny along with the narrower one) just by being detached from their place within a religious tradition. Religions, as responses to experiences of and ideas about transcendence, are constructions, and are constructed out of human materials, so to speak. The materials for their construction are myths, symbols, rituals, laws, precepts and so on. These are the means through which human beings express and explore their seriousness about the world, the means through which they respond to the demands and experiences of the world, in all its wonder and mystery.

These materials, while not exclusive to religion in the organized or institutional sense, are wherever they occur the seeds of religion. Without them, there would be no religion; with them, religion is inevitable. If it is said that secularists have much to learn from religion about how the visual arts can teach human beings how to live finer lives, what is still in question is the source of the artistic insights and impulses that inspire and produce visual and other forms of art in the first place. In most societies the arts have been intimately bound up with religion, not just because religious institutions have dominated these societies but because in the arts, and not only in explicitly religious art, the sacred is either sought or manifest. Even if a work of art merely alludes to the sacred – indeed, even if the sacred is in some way denied or mocked – the sacred nevertheless remains a condition of art. This is why those totalitarian rulers who know what they are doing will seek to take control of literature and the arts, just as they have of the political and religious institutions of a society. Likewise, they will seek to take control of law, education, science, and even sport.

ALTHOUGH OVER the centuries individual religions inevitably disappear or change beyond all recognition, the impulses, experiences, theories and values from which religions are constructed remain ever-present within human society. Even if every institutional expression of religion were somehow to be forgotten or suppressed, these elements would persist as the potential building blocks of new forms of religion. The human condition is defined by its quest for meaning and order; by its instinct for praise, thanksgiving and celebration; and by its desire to connect with what may lie beyond this world or beyond this mortal life.

The idea that religion is perennial would be endorsed even by those religions whose origins are located in some kind of uniquely revealing event or individual. For the truths or realities these historically unrepeatable events are understood to reveal are not seen as dependent on them, nor as dependent on a historically conditioned institution or tradition. If a particular truth or reality, thought of as having been revealed at a particular time and place, were to be forgotten or in danger of being forgotten, it could presumably be renewed from the self-same transcendent source. This is how Islam sees its own revelation in relation to the earlier revelations of Judaism and Christianity and of even earlier religions. The idea of an eternally repeating divine self-revelation is deeply inscribed in Hindu mythology. And in the Buddhist tradition we find the most instructive example of endlessly repeated religious truth. With perfect consistency, Buddhism regards the degradation and eventual disappearance of the Buddha's teachings

(Dhamma) as one further instance of the truth that all conditioned things are transitory. On the other hand, the nature of the universe is such that eventually the truth will out again. The path to full enlightenment will be rediscovered in the distant future, just as it was by the historical Buddha and the many Buddhas who preceded him. What is interesting, and ironic, about Buddhism's view of its own transience is that it has encouraged Buddhists over the centuries to survive and flourish by developing new ideas and practices to meet new historical situations.

Ideas about a God periodically intervening in human history, or of Buddhas being periodically reborn, mythologize the idea that – to put it as generically as possible – the nature of the universe is such that religious truth is never permanently lost to humankind. Or perhaps it could be said that the universe will always speak to humankind if humankind is in the mood to listen. When it listens in a serious and systematic way, communally rather than individually, we have the phenomenon of religion. In this sense at least, religion will no more be lost than will art or music, sport or education, law or politics, or all the rest. And yet individuals, communities, whole nations and even entire generations can nevertheless lose religion in the sense of losing sight of it, or missing out on it. This may have happened through their having deliberately ignored or rejected religion (or what is left of it), or it may have been due to circumstances beyond their control, or indeed before their birth.

There are, of course, more serious ways of missing out on religion than by deliberately rejecting it, or by being cut off from it by circumstances not of one's own choosing. For one can lose one's religion within the coils of religion itself. Such a loss – a loss of which one is likely to be entirely unaware – can actually come from certain ways of 'being religious'. Extreme examples would include the loss of religion suffered by zealots and fundamentalists whose religiosity is expressed through hatred or contempt for other religions, or whose religiosity creates the justification for persecuting and even killing the adherents of other religions. More moderate examples, already discussed in earlier chapters, are provided by the religiosity of those who make 'idols' of the ideas, images, precepts, laws, leaders and institutions of religion, which are only the means to realizing the truths or realities that are the authentic goal of religion.

If, in missing out on religion in whatever way, people have been deprived of the means of living life to the full or of the resources to meet the joys and challenges of a mortal existence, one could (from a religious point of view) say that they have been disinherited as surely as if they had missed out on the benefits of education, for example, or on the development of their artistic, musical or sporting talents. Those whose lives do miss out on religion as conventionally or traditionally understood may nevertheless find ways and means of satisfying in some degree the perennial human need to find meaning in the world, to offer thanks or praise for the good things of life, and to mark the key stages of life with ritual and ceremony. Some of these ways and means will in effect assume religious status, not just because they exist in the shadow of the religious forms they may deliberately imitate or replace, but because in feeling bound by them, or in finding order and consolation through them, or in building up on their basis a sense of life's meaning, they are connecting with those very elements that constitute religion as it is conventionally understood. No serious person can ever be completely religionless.

TWELVE

REINVENTING RELIGION

A story from the Zen tradition tells of a young man, aimless and disillusioned with life, who goes to a remote monastery to inquire of the revered Master there whether there is any way of gaining enlightenment without the long years of meditation and austerity associated with such a quest.[1] Asked by the Master what he has really concentrated on in life, the young man replies that he comes from a comfortable background and has never had to work, and that the only thing he ever took seriously was chess. The Master thinks for a moment and then tells his attendant to call for a particular monk, asking that he bring with him a chessboard and pieces. He brushes aside the attendant's comment that the monk in question is no good at chess. The monk arrives and the Master introduces him to the young man, telling them that they are to play a game of chess together. Then the Master shows them his sword, explaining that whoever loses the game will also lose his head. He reminds the monk that he has vowed complete obedience to him, and he tells the young man that if he loses the only thing he is good at he deserves to lose his head as well. They look at the Master and then at each other, realizing that the Master is absolutely serious. How on earth, the young man asks himself, did a sincere request for spiritual guidance turn into a potentially fatal game of chess?

The game begins, and for both players the chessboard on which they now concentrate becomes the whole world. Very soon the monk makes a bad move, and then another, and the young man scents that victory will soon be his. He steals a quick glance at the monk, and what he sees in the face of his opponent is calm and dignity born of absolute dedication to his austere way of life. A surge of compassion overwhelms the young man, and he deliberately makes a bad move, and then another, opening the way to his own defeat. The Master, who has been patiently watching the game, suddenly leans forward, and with a sweep of his arm scatters the chess pieces across the floor, leaving the two players dumbfounded. There is no winner and no loser here, he declares. Turning to the young man, he tells him that he has just shown a willingness to sacrifice his life for another, and that the game has proved his capacity to manifest two great virtues of the Buddhist path – concentration and compassion. If he continues to develop these virtues he is sure to find his way to enlightenment.

What this story illustrates, albeit within a particular religious and cultural setting, is a universally important point about religion – namely, that if it is to engage us it must connect with us as we are, and not as we, or others, think we should be. Religion is commonly thought to be, and often presents itself as being, a set of beliefs and practices to which individuals must measure up before they can participate. This makes no more sense than asking one's guests to be sure they've eaten well before coming to supper. It is an approach that clearly would not have worked with the young man of this story. Had the Master merely lectured him on Buddhist doctrine and practice, or turned him away as a worthless person who should return when he had made good his defects, then the young man would very likely have come away confirmed in his lack of self-esteem. What the Master actually does is to start where the young man actually is. This does not mean that the Master has watered down the message. What the Master is doing – quite apart from showing exactly the kind of compassion the young man is soon to surprise in himself – is to fit the method to the need, match the means to the end. What his method proves is that the resources with which religion works are already present in those who have lost or not yet found their way.

This story also demonstrates that there can be a positive relationship between individual spirituality and institutional religion. The young man comes to the monastery, whether or not as a last resort, because he knows this to be – in that phrase of Philip Larkin's – a 'serious house', one traditionally associated with finding the way to meaning and enlightenment. The Master himself knows that the accumulated resources of the Buddhist tradition are worthless if they cannot somehow be made relevant to the young man in his present existential crisis. If the young man is led to reinvent himself in the light of his 'fatal game of chess', this is because the Buddhist tradition is itself being reinvented for him, and for every individual who sincerely asks a question of it or comes to draw upon its resources in some way. The same is potentially true of all religions, in so far as they claim to have a beneficial message for humankind.

TO APPRECIATE the full meaning of the idea of reinvention, we need to look first at the primary idea of invention, which in the fullest range of its meaning indicates discovery, innovation, creation, fiction or fabrication. The original meaning of the word 'invention' is almost the opposite of its meaning for most people nowadays. The word derives from the Latin verb *invenire*, to find or to come upon something – something already there. In other words, it meant more or less what we now mean by discovery. In modern usage, however, the word 'invention' is mainly used in the sense of 'coming up' with something – something novel or original, be it a technological device, an artistic or literary creation, or a deliberate falsehood.[2] Likewise, when we describe people as 'inventive', we usually mean, admiringly, that they are creative or ingenious in some way – that they have come up with something new. The word can also be used disparagingly, to refer to a lie or a story made up from some less than worthy motive. A description of something as 'pure invention' is not usually intended in a complimentary sense.

When it comes to reinvention, then, we can see that this can either mean the rediscovery of what has been forgotten, or an adaptation to new or changing circumstances. Thus one often hears talk about people reinventing themselves, perhaps after some dramatic change of personal circumstances (bereavement or bankruptcy, for instance), or because they wish to start off on a new track or make the most of new opportunities. To speak of invention or reinvention in the context of religion, however, will for many religious people seem odd and even inappropriate – partly because these terms conflict with the popular image of religion as something fixed for all time, but mainly because the association of 'religion' and 'invention' seem to imply that religion is, as so many sceptics and critics of religion assert, something fabricated by human beings rather than delivered by the gods.

And yet religions, as institutionalized systems of theory and practice, are indeed inventions or constructions – institutions that continuously reinvent themselves in the course of their history. If religions did not constantly reinvent themselves they would not have a history. In any case, what would a religion that was *not* constructed or invented look like? But this is to present only one side of the picture, and to leave it there might suggest a purely reductionist account of religion. The other side of the picture is equally important. For just as physical constructions and technical innovations are based upon pre-existing ideas and materials, so are religious systems based on pre-existing ideas and materials in the form of the various events, insights and experiences cherished within religious traditions.

What I am arguing for here is not the truth of religion, or of any particular religion, but simply a properly balanced understanding of the experience and phenomenon of religion. The crucial point is that the constructed or invented character of religion does not entail the falsity of its theories or its practices. Analogously, the constructed or invented character of the novels of Jane Austen does not make these literary works false works of history or biography, for the simple reason that they do not present themselves as history or biography in the first place. They are, however, based on truths – truths about human psychology and human society, for example. Austen's novels illuminate these truths for us in ways that psychologists and sociologists perhaps cannot.

Given the inevitably constructed nature of a religion, even in the case of a religion constructed in response to what is regarded as some kind of divine revelation, it makes perfect sense to think of religions as periodically if not continuously reinventing themselves, whether in response to changing historical circumstances, welcome or unwelcome, or in line with the cumulative experience of their adherents, or indeed in the light of new divine revelations. In the construction of Buddhism, Christianity and Islam, for example, one can see all these factors in play in the earliest centuries of their history. To say, as some adherents are tempted to do, that the construction and the reinvention, as well as the original revelation, were all divinely ordained or initiated is to remove questions about religion from all rational discourse, sympathetic or otherwise. It leaves no room for critical comment or even for questions. Nevertheless, conservative tendencies within religions lead them to represent themselves, or to be represented by others, as unchanging entities in a sea of change. No one familiar with their history, however, can deny that religions have been in continuous transformation, and that many a doctrine, practice or institution labelled 'traditional', in the sense of ancient or unchanging, will have its own specific origins and history.

Even so, change within a tradition or system is not incompatible with the idea of fidelity to first principles or with the preservation of identity through change. Radical change, or a 'return to roots', is after all one of the primary motives for reform in religious traditions, the aim being the recovery or reaffirmation of essential principles lost within, or compromised by, the changes that have taken place. The fact that such reformations never do and never could return a tradition to an earlier stage of its identity is hardly the point. The point is that movements of reformation within religion, whether looking backward or forward, illustrate the meaning of reinvention either as a rediscovery of what has been lost or neglected or as an adaptation to new circumstances, or to both these things simultaneously. For example, the movement in some Christian denominations to ordain women as priests exemplifies reinvention in both these senses. The appeal has been on the one hand to modern views about gender equality and on the other to early Church traditions in which women did in fact have pastoral and administrative roles withdrawn from them in later centuries.

Other important sites of reinvention in religion have been the related areas of textual interpretation and doctrinal reformulation, both of which play a determinative role in the reinventions that take place in other dimensions of religion. In the case of texts and doctrines, the processes of reinvention are easier to see precisely because both the arguments for change and the changes themselves will often become matters of written record, and because one can compare later interpretations and formulations with earlier ones. In the case of changes in religious practice, the processes of reinvention are, for obvious reasons, less easily demonstrated, the earlier forms being displaced by or subsumed into the newer forms.

Historically and institutionally, then, the life of religion has been one of both invention and reinvention. If the truths and realities central to a religion are regarded as inventions in the sense of being discoveries every bit as real and important as the discoveries of technology and science, then the theories, practices and institutions through which these truths and realities are mediated and preserved can be regarded as inventions in the sense of human constructions. And whatever is an invention in either sense will also be subject to reinvention – whether this means the discovery of new aspects or implications of the truths and realities in question, or the construction of new ways of communicating these truths and realities or of putting them into practice.

RELIGIONS HAVE constantly reinvented themselves, but sometimes they are slow to change or resistant to change. In some cases such resistance comes to be seen as a virtue in itself, but for every person for whom the unchanging (or apparently unchanging) nature of a religion is part of its appeal, there will be many others for whom it will be a reason for staying away. It is the common complaint of many people that religions have become meaningless or irrelevant to them, by not connecting with their needs or their experience of the world. Even if the reason why people find a religion meaningless or irrelevant is that it is they themselves who have lost touch with religious truth and realities, or who have failed to live up to the demands or ideals of a religion, the onus is still upon the religion to find new ways to engage with the persons thus alienated or disaffected. It is for this reason, no doubt, that religions have sometimes shown themselves over-eager to please or too quick to change, as when they adopt language or theories which age more quickly than the forms they replace, or when engaging with movements or methods that do little or nothing to help people cultivate a genuinely spiritual life.

Alternatives to the more creative and forward-looking kinds of reinvention will mainly take the form either of 'fundamentalism' or else of what I shall call 'compartmentalism'. The first of these terms has been used in a number of ways, but in this context it refers to an insistence upon fixed (and typically 'literalist') interpretations of religious texts, ideas and practices to the exclusion of all others. Ironically enough, such fundamentalism is in itself highly reinventive, both in the sense that it generally arises in reaction to what are perceived to be invalid doctrinal or practical innovations within a tradition and in the sense that it has little or no resemblance to a religious stance of earlier centuries that typically it will claim to be reasserting or re-establishing. For instance, the early Christians were not biblical literalists, such literalism being a decidedly modern way of understanding a text.

The beliefs and practices fastened upon by fundamentalists will tend to dominate all other aspects of their lives. By contrast, those I call compartmentalists try, with varying degrees of success, to live their lives thinking (and perhaps acting) in one way where religion is concerned, and in another where everything else is concerned, thereby avoiding awkward questions about how their religious ideas about the world join up with the ideas they share with the non-religious about everything else. This strategy is also reinventive, in so far as, in the past, religious ideas and practices were not generally separated out from other concerns. It does, however, reflect the natural (self-defensive) capacity of the human mind to compartmentalize itself when dealing with the challenges and complexity of experience.[3]

Those whose minds are neither imprisoned within fundamentalism nor compromised by compartmentalism will generally agree that, in order to survive and be taken seriously in the modern world, religions must make greater efforts to reinvent themselves. This process of reinvention must take place within every dimension of religion. To begin with, the certitude that religions have in the past offered their adherents, and which adherents in turn have come to expect of their religious institutions, could profitably be tempered by the renewed virtues of 'unknowing'. Correspondingly, the propositional function of doctrines needs balancing with a greater emphasis on their equally important performative and instrumental functions. The pluralism of theoretical expression – whether in the form of myths, symbols or doctrines – rather than inviting attempts to edit or iron out inconsistencies should be seen as revealing the provisional nature of these forms. Likewise, the varieties of religious experience should be valued not so much as constituting actual or potential empirical proofs of religious truths or realities but rather as the partial and variable representations of these truths and realities within the psyche of particular historical individuals. As for religious practices such as meditation, prayer or the rituals of worship, which are commonly regarded as a means to an end rather than as ends in themselves, many of these can be reinvented as habitual forms of life no less enriching than any of those by which purely secular lives are defined. Finally, in regard to the reinvention of religious institutions, the continuing credibility of religions surely depends both on the detachment of their institutions from the political entanglements to which they have been subject over the centuries and on the recovery, or renewed emphasis, of more democratic forms of organization.

In all these areas the reinvention of religion is well under way. But three particular issues challenging the successful reinvention of religion are worth identifying here. The first is the individualism integral to modern secular society, the second is the religiously plural character of this society (including the pluralism within religions), and the third is the 'disenchantment' to which religious cosmologies have been subject. The last named issue arguably presents the most serious challenge given that it is as cosmologies (and eschatologies) that religions have their most profound impact on the human imagination. I will comment briefly on each of these three issues.

As regards the first issue, increasing recognition of the rights and equalities of all individuals, regardless of age, gender or ethnicity, have inevitably brought changes to the ways religions are practised and organized. This much is a commonplace in the history and sociology of religion. But these reinventions of practice and institution do not necessarily reach what is most profound in the challenge posed by modern individualism. One crucial consequence of modern individualism is identified by the sociologist Peter Berger. In past centuries, he says, it was in effect impossible for people not to believe – that is, impossible not to believe in the prevailing religion of one's culture. Then, with the Enlightenment and the rise of modernity, came the possibility of not believing, or at least of not believing in accordance with cultural norms and expectations. Within this situation, says Berger, emerges the further possibility of choosing alternative beliefs. This he characterizes as 'the heretical imperative', the imperative to choose one's own worldview precisely because one is now psychologically and culturally free to do so.

Arguably, the process described by Berger has now been capped by a further development – namely, by the *impossibility* of believing that seems to have become the lot of many secular individuals today. Alternatively, and more subtly, it may be not so much that such individuals can no longer believe as that they can no longer believe publicly or socially in the ways they would have done before. Religion becomes an entirely private matter, thereby encouraging the compartmentalizing stance described earlier. Even more subtly, perhaps, people who find themselves unable to believe may be happy to let others in effect do their believing for them. They may simply be happy that there are others, even within their own social circle, who do still believe. In any case, the challenge for religious institutions is to abandon their previous tendency to make assumptions about their appeal to, or authority over, their adherents or would-be adherents. In the future they must reinvent themselves, in part at least, as repositories of knowledge and technique, and as places of refuge, solace or inspiration, for all people. Such reinventions would in many respects restore roles religion fulfilled in earlier centuries.

The second challenge to religious reinvention is a greater social and intellectual awareness of religious pluralism. Religious pluralism has on the one hand provided rich resources for the exercise of Berger's 'heretical imperative' but on the other encouraged doubt and scepticism about the claims and authority of religion as such. How can we be sure that this religion or denomination rather than that one is 'authentic'? Might it not be more rational to suppose that all of them have some claim to the truth – or alternatively that they are all equally fallible? The facts of religious pluralism, whether 'domestic' or global, can function as a valuable brake on claims made by any one religion or denomination to have complete or exclusive access to religious truth. Attention to the claims made by 'other religions', and to the ways of life they promote, has certainly made a difference to how the various religions see themselves. Unfortunately this difference has not always been a positive one. In some quarters it has led to a recrudescence of exclusivism or fundamentalism, in others to a cheerful and often sloppy ecumenism in which important distinctions are ignored or brushed aside.

Undoubtedly the best responses to the facts of religious pluralism are those which acknowledge the separate identity of each tradition, and the many important differences between traditions, while recognizing the convergences between them. But what this requires is not just the exercise of tolerance towards other traditions and of cooperation with them on issues of common interest. What is required is that these 'other religions' should be treated as equals at least in the sense of recognizing their validity as coherent attempts to invent appropriate responses to experiences of the sacred or transcendent. It is also a matter of recognizing in 'other religions' truths or formulations of truths lacking in or neglected by one's own religion. Such recognition does not challenge the right of religious people to express a patriotic attitude towards their own religion – though it does not square with the more chauvinistic attitudes that have long marred and continue to mar relations between some religions. Still less does the recognition of equality between religions justify attempts either to force into existence more rational or more comprehensive forms of religion, or to cream off universal spiritual truths considered capable of surviving independently of their originating traditions.

The third challenge to religious reinvention concerns the shrinking of religious cosmology (and eschatology) in the face of modern scientific cosmology. Where science is concerned, religion clearly needs to proceed with caution, given past histories of conflict and misunderstanding. Religious thinkers need not think of religious cosmologies as in competition with, or even as comparable with, the narrowly physicalist cosmologies of modern science. Even so, all truths about the world are universal truths, and any complete view of the universe would not only include religious and scientific truths alike, but would have to demonstrate the connections between these truths. Moreover, the importance of cosmology for religion is as much social as it is theoretical. In an increasingly globalized culture, human beings have no shared cosmology, and in particular no shared eschatology, which either enables or encourages them to think beyond the here and now of human life, no shared worldview within which to situate their hopes, instincts or experiences concerning what in earlier centuries would have been called their destiny. There is no overarching intellectual structure to throw any light on the significance their lives might have in terms of some larger whole. Consequently many people accept or assume that no larger order exists within which their individual lives could have significance, either here or hereafter.

The nearest thing to a collective or unifying worldview is the one constructed by secular humanism from current scientific cosmology and evolutionary theory. This modern worldview, which has assumed the status almost of a cultural lingua franca, provides a terminology to which even religious thinkers are expected, or feel obliged, to conform when formulating or expounding their own more partisan worldviews. This dominant secular and materialist worldview is critical if not dismissive of any ideas concerning beings, powers or orders of reality existing beyond the immediacy of the here and now. Its dominating influence as the orthodoxy of secular humanism means that any instinct for transcendence, any 'rumour of angels',[4] and any questions about the possibility of a life beyond death (or before birth), tend to be excluded from the common discourse and collective 'spaces' of modern society. Such interests and impulses – refugees from the process of disenchantment that is present even within the religions – are liable either to be repressed, or else to find vicarious but never fully satisfied expression through other channels, such as political and social activism, sport, travel and recreation, or the arts.

Rather than accommodating their messages to the prevailing secular worldview, religions would do better to reaffirm the empirical and experimental nature of their own foundations – their traditions of prayer, meditation, mysticism and so on – and to begin the rehabilitation or reconstruction of their own cosmological traditions. In particular, there is a need for the restoration of what can be termed 'intermediate cosmology', that immense middle ground between earth and heaven in which so much of the drama of religion is played out – for example, in worship and meditation, in mythology and iconography, and in popular religious customs.

In recent centuries the subject matter of intermediate cosmology has become something of a no-man's land between the territories now occupied by science and religion, science claiming authority over all things physical and religion over all things spiritual. This no-man's land of 'intermediate cosmology' consequently tends to be avoided by both sides – by science because it is perceived as too 'spiritual' and by religion because it is perceived as too 'material'. It is easily objected that attention to this area diverts attention from the real or the highest aims of religion, encouraging precisely that magical or superstitious image that religions have struggled to escape, but the use of the term 'intermediate' itself indicates that the beings, powers, practices and ideas in question can be regarded, as they are in many religions, as 'condescensions' of the sacred that point towards higher goals. The experiences and phenomena associated with intermediate cosmology, while not of ultimate religious concern, certainly play a greater part in religious life than many are prepared to admit.

The almost snobbish neglect by religious thinkers of intermediate cosmology (and, along with this, intermediate eschatology) both expresses and encourages a sharply dualistic religious worldview, one that divides the material world down here from the spiritual world up there, with God as its remote if not retired occupant.[5] The relative if not complete neglect of intermediate cosmology and eschatology helps explain the rapid growth in some quarters of new religious movements and the widespread disaffection with any kind of religion in others. Abandoned by the traditions that originally gave it context and meaning, the experiences and phenomena associated with intermediate cosmology tend to assume an exaggerated importance when made the basis of new religious movements. It is no wonder that many of those suffering bereavements from the carnage of the First World War, finding that the various Churches had little or nothing to say about the hope or nature of an afterlife, should have turned for consolation to movements such as Spiritualism. Here the dead are no longer seen in a wider cosmological and eschatological content. Instead they have themselves become that context.

DISCUSSION ABOUT the ways religions as institutionalized systems of theory and practice succeed or fail in reinventing themselves does not yet reach the heart of the idea of reinventing religion. Doctrinal or institutional reinventions, however extensive, will be of little moment if they do not accommodate the attitudes and experiences of individual adherents or would-be adherents. Therefore, to ideas about religions as historical inventions, which over time are subject to reinvention, must be added ideas about the reinvention of religion in the lives of its individual adherents. In the case of the Zen tradition, for example, we can say not only that Zen is a reinvention of earlier forms of Buddhism within the constraints and opportunities of the Chinese and Japanese cultures, but that it has the resources that allow people to reinvent themselves, as was illustrated in the story that opened this chapter.

Many people share the existential situation of the young man in this story, in so far as they are aware that something vital is missing in their lives. Unlike him, they may not be aiming for some advanced spiritual goal. But they are at least seeking a meaning and purpose to their lives such as is lacking in the prevailing secular worldview. They may also seek ways of marking, and celebrating with others, the defining events of their own and others' lives. In their desire to situate their lives within a larger order of meaning than that envisaged by any secular philosophy, their quest can be said to be a religious one, regardless of whether it leads them towards (or, for that matter, away from) this or that institutionalized form of religion. Undoubtedly some people find order and meaning in interests and activities conventionally regarded as 'secular', in which case these might themselves be described as, in the broadest sense, religious. If religion is based upon what it claims to be based upon, then access to the sacred or transcendent will not be confined to the institutionalized human constructions we call religions. Ultimately, however, religious insights and instincts need to be intellectually articulated, and also to be acted out in some way, and it is through institutional religion in some form that these things have typically reached their fullest and finest forms of expression. Religion, moreover, is necessarily a social activity, and relatively few individuals will be able to survive on the basis of some socially unexpressed personal spirituality. Even those forms of religion described by sociologists and others as 'invisible' or 'implicit' have social as well as intellectual and practical dimensions.

As we saw earlier, explanations can be found for why many people are no longer able to believe, let alone to give practical and public expression to belief. At the same time, even those who do acknowledge in themselves religious instincts or aspirations find it difficult if not impossible to associate with institution-alized forms of religion, except perhaps in a purely bookish or intellectualist way. There are various reasons for this, but one of them takes us back to the problem of individualism in modern society. For one salient by-product of this individualism, at least in the modern West, is what might be called an overdeveloped sense of sincerity. Religion is widely regarded as an essentially personal matter, which in effect means that it is also an essentially private one. Sincerity of belief in, commitment to, or practice of religion becomes paramount, which in turn means that those without absolute or unquestioning conviction or commitment will often feel uncomfortable in their religion and even obliged to withdraw from it. Ironically enough, the reluctance or refusal of non-religious individuals to participate in religious practices sometimes betrays an almost superstitious fastidiousness – one they are less likely to manifest in other contexts. They would not have such feelings if persuaded to attend an opera when they did not much care for opera or a football match if they had no real interest in football.

Likewise, those who are drawn to a religion but who have doubts or reservations about some of its tenets or practices may forever hesitate to participate in its life, for fear of being thought – if not for fear of actually being – insincere or hypocritical. This either/or mentality, which religions themselves have done much to encourage, is widely assumed to be a necessary characteristic of all religion. In few if any other contexts, however, do we main-tain or even attempt such strict standards of consistency or sincerity. Many of those who give the impression of having the conviction and commitment one lacks oneself, or whom one assumes must have such conviction and commitment, may be closer to one's own situation than might appear. In any case, there is no reason why one should not become or remain associated with religious ideas, practices or institutions that one does not fully understand or find completely convincing. One is not asked at the door of the art gallery whether one fully understands and approves the principles of abstract expressionism or at the door of the opera house whether one fully endorses the musical theories of Wagner. Surely one can explore, or taste, what a religious tradition has to offer without putting one's integrity on the line, or without somehow offending or embarrassing the committed adherents of the religion in question. Imagine such hesitations or reservations arising in the contexts of education, sport or the arts, for example. How, if they did, could one ever attain proficiency in a foreign language, or develop one's skill or fitness as an athlete, or paint a good picture?

EPILOGUE

What Nathaniel Hawthorne said in 1856 about his friend and fellow novelist Herman Melville that 'He can neither believe, nor be comfortable in his unbelief,' could also be said about millions of people today.[1] Agonizing over what one can or cannot believe may well be a more honest expression of religious sensibility than the parading of certainties that characterizes many a religious 'believer' or atheistic 'unbeliever', but at the same time it bears witness to the over-cerebral religiosity that is itself part of the modern crisis of religion. What is more, the emphasis in many religious contexts on believing in hand-me-down doctrinal propositions about the nature, attributes and actions of various supernatural beings has encouraged unnecessary competition and confusion between religion and science. Doubting and questioning are as much a part of religious life and thought as they are of political, ethical or artistic life and thought, but in none of these other fields of human interest is it assumed that all doubts and questions must be resolved before any form of participation is possible. On the contrary, one participates precisely in order to engage with one's doubts and questions.

How is one to convince people that the situation in the case of religion need be no different from the situation in any other sphere of human life? Some religious people have made almost a fetish of expressing their 'honest doubt' and 'religious struggle', as if these were somehow a hallmark of genuine faith. What I have tried to do in this book is to show, in the context of each of the four dimensions of religion, how there are ways both of acting and of thinking that do not need to get caught up in these kinds of religious agonizing or dogmatizing. Looking back on all that has been said in this book, there are several points about religion worth emphasizing by way of conclusion.

To begin with, and contrary to the popular idea that religion is somehow a way of being and thinking that goes against the grain of our natural interests and impulses, what we find in all serious religious thought is the idea that religion offers a path to becoming fully human. Terms widely used in religions, such as 'liberation', 'salvation' or 'enlightenment', are not about being rescued or released from one's humanity, but rather about the fullest realization of this humanity. In Buddhism, the literal meaning of the term usually translated as enlightenment (*bodhi*) is 'waking up'. Far from being the comforting narcosis suggested by Marx's famous formula, the true goal of religion could be said to be closer to a detoxification. Or at least it is meant to be such, for all too often Marx's description does represent the actual situation of religion.

What we might more simply say is that the natural or proper state of being human is holiness – that is, a state of wholeness. This is quite other than the popular idea of holiness, according to which a holy or saintly person is merely someone who is 'very good' or 'morally perfect'. On this definition, saintly or holy persons are identified as those whose moral rectitude (assuming it is not actually a facade) makes them rather dull as well as liable to act or appear 'holier-than-thou'.[2] In the world's great religious traditions, however, genuinely holy or saintly persons do not stand apart, or see themselves as standing apart, from others. True holiness is always incognito. To become fully human is also to participate fully, and selflessly, in the human condition. That is to say, becoming fully human is a social as well as a personal achievement. This is why so many of the forms of spirituality that set themselves up as alternatives to religion, if not in opposition to it, so often get off on the wrong foot, encouraging in their unwary followers various forms of self-importance and self-absorption.

The natural state of human wholeness or holiness is also a state in which one perceives, respects and serves the holiness or wholeness of everything and everyone with which or with whom one comes into contact. In particular, a right relationship with the natural world depends on recognizing the sanctity of Nature. It is surely significant that the best term for the natural world that modernity can come up with is the word 'environment'[3], and with it the idea that human beings are the accidental but lucky biological products of this environment, which in turn becomes a quarry supplying further products for human use and pleasure – a mere 'resource' requiring appropriate human domination and management. When we treat the world as a quarry, it rapidly becomes such. Nor is the deification of Nature affirmed by some New Age or neo-pagan enthusiasts an authentic corrective to humanity's abuse of the natural world, however well-intentioned it may be (and very often is). As G. K. Chesterton puts it, nature is not our mother but our sister.[4] Those with protective instincts towards Nature should find this image more than sufficiently inspiring.

The term 'environment', already deficient as a general term, is all the worse for stopping short at the physical world – however far out into the universe our vision of the physical world might extend. For religions have traditionally regarded humankind and the world it inhabits as part of a larger order of reality no less natural than the physical world but also 'supernatural' in the sense that it overarches and illuminates our particular place within it. Unfortunately, many of the religious thinkers who continue to acknowledge this wider order of reality have ignored its continuities with the immediate world of the senses, thereby relegating the 'supernatural' subject matter of religion to a separate and distant realm that might as well be purely imaginary. But our true natures cannot be comfortably confined within the world as narrowly conceived by so many modern thinkers, including many religious thinkers. And even if we accept the misleadingly dualistic language of body and soul, which tends to 'spiritualize' religion away into a corner, our souls and our bodies remain inextricably one.

This brings us finally to that aspect of cosmology known as eschatology – the understanding of our life on earth as just one stage within a larger existence. Religious worldviews have a temporal as well as a spatial dimension: eschatology is to cosmology what history is to geography. For human beings mindful of their mortality there will always be the question as to what kind of life, if any, is to succeed their earthly life (and, indeed, the question about what kind of life might have preceded it). Thus religious worldviews do not stop at being theories of the universe comparable in some respects to scientific theories of the universe; they are also like maps – maps for living and dying. The sense of meaninglessness so widely experienced today thrives on the lack of any adequate eschatology.

If the existence and meaning of our immediate sensory world and of our present lives is indeed dependent on a wider order of reality, then the persistence of religion could itself be regarded as part of the natural condition of humanity. In theory, of course, it is possible that some individuals, groups or even whole nations could cut themselves off from any acknowledgement of, or relationship with, a wider transcendent order on which they were in fact dependent. In practice, however, the transcendental order, in virtue of being such, would hardly cease from making itself known to human beings 'at sundry times and in divers manners'.[5] Whether or not we human beings are capable of giving up on transcendence, transcendence is by definition not something that could ever give up on us. Hence religion, whatever the champions and prophets of secularism might say, is likely to remain a constant within all human culture. The real issues concern how to understand, live with and make the most of religion in its various forms.

Sceptics will always be demanding hard evidence for all of this. Reasonably or unreasonably, what these sceptics want is empirical evidence, unambiguous, repeatable and readily comprehensible. Such evidence is in fact available in copious quantities should they care to expose themselves to it. But most sceptics are not so willing. If they were, they might at least concede that the profound experiences of mystics and other religious explorers seem to offer direct glimpses of other worlds or other levels of being that should at least give them pause. Nor should one dismiss – as many religious specialists rather snobbishly do – those less profound experiences that are better described as psychic or paranormal. The latter are valuable, even in a religious context, in so far as they challenge reductionist views of human existence and make explicit the continuities between 'ordinary' and 'extraordinary' levels of human experience. One well-documented ghost could be enough to cast doubt on a whole cosmology. Those reporting out-of-body and near-death experiences may not be enlightened mystics, but they might well have clear evidence that our conscious existence is far more than a function of human biology.

But instead of the kind of piecemeal empirical evidence that tends after all to be of a personal character, perhaps what is really required are more general considerations. Might not the fact that people search for meaning in the world around them itself suggest that there is meaning to be discovered? Could the desire of many people to connect the defining events of their mortal lives with a wider order of existence through ritual and the like intimate the reality of such an order? And if there were indeed a wider order of reality to which our individual lives were integrally related, would it not be reasonable to suppose that some indication of this fact would be revealed in our own psychology and constitution, and in particular in various experiences that we might under certain conditions have? Why should the sentient properties of the universe not offer as much of a clue as to the nature and order of the universe as any of the insentient properties on which scientists concentrate? Why should the ideas, ideals, gestures, experiences and achievements of humankind not constitute as much evidence for the real nature of the universe as any of its more primitive features?

Secular humanism generally represents itself with the same kind of confidence typical of many religious positions. For Richard Holloway, the life of each individual, like that of human history as a whole, is no more than a spark in the dark:

When the map of our life is complete, and we die in the richness of our own history, some among the living will miss us for a while, but the earth will go on without us. Its day is longer than ours, though we now know that it too will die. Our brief finitude is but a beautiful spark in the vast darkness of space. So we should live the fleeting day with passion and, when the night comes, depart from it with grace.[6]

Despite the references to beauty, passion and grace, and the self-evident truth that we need to make the most of our brief lives on earth, the philosophy here is bleakly reductionist and seemingly oblivious to the rich possibilities held up by the religions and the sciences alike. How, apart from the rhetoric and the exhortation, is the thumbnail cosmology here any different from Samuel Beckett's terse summary of human life: 'They give birth astride of a grave, the light gleams an instant, then it's night once more.'[7] And what about the millions of people unable, for one reason or another, to depart from this life 'with grace'?

What Holloway says is one with the less sentimental but equally reductionist view expressed by Stephen Hawking: 'We are just a slightly advanced breed of apes on a small planet orbiting a very average star. But we can understand the universe, and that makes us something very special.'[8] This in its own way is no less emotional a statement than Holloway's. Both statements, moreover, could also be considered a touch arrogant, flying confidently in the face of the ideas, experiences and instincts of millions of thoughtful people around the world. How can Hawking and Holloway, like so many other secular thinkers, be so sure that nothing exists of us, or for us, behind, before or after our fleeting lives on earth? In these and in many other expressions of a secular worldview there appears to be an undercurrent of disappointment and even bitterness, suggesting that their authors may have unfinished business with religious questions.

There is no real evidence for the post-romantic and pseudo-scientific idea of a coldly indifferent and fundamentally impersonal universe of which human beings are merely the puzzled – as well as puzzling – accidental inhabitants. If anything, our irreducibly personal experience within this universe is prima facie evidence against such a theory. The idea, which now has the status of a doctrine, that human beings are the accidental products of evolutionary processes is a highly presumptuous one which finite beings like ourselves could never establish with anything approaching certainty. Moreover, those ready to accept this theory in the name of science or humanism should reflect on just how large the nothing is at the heart of the theory. For what the theory essentially claims is that human consciousness, along with everything that this entails for human culture and values, is a chance ephemeral product, a mere epiphenomenon, of physical processes thst are themselves the chance ephemeral products of underlying physical forces. Are we not selling ourselves drastically short here? At the very least, one would have to acknowledge the irony of the fact that the evolutionary processes in question have produced beings who think and act as if the theory is completely false.

Religion is what happens when human beings respond to what, in generic terms, can be called the sacred or the transcendent. More specifically, religious systems and institutions are what results from human beings acknowledging, thinking about and acting upon their sense of the sacred or their awareness of transcendence. In an ideal world, perhaps, what is typically separated out as a 'religious' response, or institutionalized in the form of this or that 'religion', would be distributed equally among every human activity – eating and drinking, lovemaking and family life, artistic creativity and enjoyment, education and cultural life, agriculture and industry, and so on. In a society of saints it might well be that there would exist no obviously separate religious ideas, practices or institutions for theologians, historians, sociologists and others to study. As it is, and for the foreseeable future, we must make do with religions as institutions, as well as with the idea of religion as a separate category of human thought and activity, along with art, law, politics, science and all the rest.

Religions may be in crisis today, even as they are also flourishing, but history shows that they have always been in crisis, or subject to crisis. Being in crisis is not necessarily a bad thing; on the contrary, it can have very positive effects. One effect is in encouraging people to sift the essential from the accidental, to return to first principles; another is that it encourages people to recover neglected methods and insights from the past. This is where the idea of reinventing religion comes in. The observation that there is nothing new under the sun applies as much to religion as to anything else. Quarrels between religions are unnecessary; all the great themes of religion are manifest in every religion – sacrifice, incarnation, revelation, celebration, transfiguration, redemption. No religion has a monopoly on these themes, although each may express them through different symbols. The pluralism of religions, which may once have presented a challenge or even a threat to individual religions, should today be recognized as a collective human legacy. One would expect no less in any other area of human concern.

REFERENCES

Introduction

1 See, especially, Johannes Quack and Cora Schuh, eds, *Religious Indifference: New Perspectives from Studies on Secularization and Nonreligion* (New York, 2017).

2 See Francis Wade, *Myanmar's Enemy Within: Buddhist Violence and the Making of a Muslim 'Other'*, 2nd edn (London, 2019).

3 A. C. Grayling, *The God Argument: The Case against Religion and for Humanism* (London, 2014), p. 147.

4 According to sociologist David Martin, for example, the evidence suggests that 'there is no consistent relation between the degree of scientific advance and a reduced profile of religious influence, belief and practice.' *The Future of Christianity: Reflections on Violence and Democracy, Religion and Secularization* (London and New York, 2016), p. 119.

5 On this topic, see Davíd Carrasco, *City of Sacrifice: The Aztec Empire and the Role of Violence in Civilization* (Boston, MA, 1999). Of course, moral judgements about a particular ritual practice are not incompatible with trying to understand its function within a particular religious system, nor indeed with appreciating what social and economic factors might help to explain it.

6 Memphis Barker, 'Asia Bibi: Pakistan Court Overturns Blasphemy Death Sentence', *The Guardian*, 31 October 2018.

7 For three rather differently motivated critiques of the idea of 'religion', see Wilfred Cantwell Smith, *The Meaning and End of Religion: A New Approach to the Religious Traditions of Mankind* (New York, 1963); Russell T. McCutcheon, *Manufacturing Religion: The Discourse on Sui Generis Religion and the Politics of Nostalgia* (New York, 1997); and Timothy Fitzgerald, *The Ideology of Religious Studies* (New York and Oxford, 2000).

8 According to one apologist for the legitimacy of approaching religion from a Western perspective, '*religion* is a "construction" and if other

cultures have other constructions with which they understand themselves and others, so may Western science be allowed to have its own "indigenous" concepts in order to make sense of certain specifiable forms of human behaviour. If this is an ethnocentric view, then so be it – no need to abolish science or close down philosophy departments just because some cultures do not have equivalent terms.' Jeppe Sinding Jensen, 'Is a Phenomenology of Religion Possible? On the Ideas of a Human and Social Science of Religion', *Method and Theory in the Study of Religion*, 5 (1993), pp. 109–33 (pp. 110–11).

9   The allusion here is to the famous opening sentence of L. P. Hartley's novel *The Go-between* (London, 1953).

ONE: Religion Undefined

1   Henry Fielding, *The History of Tom Jones, a Foundling* (London, 1749), I, p. 109 (Book III, ch. iii).

2   William James, *The Varieties of Religious Experience: A Study in Human Nature* (London, 1902), p. 31. There are many modern editions of this text, which has never been out of print.

3   Friedrich Schleiermacher, *The Christian Faith*, 2nd edn [1830–31], trans. and ed. H. R. Mackintosh and J. S. Stewart (Edinburgh, 1928), pp. 12–16. See also 'Second Speech: On the Essence of Religion' in Schleiermacher's earlier work, *On Religion: Speeches to Its Cultured Despisers* [1799], trans. Richard Crouter (Cambridge, 1988), pp. 96–140.

4   Paul Tillich, *Christianity and the Encounter of the World Religions* (New York, 1963), p. 4.

5   'Sometimes, what I call quasi-religions are called pseudo-religions, but this is as imprecise as it is unfair. "Pseudo" indicates an intended but deceptive similarity; "quasi" indicates a genuine similarity, not intended, but based on points of identity, and this, certainly, is the situation in cases like Fascism and Communism, the most extreme examples of quasi-religions today.' Ibid., p. 5.

6   'In the secular quasi-religions the ultimate concern is directed toward objects like nation, science, a particular form or stage of society, or a highest ideal of humanity, which are then considered divine.' Ibid., p. 5.

7   See, for example, Ninian Smart, *Worldviews: Crosscultural Explorations of Human Beliefs*, 2nd edn (Englewood Cliffs, NJ, 1995).

8   James Martineau, *A Study of Religion: Its Sources and Contents*, 2nd edn, vol. I (Oxford, 1889), p. I.

9   R. R. Marett, *The Threshold of Religion*, 2nd edn (London, 1914), p. xxxi.

10 James G. Frazer, *The Golden Bough: A Study in Magic and Religion*, 3rd edn (London, 1911), I, p. 122.

11 Anthony Wallace, *Religion: An Anthropological View* (New York, 1966), p. 107.

12 Immanuel Kant, *Religion within the Boundaries of Mere Reason, and Other Writings*, ed. and trans. Allen W. Wood, George Di Giovanni and Robert Adams (Cambridge, 1998), p. 130.

13 Matthew Arnold, *Literature and Dogma: An Essay Towards a Better Apprehension of the Bible* (London, 1873), p. 18.

14 Emile Durkheim, *The Elementary Forms of the Religious Life* [1912], trans. J. Swain (New York, 1965), p. 261.

15 Alfred North Whitehead, *Religion in the Making* (Cambridge, 1926), pp. 6, 7. 'Collective enthusiasms, revivals, institutions, churches, rituals, bibles, codes of behaviour, are the trappings of religion, its passing forms. They may be useful, or harmful; they may be authoritatively ordained, or merely temporary expedients. But the end of religion is beyond all this' (p. 7).

16 Melford E. Spiro, 'Religion: Problems of Definition and Explanation', in *Anthropological Approaches to the Study of Religion*, ed. M. Banton (London, 1966), p. 96.

17 Durkheim, *The Elementary Forms of the Religious Life*, p. 62.

18 J. M. Yinger, *Religion, Society and the Individual: An Introduction to the Sociology of Religion* (New York, 1957), p. 9.

19 Clifford Geertz, *The Interpretation of Cultures* (New York, 1973), p. 90.

20 I have explored the idea of religions as systems in greater detail in 'Religions as Systems', in *Aspects of Religion: Essays in Honour of Ninian Smart*, ed. Peter Masefield and Donald Wiebe (New York, 1994), pp. 39–57.

21 Cult, from the Latin *cultus*, is essentially an agricultural metaphor for describing devotion to or worship of a god or saint. Thus one can talk about the cult of Krishna in the Hindu tradition or the cult of saints in the Roman Catholic tradition. Cognate secular usages occur in descriptions of people being 'cultivated' (well developed or refined) and, in social life, about 'cultivating' (attending to) someone in order to gain some advantage. It is unfortunate that the term 'cult' is also commonly used, both in journalism and in sociological discourse, to refer to any extreme religious group based on uncritical devotion to a charismatic leader.

22 The etymology of the Latin *religio*, closely associated with religion in the sense of duty, reverence, obligation and hence also with religious law, remains obscure; but it could be derived from *ligare*, to bind or connect, in the sense of rebinding or reconnecting (*re-ligare*).

23 There is, indeed, an interesting reverse argument used by Christian and in particular Protestant theologians (such as Karl Barth) to the effect that the divinely revealed Christian gospel is not a religion but the 'end of religion', the term 'religion' designating all those merely human attempts to reach up to God.

24 The origins of this quip, as of a similar one about Homer, are uncertain. See Garson O'Toole, 'The Plays of Shakespeare Were Not Written

by Shakespeare But by Another Man of the Same Name', *Quote Investigator*, https://quoteinvestigator.com, 19 August 2014.

25 Even the composite term 'magico-religious' sometimes used by anthropologists seems to endorse an irreducible distinction between its two component terms.

TWO: Overcoming Belief

1 Lewis Carroll [Charles Lutwidge Dodgson], *Through the Looking-glass, and What Alice Found There* (London, 1872), p. 100.

2 Tertullian's actual words occur in a text on the doctrine of the Incarnation (*De carne Christi* v.4), where his ideas are rather subtler than that in any variation of the maxim attributed to him – albeit still likely to offend the hardened rationalist. Tertullian states that the death of Christ is credible because unfitting (*credibile est quia ineptum est*), and his resurrection certain because impossible (*certum est quia impossibile*). For more on the meaning of Tertullian's words and on their later distortion, see Robert D. Sider, 'Credo quia absurdum?', *Classical World*, LXXIII (1980), pp. 417–19; and Peter Harrison, '"I Believe Because it Is Absurd": The Enlightenment Invention of Tertullian's Credo', *Church History*, LXXXVI (2017), pp. 339–64.

3 Mark Twain, *Following the Equator: A Journey Around the World* (Hartford, CT, 1897), p. 132. This schoolboy's definition of 'faith' is cited from the fictional *Pudd'nhead Wilson's New Calendar*, brief quotations from which head each chapter of what is a serious travelogue critiquing various forms of oppression, intolerance and prejudice around the world.

4 Richard Dawkins, *The God Delusion* (London, 2006), p. 308.

5 'It may be that there are still people – I cannot vouch for this but suspect it to be true – who take down a belief every Sunday morning but have it tucked away again comfortably by half-past twelve.' William Golding, 'Belief and Creativity', in *The Moving Target* (London, 1984), pp. 185–202: p. 189.

6 See, for example, 'Why Didn't the Greeks Climb Mt Olympus (Mytikas) and See that There Weren't Any Gods Up There?', www. quora.com, updated 16 May 2019, accessed 19 January 2020. See also Paul Veyne, *Did the Greeks Believe in Their Myths?* (Chicago, IL, and London, 1988).

7 See, for example, Tim Whitmarsh, *Battling the Gods: Atheism in the Ancient World* (London, 2016).

8 Graham Greene, *Ways of Escape* (London, 1980), p. 257.

9 This statement by Anselm (1033–1109) appears at the end of the first chapter of his work *Proslogion* (1077–8): 'I do not seek to understand so that I may believe, but I believe so that I may understand; and what is more, I believe that unless I do believe I shall not understand' (Neque enim quaero intelligere ut credam, sed credo ut intelligam.

Neque enim quaero intelligere ut credam, sed credo ut intelligam. Nam et hoc credo, quia, nisi credidero, non intelligam). See Benedicta Ward, trans., *The Prayers and Meditations of Saint Anselm* (Harmondsworth, 1973), p. 244.

10 For more on this doctrine, or principle, see Paul Dundas, *The Jains*, 2nd edn (London and New York, 2002), pp. 229–32.

11 Tom Stoppard, *Jumpers* (London, 1972), p. 69.

12 Søren Kierkegaard, 'Concerning the Dedication to "The Single Individual"' [1846], in *The Point of View* (London, 1939), p. 110.

13 Mary Lutyens, ed., *The Krishnamurti Reader* (London, 1970), p. 35.

THREE: Religion as Practice

1 Karen Blixen, *Out of Africa* (London, 1937), p. 57.

2 Is it wrong to try and impress people, or to be on one's best behaviour? Is it hypocritical to tidy a normally untidy house before a guest arrives? Is it wrong to warn a school or hospital of a forthcoming official inspection and even to allow staff the time to prepare for it?

3 Frustration with this kind of situation is no doubt what prompted the quip about some technique being 'all very well in practice, but what about in theory?'

4 Gaston Burridge, 'Does the Forked Stick Locate Anything? An Inquiry into the Art of Dowsing', *Western Folklore*, XIV (1955), pp. 32–43. See also Matthew Weaver, 'UK Water Firms Admit Using Divining Rods to Find Leaks and Pipes', *The Guardian*, 21 November 2017.

5 As quoted in the *Sunday Times*, 20 January 1982.

6 What is common to these otherwise very different kinds of practice is their interpersonal character. The verb 'to pray' is but an older word for 'to ask' or, more strongly, 'to implore'. Most of the praying in Shakespeare's plays, for example, is secular in nature. For instance, 'I pray you, do not fall in love with me, for I am falser than vows made in wine' (*As You Like It*, III.v).

7 The chi-rho symbol combines the Greek letters X and P, the first two letters of 'Christ' in Greek. There are different stories explaining how Emperor Constantine came to adopt this symbol into his military insignia. According to Lactantius, Constantine was instructed to do so in a dream. According to a later account, by Eusebius, Constantine had a celestial vision (also witnessed by others) featuring a symbolic cross (of which the chi-rho was one type) and the words 'In this sign, you shall conquer'.

8 See Nicole M. Hartwell, ed., *Religion, War, and Ethics: A Sourcebook of Textual Traditions* (Cambridge, 2014), pp. 583–6. See also Daniel W. Kent, 'Onward Buddhist Soldiers: Preaching to the Sri Lankan Army', in *Buddhist Warfare*, ed. Mark Juergensmeyer and Michael K. Jerryson (New York and Oxford, 2009), pp. 157–78.

9 Technically, the distinction between 'rites' and 'rituals' is the distinction between the words and the actions accompanying the words. In modern parlance, however, the term 'rite' tends to be used synonymously with 'ritual'.

10 To take a very simple example, when people think of incense they think of religious ritual; and yet incense has long been used throughout the world as much in secular as in religious contexts – and used as much to mask unpleasant odours as to give aesthetic pleasure.

11 Talcott Parsons differentiates rituals as 'religious in so far as the goal sought is non-empirical, magical, so far as it is empirical': *The Social System* (London, 1991), p. 252.

12 Mary Douglas, *Purity and Danger: An Analysis of Concepts of Pollution and Taboo* (London, 1966), p. 59.

13 It is interesting to compare three of the several senses of this word given by the OED. Its primary meaning, virtually synonymous with the primary meaning of 'ritual', is 'An outward rite or observance, religious or held sacred; the performance of some solemn act according to prescribed form.' But it can also have a closely associated disparaging sense: 'A rite or observance regarded as merely formal or external; an empty form.' Finally, it is also used in a well-established secular (or secularized) sense: 'A formal act or observance, expressive of deference or respect to superiors in rank, or established by custom in social intercourse; a usage of courtesy, politeness, or civility.' Uses of the word in this sense are as early as uses in its primary sense (fourteenth century).

14 Daniel Dennett, *Breaking the Spell: Religion as a Natural Phenomenon* (London, 2006), p. 10.

15 For more on this theme, see, for example, Carmen Blacker and Michael Loewe, eds, *Ancient Cosmologies* (London, 1975).

16 On the other hand, Dennett says better than he knows here. Some forms of mystical or contemplative prayer might well be characterized as 'talking to oneself' if, as in many traditions, such practices are understood to help one realize the identity of the individual with the Absolute or Universal Self.

17 As one teacher says about the zazen meditation technique, 'If the practice is truly carried out, then one session of meditation is one session of being Buddha, a day of meditation is a day of being Buddha. Or as an Ancient has said: "One inch of meditation, one inch of Buddha; so inch by inch, make the six-foot form of Buddha."' Edward Conze, *Buddhist Scriptures* (Harmondsworth, 1959), p. 135.

18 Douglas, *Purity and Danger*, p. 79.

FOUR: Religion as Theory

1 According to German philosopher Martin Heidegger (1889–1976), human existence is defined by the condition of 'thrownness'

(*geworfenheit*), a term describing the way in which we find ourselves existing in, and alienated by, an ongoing world not of our own choosing or making.

2 This word strictly refers to the study or understanding of myth, but is also used to refer to an actual body of myths – as in 'Greek mythology' or 'Norse mythology'.

3 That this phrase will jar with some Christians is testimony to the long-engrained idea of a myth as a fanciful story. These same Christians, however, will happily talk about 'Hindu mythology', 'Greek mythology' and so on.

4 See Loyal D. Rue, *Amythia: Crisis in the Natural History of Western Culture* (Tuscaloosa, AL, and London, 1989).

5 Aristotle in *Poetics* 9 argues that tragic drama is truer to reality than history because it demonstrates what is universal.

6 Frederick Franck, trans., *Messenger of the Heart: The Book of Angelus Silesius, with Observations by the Ancient Zen Masters* (Bloomington, IN, 2005), p. 99.

7 Fairy stories are more likely to be related to myth, and folktales to legend.

8 This legend is the basis for William Blake's famous poem 'And did those feet in ancient time' (1804), better known through Hubert Parry's musical setting of the poem under the title 'Jerusalem' (1916).

9 Fairy stories can sometimes be shown to be literary versions of myths now isolated from their original ritual or religious contexts. As J.R.R. Tolkien has argued, fairy stories can have powerful salutary (consoling and revelatory) effects on their readers. See Verlyn Flieger and Douglas A. Anderson, eds, *Tolkien on Fairy-stories* (London, 2014).

10 These include the distinctions made between literal and symbolic, literal and metaphorical, rational and suprarational, and natural and supernatural.

11 Karen Armstrong, *The Battle for God: Fundamentalism in Judaism, Christianity and Islam* (London, 2000), pp. xv–xvii.

12 Bruce Lincoln, 'Gendered Discourses: The Early History of "Mythos" and "Logos"', *History of Religions*, XXXVI (1996), pp. 1–12; Robert L. Fowler, 'Mythos and Logos', *Journal of Hellenic Studies*, CXXXI (2011), pp. 45–66.

13 On this theme, see George Steiner, *Real Presences: Is There Anything in What We Say?* (London and Boston, MA, 1989).

14 'Symbols', says Paul Tillich, 'have one characteristic in common with [conventional] signs; they point beyond themselves to something else.' But the decisive difference between a conventional sign and a symbol is 'the fact that signs do not participate in the reality of that to which they point, while symbols do. Therefore, signs can be replaced for reasons of expediency or convention, while symbols cannot.' *Dynamics of Faith* (London, 1957), p. 42.

15 OED: a material object representing or taken to represent something immaterial or abstract, as a being, idea, quality, or condition.

16 It is worth attending to the etymology of the original Greek word σύμβολον (*symvolon*), which means a mark or token, and which seems to be related to the verb συμβάλλω (*symvallo*), meaning to unite or reunite – literally, to 'throw together' – two separate or separated entities (for instance, two halves of a broken plate, or two matching cloakroom tickets). This supports the idea that the function of the symbol is not to conceal but to reveal and embody some truth or meaning.

17 This particular example of an originally Judaic symbol, however, serves also to reintroduce the idea of religious symbols as culturally constructed, since in Christian tradition the image of the 'bush that burnt yet was not consumed' came to be read as, among other things, a symbol of the mystery of Mary as 'God-bearer' (*Theotokos*). As Gregory of Nyssa (335–394) puts it (although he is not the earliest writer to use this symbolism): 'From this we learn also the mystery of the Virgin: the light of divinity which through birth shone from her into human life did not consume the burning bush, even as the flower of her virginity was not withered by giving birth.' See Abraham J. Malherbe and Everett Ferguson, trans., *Gregory of Nyssa: The Life of Moses* (New York, 1978), p. 59.

18 Some readers may need to be reminded that the Fifth Amendment of the u.s. Constitution, one of the ten amendments making up the Bill of Rights, protects an accused person against self-incrimination (among other things), stating that no person 'shall be compelled in any criminal case to be a witness against himself'.

19 'Ayacana Sutta: The Request' (*Samyutta Nikaya* 6.1), translated from the Pali by Thanissaro Bhikkhu. *Access to Insight*, www.accesstoinsight.org, 30 November 2013.

20 What is meant here is 'supernatural' in the theological rather than the merely 'spooky' sense. Even so, as the German theologian Rudolf Otto points out, in his *The Idea of the Holy* (*Das Heilige*, 1917), the spooky or ghostly belongs within the same continuum of numinous experience whose highest form is that of the holy or (theologically) supernatural.

21 'Wholly other' (*ganz andere*) is a term used by Otto to characterize the transcendental nature of divine reality.

22 Robert Browning, 'The Year's at the Spring', in *Pippa Passes* (London, 1841).

FIVE: In Experiences We Trust?

1 *House, MD*, 'House vs. God' (series 2, episode 19; first broadcast 25 April 2006).

2 According to James, 'we learn most about a thing when we view it under a microscope, as it were, or in its most exaggerated form. This is as true

of religious phenomena as of any other kind of fact. The only cases
likely to be profitable enough to repay our attention will therefore be
cases where the religious spirit is unmistakable and extreme. Its fainter
manifestations we may tranquilly pass by.' William James, *The Varieties of
Religious Experience* (London, 1902), p. 39.

3 The term 'mystical', despite its specifically Greek origin and subsequent
Christian usage, has long been accepted as a generic epithet for a wide
range of intense ecstatic or profound contemplative experiences, such as
are susceptible of theistic and non-theistic interpretations alike.

4 James, *The Varieties of Religious Experience*, pp. 398–9.

5 It is recounted of Thomas Aquinas (1225–1274) that following an ecstatic
experience, towards the end of his life, he never wrote or dictated
anything more. Pressed to explain why he would not continue work on
his great opus *Summa theologica*, he told his secretary that 'All that I
have written seems to me like so much straw.' See James A. Weisheipl,
Friar Thomas D'Aquino: His Life, Thought, and Work (Garden City, NY,
1974), p. 321.

6 Mary Austin, *Experiences Facing Death* (Indianapolis, IN, 1931), p. 24.

7 Richard Swinburne, *The Existence of God* (Oxford, 1979), pp. 244–76.

8 See William L. Rowe, 'Religious Experience and the Principle of
Credulity', *International Journal for Philosophy of Religion*, XIII (1982),
pp. 85–92; and Peter Losin, 'Experience of God and the Principle of
Credulity: A Reply to Rowe', *Faith and Philosophy*, 4 (1987), pp. 59–70.

9 It cannot rationally be denied that innumerable people have
had experiences of ghosts or apparitions, most of which differ
phenomenologically from delusionary experiences featuring non-
existent persons. It is of course perfectly legitimate to deny that ghosts
have a veridical presence or real 'existence' in this world (however
ephemerally) as persisting or returning representations of the dead.
But if we do deny this, we are logically obliged either to offer some
alternative explanation that fits the facts at least as well, or else to
say (rather feebly) just that we don't know or can't know what such
experiences really mean.

10 *The Cloud of Unknowing*, trans. Clifton Wolters (Harmondsworth, 1961),
p. 122 (ch. 57).

11 Teresa of Avila, *Interior Castle* VI: 9, in *The Complete Works of St Teresa of
Jesus*, trans. E. Allison Peers (London, 1946), II, p. 316. See also *The Cloud
of Unknowing*, pp. 113–17 (chs 51–3).

12 See Chögyam Trungpa, *Cutting Through Spiritual Materialism* (Boston,
MA, 1973), pp. 13–22.

13 Several traditions concur with the *Cloud* in saying that 'those who
engage in the work of contemplation find that it has a good effect on
the body as well as on the soul, making them attractive in the eyes of all
who seem them', *Cloud,* ch. 54 (see also ch. 61), p. 117 (p. 127). Compare
this with the description of the newly enlightened Buddha given by the

monk Upaka, who encountered him on the road shortly after the event: 'Your faculties are serene, friend; the colour of your skin is clear and bright. Under whom have you gone forth? Or who is your teacher? Or whose Dhamma [doctrine] do you confess?' Bhikkhu Ñāṇamoli, *The Life of the Buddha According to the Pali Canon* (Kandy, 1992), p. 40.

six: Here Be Authorities and Institutions

1 *Merriam-Webster Dictionary*. This definition is in the same tradition as that of Durkheim's: 'Religions are unified systems of beliefs and rituals relative to conceptions of the sacred (that which is set apart and/or forbidden), beliefs and rituals that encourage individuals to subordinate their apparent self-interest in relation to the collectively expressed interest of sovereign organizations.' Emile Durkheim, *The Elementary Forms of the Religious Life* [1912], trans. J. Swain (New York, 1965), p. 326.

2 The term 'institution' has had a particularly wide range of meanings and associations. In one of its uses it comes close to being synonymous with 'organization': 'An establishment, organization, or association, instituted for the promotion of some object, esp. one of public or general utility, religious, charitable, educational, etc.' (OED). It is also used to refer to something within a social organization or institution: 'An established law, custom, usage, practice, organization, or other element in the political or social life of a people; a regulative principle or convention subservient to the needs of an organized community or the general ends of civilization' (OED).

3 Thomas F. O'Dea and J. Milton Yinger, 'Five Dilemmas in the Institutionalization of Religion', *Journal for the Scientific Study of Religion*, 1 (1961), pp. 30–41.

4 'Organized religion acts unethically whenever it compromises its prophetic role for the sake of institutional self-preservation, prestige, or power. Its dilemma arises from the fact that it must interact with the power structures in society which, as well as its own adherents, often seek to use religion to support their own interests instead of responding to its insights.' Paul C. Empie, 'Can Organized Religion be Unethical?', *Annals of the American Academy of Political and Social Science*, 363 (1966), pp. 70–78.

5 For more on this concept, see Robert N. Bellah and Phillip E. Hammond, *Varieties of Civil Religion* (San Francisco, CA, 1980).

6 Worth mentioning here is Max Weber's influential theory of the 'routinization of charisma', whereby the original, personal authority of a leader comes to be replaced by less personal and more predictable means of organization. For Weber, charismatic authority in its purest and most personal form exists only at the beginning of a tradition. Thereafter, in the interests of the stability and continuity of the institution thus established, charisma becomes to a greater or lesser degree rationalized

and bureaucratized. See Max Weber, *The Theory of Social and Economic Organization* (New York, 1968), pp. 363–4.

7 The 'official' target of the joke is, of course, Jesuitical argumentation.

8 Perhaps part of the enjoyment of this joke is that Gagarin didn't keep quiet – and that this is why we have the story. The joke is, after all, at the expense of both president and pope.

9 One common development in institutional religion, given the very different personal qualities of those who emerge to lead it, is a sharpening of the distinction between office and office-holder, so that (in theory at least) the defects of the latter in no way damage the credibility of the former.

10 Aside from the obviously fallacious nature of arguing from the mere antiquity of a belief or practice to its truth (or value), many of the traditions described as 'ancient', 'time-honoured' or 'long-established', whether in religion or in any other context, can be shown to be of relatively recent origin. The 'traditional' Christmas, for example, furnishes several illustrations. So does so-called 'fundamentalist Islam', a modernizing version of Islam heavily influenced by Protestantism. See also James R. Lewis and Olav Hammer, eds, *The Invention of Sacred Tradition* (Cambridge, 2007).

11 'Do not go upon what has been acquired by repeated hearing; nor upon tradition; nor upon rumour; nor upon what is in a scripture; nor upon surmise; nor upon an axiom; nor upon specious reasoning; nor upon a bias towards a notion that has been pondered over; nor upon another's seeming ability; nor upon the consideration that the person is our teacher.' Kalama Sutta: The Buddha's Charter of Free Inquiry, translated from the Pali by Soma Thera (1994); *Access to Insight*, www.accesstoinsight.org, 30 November 2013.

12 Bhikkhu Ñāṇamoli, *The Life of the Buddha According to the Pali Canon* (Kandy, 1992), p. 300.

13 Mark 2:27; F. W. Beare, 'The Sabbath Was Made for Man?', *Journal of Biblical Literature*, LXXIX (1960), pp. 130–36.

SEVEN: No Good Being Religious

1 This phrase comes from Immanuel Kant's *Idea for a General History with a Cosmopolitan Purpose* (1784), Proposition 6 of which states: 'Out of the crooked timber of humanity, no straight thing was ever made.' The phrase became well known after Isaiah Berlin used it in the title of his book *The Crooked Timber of Humanity: Chapters in the History of Ideas* (London, 1990).

2 This is my own variation of a parable of which various versions exist.

3 Of the many Hebrew words that have been or could be translated as 'sin', the three most common are *ḥeṭ'*, *pesha'* and *'awon*. The first connotes a mistake or failure, the second a deliberate 'breach' or

transgression of God's Law, and the third knowingly 'crooked' or immoral behaviour of some kind. For a useful overview, see David Daube, *Sin, Ignorance and Forgiveness in the Bible* (London, 1960).

4 According to Judaism, human beings are free to follow either *yetzer hara*, the impulse or inclination towards evil, or *yetzer hatov*, the impulse or inclination towards good, with the former often seen as the stronger. Scriptural sources for this idea occur in Genesis 6:5 and 8:21.

5 The ultimate 'ontologization' of good and evil is found in those mythologies where good and evil are reified, if not deified, as two antithetical forces or principles, to which may then be attributed the corresponding conflicts between good and evil evident in human history and within each individual self.

6 Augustine, *Confessions* II, iv, 6.

7 For more on the context of this story, see Jacob Neusner, trans., *Talmud Bavli Shabbat* (Atlanta, GA, 1992).

8 See Jeffrey Wattles, *The Golden Rule* (New York and Oxford, 1996).

9 Matthew Arnold, *Literature and Dogma: An Essay Towards a Better Apprehension of the Bible* (London, 1873), p. 18.

10 T. K. Abbott, trans., *Critique of Practical Reason and Other Works on the Theory of Ethics*, 6th edn (London, 1954), pp. 226–7.

11 'The Greek term *hosion* means knowledge of the proper ritual in prayer and sacrifice and of course its performance (as Euthyphro himself defines it in 14b). But obviously Euthyphro uses it in the much wider sense of pious conduct generally (e.g., his own), and in that sense the word is practically equivalent to righteousness (the justice of the Republic), the transition being by way of conduct pleasing to the gods.' G.M.A. Grube. trans., *Plato: Five Dialogues*, 2nd edn (Indianapolis, IN, 2002), p. 1.

12 Latinized as Mencius.

13 D. C. Lau, trans., *Mencius* (Harmondsworth, 1970), p. 79.

14 The ancient Chinese character for *Tian* literally reads 'Great Man', meaning the Ruler who lives in Heaven; but the term has been used, or interpreted, in rationalistic and naturalistic as well as in religious or mystical ways.

15 See, for example, Stuart Hampshire, *Spinoza* (Harmondsworth, 1951), pp. 30–55.

16 The familiar titles were systematically introduced with the invention of printing, after the more or less continuous texts of scroll and codex were divided up into the chapters and paragraphs familiar to modern readers.

17 In the Jerusalem Bible, the parable is entitled 'The lost son (the "prodigal") and the dutiful son'.

18 According to the law of the time, a younger son would inherit only one-third of the estate, but to receive this inheritance before the father's death would have been unusual, though not impossible. Faced with such a request, the father would have had either to liquidate assets from the

estate or even to sell or mortgage part of the estate to a third party. It would have been unthinkable for an elder son as main inheritor to have made such a request.

19 Richard Dawkins, *The God Delusion* (London, 2006), p. 211.

20 The corresponding Greek word σωτηρία (*sotiria*), from which we get the term 'soteriology', has a similar range of meanings. Cognate with the verb σώζειν (*sozein*), to save, preserve or rescue, σωτηρία can refer to bodily health and well-being as well as to deliverance from danger or restoration to a state of safety.

21 Gautama Buddha is sometimes described as a physician, and represented in iconography holding out a jar containing a remedy for those seeking to be cured. Christ is also referred to as a physician (quite apart from being called a healer through miracles), in the New Testament referring to himself thus: 'Those who are well have no need of a physician, but those who are sick. I came not to call the righteous, but sinners' (Mark 2:17). See also Augustine of Hippo, 'Sermon 38 on the New Testament', *Nicene and Post-Nicene Fathers, First Series*, vol. VI, ed. Philip Schaff, trans. R. G. MacMullen (Edinburgh, 1980).

22 The modern word 'holy' comes from Old English *hālig*. It derives from the adjective **hailo-*, Old English *hál*, free from injury, whole, hale, or of the derivative noun **hailoz-*, **hailiz-*, in Old High German *heil*, Old Norse *heill*, health, happiness, good luck (OED).

EIGHT: Idolatries Ancient and Modern

1 This word makes its first appearance in the New Testament, in Paul's Epistle to the Galatians (5:20) and First Epistle to the Corinthians (10:14).

2 In Islam the Arabic term *shirk*, meaning 'association', covers both idolatry and polytheism – the common root of these sins being the attribution of divinity to someone or something beside the One God.

3 If on the other hand the image were thought to be divinely animate in some sense (if only temporarily), it would thereby be excluded from the class of the inanimate objects it would be 'idolatrous' to worship.

4 See under 'Image Makers Will Be Punished on the Day of Judgement', https://sunnahonline.com, accessed 9 August 2019. One *ḥadīth* preserved in the *Ṣaḥīḥ al-Bukhārī*, the collection made by Al-Bukhari (d. 870), records the Prophet Muhammad as saying that 'Those who make these images (*suwar*) will be punished on the Day of Resurrection, and it will be said to them, make alive what you have created.' A commentary by Al-Hafidh Ibn Hajar states: 'It is a command to do that which one is unable to do. From it we get a description of how the punishment of the image-maker will be. He will be ordered to breathe the soul into the image which he has made and he will not be able to do so. As a result his punishment will continue (unceasingly).'

5 In the Qur'ān, one of the epithets for God is the term *al-musawwir* – 'bestower of forms', or even 'artist'.

6 See also Isaiah 44:9–20.

7 In Hindu culture, for example, anything and everything can be worshipped in some sense or in some degree, which fact helps to express the omnipresence of the divine, and the relevance of religious piety to every department of life.

8 John Calvin (1509–1564) describes this distinction as a 'distinction without a difference'. John Calvin, *Institutes of the Christian Religion* [5th edn 1559], ed. John T. McNeill, trans. Ford Lewis Battles (Philadelphia, PA, 1960), vol. I, pp. 162–3.

9 To think, while engaged in an act of prayer before an image of the Holy Virgin, 'Here am I venerating the Holy Virgin, but while doing so I know, of course, that this image before me is not the Holy Virgin herself' would be like sitting in a cinema watching a film while continually reminding oneself that, of course, the events occurring on screen are not really taking place.

10 Alain Daniélou, *Hindu Polytheism* (New York, 1964), p. 364.

11 M.O'C. Walshe, ed. and trans., *Meister Eckhart: German Sermons and Treatises*, vol. I (London and Dulverton, 1979), p. 66.

12 Immanuel Kant, *Religion Within the Limits of Reason Alone*, trans. Theodore M. Greene and Hoyt H. Hudson (New York, 1960), p. 157. It is noteworthy that, in a footnote, Kant appears to acknowledge the value as well as inevitability of a kind of provisional idolatry: 'Though it does indeed sound dangerous, it is no way reprehensible to say that every man *creates a God* for himself, nay, must make himself a God according to moral concepts . . . in order to honour in Him *the One who created him*. For in whatever manner a being has been made known to him by another and described as God, yea, even if such a Being had appeared to him (if this is possible), he must first of all compare this representation with his ideal in order to judge whether he is entitled to regard it and to honour it as a divinity. Hence there can be no religion springing from revelation alone, i.e., without *first* positing that concept, in its purity, as a touchstone. Without this all reverence for God would be idolatry.'

13 George A. Panichas, ed., *The Simone Weil Reader* (New York, 1977), p. 220.

14 Ibid., p. 199.

15 Simone Weil, *Gravity and Grace* (London, 1952), p. 53.

16 Ibid., pp. 53–4.

17 This would cover both the general idea of religion itself, as well as the various traditions and denominations to which particular nations or groups of people adhere and 'in' which individuals 'believe'.

18 According to Paul Tillich, 'this idea that the human mind is a perpetual manufacturer of idols is one of the deepest things which can be said about our thinking of God. Even orthodox theology very often is

nothing other than idolatry.' *A History of Christian Thought from its
Judaic and Hellenistic Origins to Existentialism* (New York, 1968), p. 64.

19 Charles E. Moore, ed., *Provocations: Spiritual Writings of Kierkegaard*
(Walden, NY, 2002), pp. 83–6.

20 Thomas Carlyle, *On Heroes, Hero-worship and the Heroic in History* [1841]
(London, 1897), p. 15.

21 Panichas, ed., *The Simone Weil Reader*, p. 417.

22 On the Chinese Lin-Chi (Japanese: Rinzai) school of Buddhism
(eighth century CE onwards) and its unconventional methods (even by
Buddhist standards), see, for example, Alan W. Watts, *The Way of Zen*
(Harmondsworth, 1962), pp. 97–131.

NINE: Universality in Particularity

1 Christopher Hitchens, 'The Lord and the Intellectuals', *Harper's
Magazine* (July 1982), pp. 60–63.

2 A classic example of absolute exclusivism is found in the papal bull
Unam Sanctam (1302), which concludes: 'we declare, we proclaim,
we define that it is absolutely necessary for salvation that every human
creature be subject to the Roman Pontiff.' This is more narrowly
exclusive than the well-known 'No man cometh unto the Father,
but by me' (John 14:6), which is at least open to an inclusivist and
theoretically even a relativist interpretation.

3 'Had Allah willed, He would have made you one nation [united in
religion], but [He intended] to test you in what He has given you; so
race to [all that is] good. To Allah is your return all together, and He
will [then] inform you concerning that over which you used to differ'
(Qur'ān 5:48). See also Qur'ān 16:92. Saheeh International translation
(1997), available at https://quran.com, accessed 2 January 2020.

4 Emil Brunner, *The Scandal of Christianity* (Philadelphia, PA, 1951). See
also Edith M. Humphrey, *Ecstasy and Intimacy: When the Holy Spirit
Meets the Human Spirit* (Grand Rapids, MI, 2006), p. 213: 'It is not . .
. that our "religion" is superior. Instead we abide within the Christian
story and so must affirm two "scandals", to use the words of the
theologian Emil Brunner. The first offense is the scandal of particularity,
because this living God has come to us among a particular people,
the Jews, by acting in their midst and finally taking on human flesh in
the particular man Jesus. The second, related offense is the scandal of
universality, for from the beginning Christians have insisted that God's
active revelation, or his revelatory action, is for all humanity.'

5 For this and other translations, see *The Quranic Arabic Corpus*,
https://corpus.quran.com.

6 John Milton, *Areopagitica; a Speech* (1644); in *Complete Prose Works of
John Milton*, ed. Don M. Wolfe et al., 8 vols (New Haven, CT, 1953–82),
II, p. 552.

7 The wry comment of E. M. Delafield, the Sussex-born novelist, is probably no less apposite today than it was when she wrote it in 1938: namely, that 'most Englishmen, if forced into analysing their own creeds – which heaven forbid – are convinced that God is an Englishman – probably educated at Eton.' 'Preface' in Pont [Graham Laidler], *The British Character Studied and Revealed* (London, 1938), p. 9.

8 My reading of this story follows the analysis given in Leon R. Kass, 'The Humanist Dream: Babel Then and Now', *Gregorianum*, LXXXI (2000), pp. 633–57.

9 *Tao Te Ching*, 34; in Alan Watts, *The Way of Zen* (Harmondsworth, 1962), p. 38.

TEN: The Cosmological Connection

1 Thomas H. Huxley, *Westminster Review*, XVII (1860), pp. 541–70 (p. 556).

2 Letter from Darwin to Huxley (14 April 1860): 'I quite agree with letter from Lyell that your extinguished Theologians laying about the cradle of each new science &c &c is *splendid*.' Imperial College of Science, Technology and Medicine Archives (Huxley 5:115).

3 Stephen Jay Gould uses this term to describe 'a domain where one form of teaching holds the appropriate tools for meaningful discourse and resolution'. He then defines the relationship between science and religion as that of two 'Non-overlapping Magisteria'. See his *Rock of Ages: Science and Religion in the Fullness of Life* (New York, 1999), pp. 4–6.

4 One does, however, come across statements of the form: science has shown that x is really y. For example, love is just the behaviour of our hormones, smiling is really the sublimation of aggressive feelings, and so on.

5 On this subject, see Mary Midgley, *Science as Salvation: A Modern Myth and its Meaning* (London and New York, 1992).

6 That 'narratives' about the relationship between science and religion have not always been narratives about conflict is made clear in J. H. Brooke and Geoffrey Cantor, *Reconstructing Nature: The Engagement of Science and Religion* (Edinburgh, 1998).

7 Gould, *Rock of Ages*, p. 6.

8 See William R. Shea, 'Galileo and the Church', in *God and Nature: Historical Essays on the Encounter Between Christianity and Science*, ed. David C. Lindberg and Ronald L. Numbers (Berkeley and Los Angeles, CA, 1986), pp. 114–35.

9 It is worth noting here that both the German *wissenschaft* and the French *science* retain meanings much wider than that of the English word 'science', which has become too closely identified with the physical or so-called 'natural' sciences.

10 For more on this, see Mary Midgley, *Evolution as a Religion: Strange Hopes and Stranger Fears*, 2nd edn (London and New York, 2002).

11 For a sympathetic account of Ussher's efforts, see Stephen Jay Gould, *Eight Little Piggies: Reflections in Natural History* (London, 1993), pp. 181–93.

12 For many of those who use the biblical texts in this way, these texts were not 'composed' in the usual human manner or altered by historical circumstances. God, or those inspired or directed by God, could not have got the facts wrong. Nor has the essential content or meaning of these texts changed, even when translated.

13 Augustine of Hippo, *De civitate Dei (City of God)* XI:6; in *Augustine: The City of God*, trans. Henry Bettenson (Harmondsworth, 1972), p. 436. For more by Augustine on not using scripture to settle questions about natural phenomena, see his *De Genesi ad litteram*, 1:18–21 and 11:9.

14 Paul Davies, *God and the New Physics* (London, 1983), pp. 5–6.

15 Ian Hughes, 'We Are Only Human', *New Scientist*, 149 (23 March 1996), p. 60.

16 H. H. Gerth and C. Wright Mills, eds and trans., *From Max Weber: Essays in Sociology* (New York, 1946), pp. 129–56.

17 Hans Peter Rickman, 'Wilhelm Dilthey', in *Encyclopedia of Philosophy*, ed. Paul Edwards (New York, 1967), 11, p. 403.

18 Universe, meaning 'the whole world or cosmos; the totality of existing things', comes from the Latin *universum*, 'all things, all people, the whole world', a nominal use of the neuter form of the adjective *universus*, 'all together, all in one, whole, entire, relating to all'; literally 'turned into one'.

19 For a concise and comprehensive survey of this theme, see Joseph Milne, *Metaphysics and the Cosmic Order* (London, 2008).

ELEVEN: Losing Our Religion?

1 The story occurs in Plutarch's *Moralia* (III. 419B–E), in ch. 17 of his treatise 'On the Obsolescence of the Oracles' (Περὶ τῶν ἐκλελοιπότων χρηστηρίων; in Latin: *De oraculorum defectu*). See Frank C. Babbitt, ed. and trans, *Moralia*, vol. v (Cambridge, MA, and London, 1936), pp. 400–403.

2 Friedrich Nietzsche, *Die fröhliche Wissenschaft* (1887); trans. Walter Kaufmann as *The Gay Science* (New York, 1974), pp. 181–2 (§125 'The madman').

3 See William C. Placher, *The Domestication of Transcendence: How Modern Thinking about God Went Wrong* (Louisville, KY, 1996).

4 In Book V of *The Gay Science*, 'We Fearless Ones', Nietzsche describes the event more soberly: 'The greatest recent event – that "God is dead", that the belief in the Christian god has become unbelievable – already begins to cast its first shadows over Europe. For the few at least, whose eyes – the suspicion in whose eyes is strong and subtle enough for this spectacle, some sun seems to have set and some ancient and profound

trust has been turned into doubt; to them our old world must appear daily more like evening, more mistrustful, stranger, "older". But in the main one may say: The event itself is far too great, too distant, too remote from the multitude's capacity for comprehension even for the tidings of it to be thought of as having *arrived* as yet. Much less may one suppose that many people know as yet *what* this event really means – and how much must collapse now that this faith has been undermined because it was built upon this faith, propped up by it, grown into it; for example, the whole of our European morality'; Kaufmann, p. 279 (§343 'The meaning of our cheerfulness').

5 Some have attempted to revive these gods in various forms, just as others have found the pagan gods useful metaphors. See, on these topics, Ronald Hutton, *The Triumph of the Moon: A History of Modern Pagan Witchcraft* (Oxford, 2001) and *Pagan Britain* (New Haven, CT, 2013), and Jean Seznec, *The Survival of the Pagan Gods: The Mythological Tradition and its Place in Renaissance Humanism and Art* (New York, 1953).

6 Fyodor Dostoyevsky, *The Brothers Karamazov* (1880), Book v, ch. 5.

7 According to one sociologist, secularization theory was 'bedevilled by shifts in definition, and the manipulation of criteria, so that it became difficult to know when one was comparing like with like, over time and over cultural space. Worst of all . . . was a pervasive epiphenomenalism which could selectively, or even in principle, declare religion to be "really" something else as, for example, political frustration, or nationalism, in order to fit religion in to whatever the dictates of sociological theory might be.' David Martin, 'The Secularization Issue: Prospect and Retrospect', *British Journal of Sociology*, 42 (1991), pp. 465–74 (pp. 465–6).

8 This term, first used by scholars Paul Tillich and Heinrich Zimmer, is further developed in the work of Ninian Smart, who coins more elaborate terms such as 'transpolytheism', 'transpolytheistic monotheism' and even 'transpolytheistic transtheistic absolutism'. These terms serve to accommodate religious positions that, despite looking to a non-personal state or Absolute beyond the gods or God, continue to affirm the relative importance of the latter.

9 For a dramatic example of a 'counter-conversion', away from religious belief, see William James, *The Varieties of Religious Experience* (London, 1902), pp. 176–7.

10 See, for example, the opening paragraph of Julian Barnes, *Nothing to Be Frightened Of* (London, 2008): '"I don't believe in God, but I miss him." That's what I say when the question is put. I asked my brother, who has taught philosophy at Oxford, Geneva, and the Sorbonne, what he thought of such a statement, without revealing that it was my own. He replied with a single word: "Soppy".'

11 Philip Larkin, 'Aubade'; *Collected Poems* (London, 1988), pp. 208–9.

12 Larkin, 'Church Going'; ibid., pp. 97–8.

13 Sigmund Freud, *Introductory Lectures on Psycho-analysis* (1916–17), in *The Standard Edition of the Complete Psychological Works of Sigmund Freud*, ed. James Strachey et al. (London, 1953–74), XV–XVI, pp. 284–5. See also 'A Difficulty on the Path of Psycho-analysis' (1917), ibid., XVII, pp. 135–44 (p. 140).

14 See, on the sources and precursors of Weber's idea of 'disenchantment', Ian H. Angus, 'Disenchantment and Modernity: The Mirror of Technique', *Human Studies*, 6 (1983), pp. 141–66; and Sara Lyons, 'The Disenchantment/Re-enchantment of the World: Aesthetics, Secularization, and the Gods of Greece from Friedrich Schiller to Walter Pater', *Modern Language Review*, CIX (2014), pp. 873–95. For a detailed critique of the idea of the progressive 'disenchantment' of the modern world, see Jason Ā. Josephson-Storm, *The Myth of Disenchantment: Magic, Modernity, and the Birth of the Human Sciences* (Chicago, IL, 2017).

15 Max Weber, *The Protestant Ethic and the Spirit of Capitalism* (1920); and 'Science as a Vocation' (1919), in *From Max Weber: Essays in Sociology*, ed. and trans. H. H. Gerth and C. Wright Mills (New York, 1946), pp. 129–56.

16 See, for example, Thomas J. J. Altizer, *The Gospel of Christian Atheism* (Philadelphia, PA, 1966).

17 Dietrich Bonhoeffer, *Letters and Papers from Prison*, ed. Eberhard Bethge (London, 1999), p. 279. 'We are moving towards a completely religionless time; people as they are now simply cannot be religious any more. Even those who honestly describe themselves as "religious" do not in the least act up to it, and so they presumably mean something quite different by "religious".'

18 Alain de Botton, *Religion for Atheists: A Non-believer's Guide to the Uses of Religion* (London, 2012), p. 14 (author's emphasis).

TWELVE: Reinventing Religion

1 Zen Buddhism is the Japanese version of Ch'an Buddhism, which arose in China from the sixth century CE onwards and was introduced into Japan from the thirteenth century. Here and elsewhere I use the term 'Zen' generically to refer to the whole school.

2 The word 'original', too, has come to mean 'novel' rather than, as its etymology indicates, 'deriving from a source or origin'.

3 Some have suggested that mental compartmentalization is not merely inevitable but beneficial. The writer H. P. Lovecraft opens one of his short stories, 'The Call of Cthulhu', with these words: 'The most merciful thing in the world, I think, is the inability of the mind to correlate all its contents.' *The Haunter of the Dark and Other Tales* (London, 1963), p. 47.

4 'A few years ago, a priest working in a slum section of a European city was asked why he was doing it, and replied, "So that the rumour of

God may not completely disappear." The word aptly expresses what the signals of transcendence have become in our situation – rumours – and not very reputable rumours at that.' See Peter L. Berger, *A Rumour of Angels: Modern Society and the Rediscovery of the Supernatural* (Harmondsworth, 1971), p. 119.

5 This alludes to the simplified or minimalist form of monotheism known as Deism – with its idea of a creator God who does not, or cannot, intervene in His creation. It is associated in particular with leading thinkers of the European Enlightenment.

Epilogue

1 Nathaniel Hawthorne, *English Notebooks* (New York, 1941), p. 433.

2 Synonyms for this abound, both within and beyond religion: sanctimonious, pious, self-righteous, smug, complacent, self-satisfied, priggish.

3 It was Thomas Carlyle who (in 1828) launched the use of the word 'environment' to describe the setting or surroundings of something. Its only earlier use was to refer specifically to the action or condition of being surrounded or encircled (the OED gives its earliest recorded use in this sense as 1603). The first recorded use of 'environment' in the now familiar modern ecological sense was in 1956.

4 'The essence of all pantheism, evolutionism, and modern cosmic religion is really in this proposition: that Nature is our mother. Unfortunately, if you regard Nature as a mother, you discover that she is a step-mother. The main point of Christianity was this: that Nature is not our mother: Nature is our sister. We can be proud of her beauty, since we have the same father; but she has no authority over us; we have to admire, but not to imitate. This gives to the typically Christian pleasure in this earth a strange touch of lightness that is almost frivolity. Nature was a solemn mother to the worshippers of Isis and Cybele. Nature was a solemn mother to Wordsworth or to Emerson. But Nature is not solemn to Francis of Assisi or to George Herbert. To St Francis, Nature is a sister, and even a younger sister: a little, dancing sister, to be laughed at as well as loved.' G. K. Chesterton, *Orthodoxy* (London, 1908), pp. 115–16. Chesterton is writing as a Christian, of course, but the general tenor of his remarks here would be endorsed by thinkers in other religions too.

5 Epistle to the Hebrews 1:1.

6 Richard Holloway, *Looking in the Distance: The Human Search for Meaning* (Edinburgh, 2004), pp. 214–15. Holloway denies that meaning is to be found anywhere but in the ephemeral phenomena of human life, which his own cosmology seems to imply are meaningless: 'We may be no closer to understanding why there is a world, but we are now able to accept the fact that the world itself is the source of the values and

meanings we prize most, not some hypothetical transcendent reality which did none of the work yet claims all the credit' (p. 28).

7 Samuel Beckett, *Waiting for Godot: A TragiComedy in Two Acts* (London, 1965), p. 89.

8 From an interview in *Der Spiegel*, 17 October 1988: *Spiegel Online*, www. spiegel.de. Why say '*just* a slightly advanced breed of apes [emphasis mine]' rather than simply 'a slightly advanced breed of apes'? And what relevance does our being on a small planet orbiting a 'very average' star have for any judgement about our status in the universe? Hawking seems to be saying that we should not be treating the earth and ourselves as in any way special, and yet he also wants to affirm that we are indeed special because we are able to understand the universe.

SELECT BIBLIOGRAPHY

Armstrong, Karen, *The Case for God: What Religion Really Means* (London, 2009)

Beattie, T., *The New Atheists: The Twilight of Reason and the War on Religion* (London, 2007)

Bell, Catherine, *Ritual Theory, Ritual Practice* (New York and Oxford, 1992)

Berger, Peter L., *The Heretical Imperative: Contemporary Possibilities of Religious Affirmation* (Garden City, NY, 1979)

———, *A Rumour of Angels: Modern Society and the Rediscovery of the Supernatural* (London, 1970)

Botton, Alain de, *Religion for Atheists: A Non-believer's Guide to the Uses of Religion* (London, 2012)

Bowker, John, *Licensed Insanities: Religions and Belief in God in the Contemporary World* (London, 1987)

Boyer, Pascal, *Religion Explained: The Human Instincts that Fashion Gods, Spirits and Ancestors* (London, 2008)

Brainard, F. Samuel, *Reality and Mystical Experience* (University Park, PA, 2000)

Buckley, Michael J., *At the Origins of Modern Atheism* (New Haven, CT, and London, 1987)

———, *Denying and Disclosing God: The Ambiguous Progress of Modern Atheism* (New Haven, CT, and London, 2004)

Carrette, Jeremy, and Richard King, *Selling Spirituality: The Silent Takeover of Religion* (Abingdon and New York, 2005)

Clark, Stephen R. L., *The Mysteries of Religion: An Introduction to Philosophy through Religion* (Oxford, 1986)

Connolly, Peter, *Understanding Religious Experience* (Bristol, 2019)

Crane, Tim, *The Meaning of Belief: Religion from an Atheist's Point of View* (Cambridge, MA, 2017)

Critchley, Simon, *The Faith of the Faithless: Experiments in Political Theology* (London and New York, 2012)

Curry, Patrick, *Enchantment: Wonder in Modern Life* (Edinburgh, 2019)

Dark, David, *The Sacredness of Questioning Everything* (Grand Rapids, MI, 2009)

——, *Life's Too Short to Pretend You're Not Religious* (Downers Grove, IL, 2016)

Davis, Caroline Franks, *The Evidential Force of Religious Experience* (Oxford, 1989)

Dennett, Daniel, *Breaking the Spell: Religion as a Natural Phenomenon* (London, 2006)

Dupré, Louis, *Passage to Modernity: An Essay in the Hermeneutics of Nature and Culture* (New Haven, CT, and London, 1993)

Edwards, James C., *The Plain Sense of Things: The Fate of Religion in an Age of Normal Nihilism* (University Park, PA, 1997)

Fergusson, David, *Faith and Its Critics: A Conversation* (Oxford, 2009)

Gauchet, Marcel, *The Disenchantment of the World: A Political History of Religion*, trans. Oscar Burge (Princeton, NJ, 1997)

Gellman, Jerome, *Mystical Experience of God: A Philosophical Inquiry* (London and New York, 2001)

Gillespie, Michael Allen, *The Theological Origins of Modernity* (Chicago, IL, 2008)

Gould, Stephen Jay, *Rocks of Ages: Science and Religion in the Fullness of Life* (New York, 1999)

Gray, John, *Seven Types of Atheism* (London, 2018)

Grayling, A. C., *The God Argument: The Case against Religion and for Humanism* (London, 2013)

Grimes, Ronald L., *Deeply into the Bone: Re-inventing Rites of Passage* (Berkeley, CA, 2000)

Harris, Sam, *The End of Faith: Religion, Terror, and the Future of Reason* (London, 2005)

Haught, John F., *God and the New Atheism: A Critical Response to Dawkins, Harris, and Hitchens* (Louisville, KY, 2008)

Heelas, Paul, *The New Age Movement: The Celebration of the Self and the Sacralization of Modernity* (Oxford, 1996)

Hick, John, *Problems of Religious Pluralism* (New York, 1985)

Hitchens, Christopher, *God Is Not Great: How Religion Poisons Everything* (New York, 2007)

Holloway, Richard, *Looking in the Distance: The Human Search for Meaning* (London, 2009)

James, William, *The Varieties of Religious Experience*, new edn. with Introduction by Martin E. Marty (London, 1985)

Johnson, Willard, *Riding the Ox Home: A History of Meditation from Shamanism to Science* (London, 1982)

Johnston, Mark, *Saving God: Religion after Idolatry* (Princeton, NJ, and Oxford, 2009)

Kearney, Richard, *Anatheism: Returning to God after God* (New York, 2010)

Kerr, Fergus, *Immortal Longings: Versions of Transcending Humanity* (London, 1997)

Kolakowski, Leszek, *Religion*, 2nd edn (London, 1993)

Lash, Nicholas, *The Beginning and the End of 'Religion'* (Cambridge, 1996)

Lindbeck, George A., *The Nature of Doctrine: Religion and Theology in a Postliberal Age* (Philadelphia, PA, 1984)

Lindberg, David C., and Ronald L. Numbers, *God and Nature: Historical Essays on the Encounter Between Christianity and Science* (Berkeley, CA, and London, 1986)

Luckmann, T., *The Invisible Religion: The Problem of Religion in Modern Society* (New York, 1970)

Midgeley, Mary, *Evolution as a Religion: Strange Hopes and Stranger Fears* (London and New York, 1985)

——, *Science as Salvation: A Modern Myth and Its Meaning* (London and New York, 1992)

Milne, Joseph, *The Lost Vision of Nature* (London, 2018)

——, *Metaphysics and the Cosmic Order* (London, 2008)

Moore, Peter, *Where Are the Dead? Exploring the Idea of an Embodied Afterlife* (London and New York, 2017)

Nagel, Thomas, *Mind and Cosmos: Why the Materialist Neo-Darwinian Conception of Nature is Almost Certainly False* (Oxford and New York, 2012)

Numbers, Ronald L., *Galileo Goes to Jail and Other Myths about Science and Religion* (Cambridge, MA, and London, 2011)

Pals, Daniel L., *Nine Theories of Religion*, 3rd edn (New York and Oxford, 2014)

Parry, Jim, et al., *Sport and Spirituality: An Introduction* (London, 2007)

Pieper, Josef, *'Divine Madness': Plato's Case Against Secular Humanism*, trans. Lothar Krauth (San Francisco, CA, 1995)

——, *In Tune with the World: A Theory of Festivity*, trans. Richard and Clara Winston (New York, 1965)

Placher, William, *The Domestication of Transcendence: How Modern Thinking About God Went Wrong* (Louisville, KY, 1996)

Prozesky, Martin, and Gustavo Gregorutti, eds, *Religion and Ultimate Well-being: An Explanatory Theory* (New York, 1984)

Roberts, Tyler, *Encountering Religion: Responsibility and Criticism After Secularism* (New York, 2013)

Robinson, Marilynne, *When I Was a Child I Read Books* (London, 2012)

Rogers, Pattiann, *The Grand Array: Writings on Nature, Science, and Spirit* (San Antonio, TX, 2019)

Rue, Loyal D., *Religion Is Not About God: How Spiritual Traditions Nurture Our Biological Nature and What to Expect When They Fail* (New Brunswick, NJ, and London, 2005)

Saler, Benson, *Conceptualizing Religion: Immanent Anthropologists, Transcendent Natives, and Unbounded Categories* (Leiden, 1993)

Sheldrake, Rupert, *The Science Delusion: Freeing the Spirit of Enquiry* (London, 2012)

Schellenberg, J. L., *The Will to Imagine: A Justification of Skeptical Religion* (Ithaca, NY, 2009)

Smart, Ninian, *Worldviews: Crosscultural Explorations of Human Beliefs*, 2nd edn (Englewood Cliffs, NJ, 1994)

Smith, Christian, *Religion: What It Is, How It Works, and Why It Matters* (Princeton, NJ, 2017)

Smith, Huston, *Forgotten Truth: The Primordial Tradition* (New York, 1976)

Solomon, Robert C., *Spirituality for the Skeptic: The Thoughtful Love of Life* (New York, 2002)

Spong, John Shelby, *Biblical Literalism: A Gentile Heresy* (New York, 2016)

Taylor, Charles, *A Secular Age* (Cambridge, MA, 2007)

Taylor, Mark C., *After God* (Chicago, IL, and Bristol, 2007)

Vasquez, Manuel A., *More Than Belief: A Materialist Theory of Religion* (Oxford, 2011)

Wilson, A. N., *God's Funeral* (London, 1999)

Wilson, Edward O., *The Meaning of Human Existence* (New York, 2014)

Zaleski, Carol, *Otherworld Journeys: Accounts of Near-death Experience in Medieval and Modern Times* (New York and Oxford, 1987)

ACKNOWLEDGEMENTS

This book is the by-product of many years' thinking, reading and teaching about religion, and – in my own way – of practising it. As such, it owes much not only to the scholarship to which I have been fortunate enough to have had access, but more particularly to the ideas, insights and example of a diversity of friends, teachers and colleagues. In this regard, I am particularly indebted to Donald Allchin, Christopher Cherry, James Dickie, Eric Doyle, Alexander Fostiropoulos, Michael Grant, Ursula King, Joseph Milne, David McLellan, Marco Pallis, Anthony Ramsay, A. K. Saran, Leon Schlamm, Philip Sherrard, Ninian Smart and Duane Williams. The task of completing the book has been greatly assisted by the willingness of David McLellan to comment on drafts of each chapter, as well as by the unfailing support and encouragement of my wife, Maria Moore. I am also grateful to Joseph Milne and Duane Williams for helpful comments on particular sections of the text. Finally, I must thank Michael Leaman for agreeing to publish this book and his colleagues at Reaktion Books for their expertise in seeing it through all the necessary stages.

INDEX